RECLAIMING THE FIRE

How Successful People
Overcome Burnout

DR. STEVEN BERGLAS

 RANDOM HOUSE / NEW YORK

Grateful acknowledgment is made to the following for permission to reprint previously published material:

American Psychological Association: Excerpt from "If We Are So Rich, Why Aren't We Happy?" by Mihaly Csikszentmihalyi, from the October 1999 issue of *American Psychologist* (vol. 54, pp. 821–827; excerpt appears on pp. 823–824). Reprinted by permission of the American Psychological Association.

Harvard Business School Publishing: Excerpt from "Teaching Smart People How to Learn" by Chris Argyris, from the May–June 1991 issue of *Harvard Business Review.* Copyright © 1991 by Harvard Business School Publishing Corporation. All rights reserved. Reprinted by permission of Harvard Business School Publishing.

International Creative Management: Excerpt from an article by Barbara Goldsmith from the December 4, 1983, *New York Times Magazine.* Copyright © 1983 by Barbara Goldsmith. Reprinted by permission of International Creative Management.

Library of Congress Cataloging-in-Publication Data
Berglas, Steven.
Reclaiming the fire: how successful people overcome burnout / Steven Berglas.
p. cm.
Includes bibliographical references.
ISBN 0-812-99255-5
1. Burn out (Psychology)   2. Mental fatigue.   3. Success—Psychological aspects.
I. Title.
BF481 .B39 2001
158.7'23—dc21   00-045905

Random House website address: www.atrandom.com

Book design by Caroline Cunningham

For Jennifer—
my gift from God

A way of life cannot be successful so long as it is mere intellectual conviction. It must be deeply felt, deeply believed, dominant even in dreams.

—BERTRAND RUSSELL

Contents

1 People Who Hit Bottom When They Reach the Top — 3

2 Success Depression and Encore Anxiety — 28

3 Why So Many Baby Boomers Suffer Supernova Burnout — 54

4 Pyrrhic Revenge: "I Hope This Hurts You More Than It Hurts Me" — 80

5 If at First You *Do* Succeed, Try Thinking Like a Woman — 95

6 Toward Resolving the Paradox of Supernova Burnout: How the Enchantment with Success Became an Obsession — 122

7 The Goldilocks Dilemma: Embracing Challenge, Innovation, and Change — 134

8 Generativity: Developing People, Not Building Monuments — 158

9 True Happiness Is a Verb — 185

Acknowledgments — 221
Notes — 223
Index — 231

RECLAIMING
THE FIRE

CHAPTER 1

People Who Hit Bottom
When They Reach the Top

Few highly successful people contact a mental health professional unless they experience a crisis. Actually, most successful professionals, even in the throes of a crisis, are loath to admit to needing a "shrink." The vast majority of my clients are referred to me by third parties who sense that without professional help the crisis that their colleague, friend, or lover is suffering will get worse. Given the energy expended to get a successful person to accept the need for a psychotherapist, corporate consultant, or executive coach, some may find it odd that the first thing I do when meeting a new referral is attempt to illustrate the two ironies of his or her situation.

The first irony lies in the fact that no successful person I can think of became successful without conquering some form of crisis. Career success signifies an ability to overcome obstacles, to persevere in the face of competitive threats, to adapt to change, and to endure grueling periods of deprivation. Someone who succeeds must have experienced the travails of (1) acquiring a new or specialized skill, (2) perfecting skills in order to display talents and abilities in a stellar fashion, or (3) deconstructing the status quo (as an entrepreneur, artist, inventor) and creating a new paradigm or prototype of excellence. Successful people are conquerors, so when they come to see me, the first thing I do is remind them of that fact. This reminder sets the stage for helping them understand why they are at a point where they can no longer do—or refuse to do—what they once did superbly.

The second irony involves the self-defeating nuances of meaning every successful person imposes on the idea of "crisis." When I begin treating people who suffer success-induced disorders, I try to help them accept the fact that connotations can kill. I start by showing them the Chinese symbol for *crisis,* which consists of two intertwined characters: the symbol for "danger" and the symbol for "opportunity." To help successful people in crisis help themselves, my job is to move them away from focusing on danger and help them begin focusing on opportunity.

Finding opportunity in crisis is not a facile fortune cookie cure. *Crisis* need not connote impending catastrophe; it can be understood as a turning point, a choice point, an opportunity for change. One patient of mine who read tarot cards as a hobby pointed out that the "death card" has a similar duality: loss plus generative potential. As Picasso allegedly observed, "Every act of creation is first of all an act of destruction."

We suffer loss and opportunity throughout our lives, yet during our youth these events do not typically precipitate crises. When adolescents lose the protective status of being minors (at approximately the time we begin our search for identity), they typically focus on opportunity and feel elated. What freedoms adulthood holds! To drive a car. To hold an esteem-building job outside the sheltering (and at times restrictive) protection of the nuclear family. To date. It is undeniable that when something familiar dies, the loss arouses anxiety, but it is always possible to find exhilarating challenges before you. The key is to understand them as such and not focus on the potential threats they impose. Being pushed from any nest is unsettling, but contrast the entrapment of the nest with the freedom of flight!

A paradox of success lost on successful people in crisis is how constraining, tedious, and demanding their ostensibly favorable status is. There is great danger in abandoning the tried and true; to be a rookie after enjoying years as a superstar exposes you to humiliation and shame should you fail to live up to the image you've created. But what about the danger inherent in never freeing yourself from Sisyphean monotony? What about the danger inherent in not expanding your horizons or failing to actualize untapped potential? You know what they say about the tortoise who cannot get anywhere without sticking his neck out? It is safer within one's shell of success, but at what cost?

So people come to see me after a proven history of mastering crisis, yet they feel impotent to address a new one. They (or those who have referred them) seek my help to cope with perceived threats, despite knowing that they have mastered the dangers inherent in striving for success. When successful people visit me for the first time, they are aware of only the potential for loss, the potential for pain, the potential for shame. These are the concerns of people coming to grips with the syndrome I call Supernova Burnout.

SUPERNOVA BURNOUT

Supernova Burnout afflicts successful people who find that their vocations are no longer psychologically rewarding or have become threatening to their self-esteem. Our culture glorifies material success. The truth, however, is that this flawed ideal is to blame for the rising number of high-achieving men and women wanting desperately to escape their circumstances after years of arduous work to get there. I am referring to business executives with years of success begging to break the grip of golden handcuffs, professionals willing to discard advanced degrees in order to escape mind-numbing tedium, and performers including athletes, musicians, and actors who report that they are crippled by the demands of constantly needing to answer calls of "encore, encore" when what they want to scream is *Ciao!*

Everyone knows of at least one rags-to-riches-to-rags saga that ended because someone who had it all (Freddie Prinze, Vince Foster, Robert Maxwell, David Begelman) was overwhelmed by psychological demons and committed suicide. This is not Supernova Burnout. The phenomenon I have studied for over twenty years is pervasive dissatisfaction with a successful career interrupted by often nondramatic, yet incredibly debilitating, symptoms ranging from anxiety about living up to the expectations born of success to a sense of ennui born of the realization that attaining the goal you *thought* would change your life did no such thing.

Achieving what you want and realizing that no favorable psychological changes have automatically ensued is far worse than failing to reach a goal. With failure you can always go back to the drawing board, or "try, try again"—these are actually energizing conditions. With success that forces you to ask "Is that all there is?" no such second chances exist. The disappointment of exposing the myths that surround success is devastating because we are obsessed with success.

Career success is the objective common to virtually all the heroes who have shaped our capitalist culture, from Horatio Alger's protagonists through Rockefeller, Mellon, and Carnegie to today's heroes like Michael Jordan, Oprah Winfrey, Bill Gates, and Steve Case. All these whites and blacks, men and women, have risen to the top of a professional heap and earned lots of money. Yet in my experience the most compelling common denominator in this population is the vulnerability to deep emotional pain that has the potential to blow the American dream apart.

Supernova Burnout is widespread, yet in spite of the fact that it has been written about for centuries, people are loath to acknowledge its existence. George Bernard Shaw started his professional life battling feelings best described as contempt-laden despair because he felt coopted by success and recognition:

I made good in spite of myself, and found, to my dismay, that Business, instead of expelling me as the worthless imposter I was, was fastening upon me with no intention of letting me go. Behold me, therefore, in my twentieth year, with a business training, in an occupation which I detested as cordially as any sane person lets himself detest anything he cannot escape from.... [Ultimately,] I broke loose.[1]

Shaw wrote these words when he was in his seventies and was asked to reflect upon what life was like before he found, or began to practice, his true calling. Most of the professionals I have worked with in psychotherapy or executives I have coached on the job were not able to "break loose" the way Shaw did in his early twenties, a time in life when golden handcuffs are far less constrictive than they are in later years filled with familial demands and expectations.[2] In the main, professionals who suffer Supernova Burnout have long recognized that they are in vocations (or professional circumstances) that they detest, but they are unable to break free until something cataclysmic forces their hand.

There are, to be certain, many people—like the vast majority of you reading this book—who have experienced symptoms akin to those that cause Supernova Burnout and who don't need the help of a mental health professional, or a tragedy, to make adjustments to their lives.

One woman I'll call Martha—because she possessed the meticulous and somewhat obsessional organizational skills of Martha Stewart—had seemingly adjusted to the ennui she experienced after years of working as the executive vice president of finance with a Fortune 1000 corporation located near Washington, D.C. But when I met Martha—I was assessing the corporation's executive team for their readiness to initiate a takeover of a related business—I was struck by how ill-prepared for new challenges Martha seemed to be. After our initial meeting, I scheduled a follow-up session to confront her with my concerns. "You know, I don't sense that you view purchasing [the targeted corporation] as a worthwhile move for your company," I said. "In fact, when I talk with you, it strikes me that you're bracing for a set of onerous chores, not an opportunity for growth."

Her response was completely candid: "You're right, but for reasons that have nothing to do with my role here. My job *was* a dream come true when I landed it, but no longer. I'm forty-one years old, my daughters are both in high school, and I'm jealous of them; their opportunities are limitless. When I was their age, the aspirations I listed under my yearbook picture were 'future Nobel Prize laureate' and 'philanthropist.' My salary here without stock options is more than twice as much as Nobel Prize winners get, but that's not enough. Why can't I just try to do something that will make me feel like a winner, rather than a prosaic professional?"

Martha and I met several more times for brief chats, and while I can say that I was a catalyst in her decision to move, I was in no way a causal agent. I discovered that Martha had been exploring for more than a year the possibility of getting a fellowship at a prestigious economic think tank in the D.C. area (she had a Ph.D. in economics), and with my urging—and a few clarifying remarks about how normal it is to experience inertia in a career that is the envy of most professionals—she resigned her job.

The people that I describe as suffering Supernova Burnout suffer much more than the normal inertia that holds people in well-paying but psychologically unrewarding jobs. These people are trapped, or terrified of failing to live up to expectations, and suffer mightily as a consequence, but their core concerns differ in degree only, not in kind, from the ones affecting virtually all careerists. I use extreme instances of Supernova Burnout for illustrative purposes for the same reason that advertisers use beautiful women in ads for products ranging from automobiles to beer: to capture attention. The psychological forces that kept Martha in corporate America years longer than she wanted to be there are not apparent without an in-depth understanding of Supernova Burnout. The cases that I have chosen to describe in the pages that follow are designed to make the conflicts, doubts, anxieties, feelings of guilt, and hostilities that cause Supernova Burnout obvious and understandable to all.

I'm an alcoholic...I thought only losers became alcoholics.
—JASON ROBARDS (FROM A NATIONAL COUNCIL
ON ALCOHOLISM ADVERTISEMENT)

Typical victims of Supernova Burnout let their bodies do their talking. Stress-induced cardiovascular disease and clinical depression are among the most common precipitants of career change I know of. When physical disease isn't available to provide a convenient exit strategy, self-destructive behavior can be relied upon to get the job done. Have you ever wondered why there are so many well-publicized cases of Wall Street tycoons getting caught in shameful situations that involve white-collar crimes such as insider trading, illicit sexual affairs, or violence? The underlying cause of these "inexplicable" acts is often an inability to admit that living the good life is anything other than psychological purgatory.

Roughly two years ago James McDermott, the former chief executive of a major New York City investment bank (Keefe, Bruyette & Woods), was charged with insider trading and securities fraud for allegedly alerting an adult-video actress, Marylin Starr, with whom he was having a sexual relationship, to a series of impending bank mergers.[3] Can I say conclusively that what McDermott did was a quasi-intentional plea for help? Obviously not. But I can say that I have treated over twenty men with comparable wealth, status, and power who "inexplicably" ended their successful careers by recklessly infusing a disheartening day-to-day routine with the exhilaration of illicit criminal activities. While it may be true, particularly for multimillionaires, that crime doesn't pay, illegal activity can be an incredibly stimulating alternative to the monotonous ordeal their careers have become.

While a significant—and highly publicized—number of people who suffer Supernova Burnout break loose from their career imprisonment by engaging in self-immolation, I have found that the majority resort to alcohol abuse, the most reliable unhealthy mechanism there is for pulling those who detest life at the top out of their gold-plated psychological confinement. I have treated scores of men and women (who must remain anonymous) for success-induced alcohol abuse. The former Boston Bruins hockey great Derek Sanderson has allowed me to discuss his descent from highest-paid athlete on earth (displacing the soccer great Pele) to skid-row alcoholic.[4] Sanderson's travails, along with the stardom-to-sot chronicles of successful people such as Jason Robards, have given me a wonderful point of departure from which to explain how my life's work took shape.

My experience drinking alcohol and spending time in two places where it was served—catering halls and bars—played a central role in helping me understand how success can control, overwhelm, or destroy a person's professional life. In a certain sense, were it not for my questions about the effects of alcohol consumption, I would never have formulated the theory of Supernova Burnout.

FATHER KNOWS BEST, BUT NOT ABOUT BOOZE

Several years before I was legally able to enter a bar, I had my first profound lesson about alcohol. I was roughly fifteen years old, an age when many boys find that the easiest way to endure dateless weekends is by joining a group of guys trying to dull the pain of adolescence by getting drunk. On one such night, after bingeing on a premixed screwdriver concoction that sickened me so completely I was unable to sneak into my home without creating a commotion, I was confronted by my father, who counseled me in furious yet caring terms: "My son, I want only what's best for you. You need to know that only bums get drunk. Men who cannot hold jobs and cannot provide for their families get drunk. I want you to be a success and a good provider. Do you hear me? *Don't be a bum.*"

I never forgot my father's words because, to my chagrin, I was constantly being confronted by data that demonstrated just how wrong his "only bums get drunk" contention was. Out of love and respect for my father, I had to believe there was something valid in what he said, yet it was hard to reconcile that impulse with my first-hand observations of people who were the antitheses of "bums" regularly drinking themselves senseless. Long before I made a formal decision to research the etiology of alcohol abuse among successful people, I was exposed to two more experiences that convinced me of an odd relationship between grabbing life's brass ring and abusing intoxicants. The first of these was tending bar for the labor union that staffed weddings and bar mitzvahs around Long Island.

For those of you who have no idea what it is like to flaunt wealth on Long Island's South Shore, let me describe one of these upper-class celebrations: In addition to six-course meals and limitless liquor for the adults, bar mitzvah parties regularly included diversions for friends of the guest of honor such as pinball machines, rock bands, cartoonists, clowns, and magicians. One cutting-edge gala included a belly dancer. Wedding parties were even more extravagant: Table centerpieces routinely consisted of two dozen long-stemmed roses, multiple bands or orchestras were commonplace, as were outfit changes by the newlyweds and their families. There were both video and still photographers plus, strange as it sounds, extras such as sketch artists and fortune-tellers.

It didn't take long for me to conclude that not only were the folks attending these bacchanalian feasts the antitheses of "bums" but they were, in the aggregate, highly successful pillars of the community. In addition, they marked these festive occasions by getting quite drunk. During the five years I tended bar professionally, I witnessed no fewer than a dozen fistfights between tuxedo-clad combatants, as well as scores of booze-fueled screaming matches between husbands and wives. I was also regularly in a position to talk with these imbibers. But little did I realize until graduate school that the themes these partygoers discussed with me would form the basis of my theory of success-induced substance abuse.

THE CASE OF THE MAUDLIN MODEL

When I graduated from college and ended my bartending career, I began graduate training in psychology at Columbia University. Like most New York natives who return home after years away at school, I availed myself of all the resources the greatest city on earth had to offer, including the opportunity to party whenever I wanted to. A friend of mine was dating a fashion model and, given the amount of disposable income she had to squander, my student status never got in the way of having a good time whenever they invited me to an Italian restaurant near Gramercy Park. Before long the regulars at this hangout—most of whom worked with my friend's girlfriend—began to treat me like the folks at Cheers treated Dr. Frasier Crane. Soon I could claim that I was confidant and counselor to many of the most famous faces in New York City.

By December 1972, my first season as a shrink without portfolio, I experienced what every mental health professional knows well: December is a notoriously depressing month for many reasons, not the least of which are the psychological tensions and stresses associated with Christmas family reunions. Emergency visits to psychiatric counseling centers skyrocket, and psychiatrists find themselves writing more prescriptions for antidepressants than during any other time of the year. And although I had become accustomed to my model "clients" bending my ear while they were drugged out or drunk, I was not prepared for what occurred one evening a week or two before Christmas.

I was relaxing at our hangout when a woman who looked to be on the verge of complete disintegration approached me. My initial thought was that she got drunk to cope with a fear of flying she would have to confront en route to Christmas with the family. On her first attempt to sit next to me, she fell to the floor. After I lifted her to a chair, she slumped down, legs akimbo, and said nothing for more than five minutes. When I finally roused her she greeted me with "Fuck those 'Ludes" and started to ramble about her desperation.

I had never met this woman before, but I discovered that she was one of the more highly compensated models in New York City at the time. Yet despite her wealth, obvious good looks, and innate intelligence, she was despondent. To cope with her psychological pain she resorted to "pill popping," and her drug of choice was the hypnotic-sedative methaqualone, more commonly known as Quaaludes or 'Ludes. Quaaludes were once routinely prescribed to reduce agitation or manage insomnia, but, because of their extraordinary potential for abuse and popularity as a recreational intoxicant, they have long since been banned.

As that gloomy evening wore on and the effects of the drug abated, this woman became more talkative. Emboldened by her desire to share her life experiences with me, I asked her a question that now seems hopelessly naïve: "I don't get it," I said. "You have everything in the world going for you. You make tons of money. You are on everyone's A-list for openings and sold-out events. Men throw themselves at your feet. Yet you seem to be doing everything in your power to destroy yourself. What gives?"

"What gives," she raged, "is the garbage you just spewed. All you see is the outside: My beauty, an accident of my birth, is why you're talking to me. Would you pay attention to a stoned woman who was ugly? And you're so impressed with all the things I have access to, but do you know *me*? Do you look past my face for a *person* inside? *You* have relationships with people, but everyone views me as an *object*. My looks define the 'me' people deal with. What's up is that I want a life but I don't have the guts to cut up my face."

SELF-HANDICAPPING BEHAVIOR

I left New York City, Columbia University, and the crowd at the restaurant for Duke University shortly after that Christmas holiday, but the seeds of my life's work were firmly planted. I had learned that an unbelievably high percentage of extremely successful people—when success is defined in terms of material wealth—threaten their physical health and emotional well-being by using drugs or alcohol in abusive ways. But what purpose could be served by sitting atop the ladder of success and ingesting an intoxicant that will virtually guarantee one's fall? Why do so many people who strive for excellence, recognition, and material rewards ultimately come to resent what got them to their goal?

As I thought about the people I had observed on Long Island and my encounter with the Quaalude-dependent model, I was struck that the major distinction between their experiences of success and, say, the successes that people climbing the ladder experience is activity versus passivity. The model's lament was that she did nothing for what she got. While that was untrue—fashion models endure grueling workdays and must be indefatigable when starting out—those who are best known in the profession "enjoy" agents, handlers, and multiyear contracts that remove the strain from their lives.

Likewise the folks I met at weddings and bar mitzvahs. It occurred to me that the ones who acted out or quarreled at these affairs were the older folks who had made it: Not one of the incidents that had shocked me involved someone younger than thirty. I decided that there had to be some link between success acquired passively and the ennui people sought to relieve through drink or drugs.

The other insight I gleaned from years of questioning the "only bums get drunk" thesis was that there might be a value in substance abuse beyond the high or sense of relief that comes with intoxication. When I thought about the model, I realized that what she wanted was an "escape" from a role she was conscripted to enact because she was beautiful.

The maudlin model I spoke to bore no resemblance to the woman whose face had been gracing the covers of top women's magazines, and who had earlier that fall walked down a runway in Paris wearing designer dresses. This woman was incapable of standing, let alone posing for pictures. What I saw (and heard) her expressing under the influence of Quaaludes was "I'm out . . . but I'm out *because of this drug*." She strategically hedged her bet in life with the help of a mood- and mind-altering drug.

Whenever I thought about that model I was reminded of the comedian Flip Wilson, who at the time had a hit TV show and a huge following. Actually, it was Wilson's signature line, "The devil made me do it" (from the mouth of his character Geraldine), that caught my attention. Geraldine was Wilson's tawdry alter ego, talking trash and doing the stuff the "good" Flip Wilson would never do. The model didn't have a Geraldine line, but Quaaludes unleashed a "devil made me do it" freedom to be contemptuous of her life and the sycophants with whom she regularly came in contact.

The upshot of all my cogitating was the *self-handicapping* theory. It became clear to me that the most problematic aspect of sitting atop the ladder of success—in contrast with climbing to get there—was the unwanted pressure to be "in role" and "onstage" at all times.

Many people are victims of success and of those who reward them beyond their demonstrated abilities or comprehension. The drug-addled model was the prototype of this entrapment: On the one hand, she knew full well that her visage was valuable. On the other hand, she could never comprehend why so many of life's rewards allegedly linked to competence, character, or charisma should come to her because of, in her words, "an accident of birth."

Ultimately I came to two realizations: (1) that success obtained without a clear sense of having tried to achieve it by intentional, skilled, or goal-seeking behavior (for example, by inheriting wealth or being born beautiful) imposes burdensome psychological expectations, and (2) without obvious, clear-cut mechanisms for dealing with those expectations, people will go to great lengths to avoid being embarrassed or shamed by failing to perform as expected unless they can find a way to demonstrate that "the devil made me do it." My self-handicapping theory details why and how people feel the need to protect themselves from the performance pressures born of a favorable but fragile or misunderstood self-image.[5]

At its most fundamental level, self-handicapping theory details a form of strategic self-presentation—putting your best foot forward, so to speak—that, paradoxically, involves heightening the likelihood you'll trip yourself up. Self-handicappers set out to cloud judgments of responsibility for any behaviors that may fall short of the expectations others have of them by virtue of their success. Self-handicappers can do this by "embracing" external agents (alcohol, drugs, handcuffs, a ball and chain) known to inhibit skilled performance or encumber rational thinking. Once under the influence of these agents, self-handicappers have an excuse for failure.

NONCONTINGENT SUCCESS IN THE LAB

Inspired by this formulation to demonstrate the lengths people would go to escape unreasonable performance expectations, I set out to create in a laboratory setting the discomfort that the New York City fashion model endured from an ostensibly favorable "accident of birth." In a series of experiments I conducted at Duke University, undergraduate students were recruited for a bogus investigation of two drugs alleged to affect intellectual performance.[6] Subjects were told that to determine if the presumed side effects were real, they would take two forms of a very challenging intelligence test separated by the ingestion of one of the drugs. They would get their choice of drug: one that purportedly facilitated intellectual performance (Actival) or one, modeled after the effects of alcohol (Pandocrin), that purportedly disrupted intellectual functioning. The reason given for having subjects take two tests—one drug-free and one under the influence—was to determine if the presumed effects of the drugs were real. In truth, my aim was to determine if the effects of noncontingent success—the kind of success experienced by the maudlin model—could be produced in a laboratory and prove to be disturbing to normal subjects.

Contingent (ability-derived) versus noncontingent success was established by creating two similar-looking but quite distinct test batteries. While all questions were of the same type (comparable to the Scholastic Aptitude Test [SAT] verbal aptitude and analogy questions), one battery was composed of 80 percent soluble and 20 percent insoluble questions, while the other was 80 percent insoluble and only 20 percent soluble. Regardless of which test battery they received, all subjects were told the same thing after their pre-drug-ingestion test: "Congratulations. You got the highest score to date among Duke students." Thus, 50 percent of the subjects, those in the contingent success condition, were overjoyed by the feedback they received. Not so the students in the noncontingent success condition. They doubted their capacity to replicate their success since it was a function of factors not under their control.

The measure of subjects' tendency to self-handicap was reflected in their selection of either the facilitative or the disruptive drug immediately after being told how successful they were on their first test. As predicted, roughly 67 percent of the males who received noncontingent success feedback elected to receive the performance-inhibiting drug, while males who received contingent success feedback selected this drug less than 20 percent of the time. Females never manifested a propensity to engage in self-handicapping behavior in my original research or in dozens of studies that expanded the paradigm. While it is now accepted that self-handicapping theory demonstrates that "seemingly successful persons, who lack obvious financial or interpersonal problems, may be at risk for alcohol problems if they perceive that past successes were due to non-ability factors,"[7] women are clearly not as prone to using this coping strategy as men are. In Chapter 5 we will examine this and other so-called sex differences in reaction to the expectations born of success.

SUPERSTARS SUFFERING FROM SUCCESS

Shortly after I completed the original self-handicapping experiments, I moved to Harvard Medical School to pursue postdoctoral training and develop a psychotherapy practice. One of my hospital supervisors was intrigued with my model of success-induced alcoholism and began referring to me VIP patients who seemed to fit the paradigm. Before long I was treating scores of people with proven competence and a shared symptom—success that not only failed to inoculate them against psychological distress but seemed to precipitate, or at least exacerbate, emotional distress. I soon determined that it was time for a broader investigation of the myriad forms of disease linked with, or caused by, success.

THE BOYS IN THE BAND

A major boost to my development of an expanded theory of problems born of success occurred when a Los Angeles–based rock band hired me to help with their cocaine abuse problems. It soon became clear to me that not one member of the band was self-handicapping with cocaine. Their lament wasn't "No one loves us as people" or "We fear we can't live up to the expectations of our fans," their problem was just the opposite. They were distressed by the realization (conveyed by the drummer) that "we could go on stage, barf, sing 'Mary Had a Little Lamb' off key, and leave, and the kids would go wild. It's no fun anymore. Groupies could care less about which one of us they have sex with as long as they get to brag that they bagged a 'name.' "

While in technical terms the group's success was contingent upon their continued performance, it never felt that way to them since the *quality* of their work was irrelevant. What caused their psychological malaise was that they had reached the top of their profession, looked around them, and fallen victim, collectively it seemed, to a massive case of ennui. During my second meeting with them I asked the lead singer, "So it's like you struggled to get here and are now forced to ask, 'Is that all there is,' right?" He replied, "If you can cure that, Doc, you can join the band."

While I didn't actually cure the band's despondency, I did offer several suggestions to reinvigorate their careers. But they helped me as much as I helped them by alerting me to an epidemic of depression, melancholy, and, in extreme instances, self-destructive behavior that ensues from being trapped by success in an unstimulating career. From that day forward I was sensitized to view every paradoxical early retirement, abrupt resignation, or unanticipated termination from a high-powered job as similar to what this band had suffered.

Then Michael Jordan shocked the world of professional sports by announcing that after leading the Chicago Bulls to their third consecutive NBA championship, he was hanging up his Nikes. When I read about Jordan's decision, another component of my theory of success-induced disorders began to crystallize.

MICHAEL JORDAN'S SUPERNOVA BURNOUT

At the start of his career with the Chicago Bulls, long before he attained superstar status, Michael Jordan was playing in an off-season, recreational game of basketball when he injured himself. Concerned that they would lose their "franchise" player, the Bulls management sought to keep Jordan from playing recreational games. This constraint so incensed Jordan that he fought for, and won, a right to play clause in his contract, giving him complete control over if, when, and where he could indulge in his labor of love.

In the fall of 1993, despite the fact that he was still unabashedly in love with the game, Jordan retired from professional basketball. He maintained that his decision to retire was a highly personal one stemming, primarily, from the pain generated by the murder of his father earlier that year. But the public doubted this explanation. Conventional wisdom held that Jordan had problems with gambling and that the NBA told him unless he "retired" in glory, he would be suspended and forced into rehabilitation. While this view had supporters, I maintained that there was a far more compelling explanation for Jordan's inexplicable career move: Michael Jordan still loved the *game of basketball,* but he quit *professional basketball* because he was suffering from *Supernova Burnout.*[8]

I define Supernova Burnout as a psychological disorder that results when a competent person who is, or could be, successful in a professional arena experiences a state of chronic trepidation, distress, despondency, or depression attributable to the belief that he is trapped in a job, or on a career path, from which he can neither escape nor derive psychological gratification. Because of their malaise and angst, people who suffer Supernova Burnout often engage in what psychologists call acting-out or escapist behaviors: substance abuse, abandonment of families or careers, and, in extreme circumstances, self-destructive behavior. While Supernova Burnout typically affects people at or near midlife, sufferers can be young or old provided they have experienced significant success.

Supernova Burnout is easily differentiated from the typical form of burnout described in modern psychiatric textbooks.[9] Generic burnout is well known to the military; in their parlance it is battle fatigue. Characterized by exhaustion and a sense of futility, burnout is regularly accompanied by anger or contempt for others: anger at having to follow directives (but not being able to strike back), contempt for those one is fighting to help yet no longer truly cares about (a symptom also prevalent among social service workers).

Given the antisocial symptoms of burnout, the military dealt with this disorder by maximizing the group support available to troops in combat while giving them access to recreation and relaxation as often as possible. Their reasoning was that feeling appreciated and receiving the emotional support of comrades would boost soldiers' morale, help them identify with the cause they were fighting for, and foster the belief that risking their lives was worthwhile.

Is the same true for Supernova Burnout? Yes and no. Victims of Supernova Burnout feel denied emotional support but not because people have pulled away from them. Quite the contrary; those who experience Supernova Burnout feel that other people are encroaching upon them, or, in an extreme sense, using them like a "tool" by demanding that they fulfill performance expectations or sustain previously achieved levels of success.

Strange as it sounds, my take on Michael Jordan's Supernova Burnout was that his success *deprived* him of the emotional support he needed to go into battle year after year as a professional basketball player. Yet Jordan wasn't angry at anyone in particular. If you analyze any superstar's life circumstances, it is immediately apparent that, paradoxically, a history of achievement does nothing to inoculate a person against self-esteem damage. In fact, when a person perceives that she has something (status, acclaim) to lose after having succeeded, evaluations of ability are typically more threatening than when he or she was a novice.

The intense threats to self-esteem suffered by successful people evolve logically: Until a person demonstrates competence, there can be no legitimate basis for forming an expectation of how he will perform at a given task. Yet once a person achieves a level of proficiency, that "level" becomes the baseline against which someone can determine how well he has performed. Unfavorable performance expectations can always be revised upward, but favorable expectations resist downward adjustments.

This dilemma can become particularly acute in professional life. We are intolerant of any work product that falls short of expectations set by a person's previous "best effort" because we know "she can do it if she puts her mind to it." The notion that in an organization you are only as good as your last achievement is psychologically sound. A history of success heightens performance pressure by generating the expectation that a performer will meet or exceed past levels of achievement. In fact, merely to keep pace with the standards he has generated, a successful performer must either constantly improve or be judged wanting.

Michael Jordan certainly had a great deal to lose in terms of self-esteem after being credited with leading the Chicago Bulls to a championship, a repeat championship, and then a "threepeat" in successive years. Given this record and its resulting expectations for ongoing achievement, it would have been reasonable for anyone—including Jordan himself—to anticipate a "fourpeat" as business as usual, had he elected to remain with the Bulls following his threepeat season. In fact, *failure* to achieve an encore might have generated more notice than another championship, which, regardless of how difficult it was to achieve, would likely have elicited a been-there-done-that reaction.

Because he was in an everything to lose, nothing to gain predicament following the Bulls' threepeat, and because he would be unable to *gain* psychological rewards unless he met or exceeded the expectations born of his history of success, Jordan's decision to quit while he was ahead can be seen as an adaptive career move. Had he not retired when he did, Jordan would have been subjected to extraordinary performance pressures guaranteed to generate threats to his self-esteem. Whatever psychological damage he may have suffered from his untimely retirement, it was far less than he would have endured had he failed to live up to his reputation.

THE TWO FACES OF STRESS

The final issue that I saw bedeviling Michael Jordan as he looked forward to a fourpeat season was that it must have become extremely difficult for him to view basketball as a *game*. Rather than being an activity that he "played" like a child during recess, professional basketball must have become for him a monotonous job. When psychologists describe what's missing from repetitive tasks that provide few, if any, rewarding results, they often note that these activities fail to provide *eustress*, the "good stress" derived from stimulating circumstances or challenges.

Eustress—in contrast to distress, which has come to be known simply as stress—is necessary for both physical and mental health. The mind needs to be actively stimulated with inputs from the external world or it will create its own stimulation through dreams, fantasies, or, if need be, hallucinations. Performing a skilled activity you have mastered in an environment that is wholly familiar can block stimulation and the experience of eustress almost as effectively as blindfolds, earplugs, and swaddling block out sensory stimulation. If you're a golfer, imagine playing the same hole for life. The feeling would be more akin to the torment suffered by Sisyphus pushing his boulder up a mountain for eternity than to the challenge experienced by Tiger Woods putting for a championship at the eighteenth hole at Pebble Beach.

Striving for success captures the essence of play, whereas *sustaining* success is work, pure and simple. A person who strives for success has an opportunity to continually reaffirm her self-worth, whereas a person sustaining success has no such thing. When you strive for success, you feel energized, alert, and activated because you can see yourself adding value to an entity or enterprise that has yet to realize its full potential. In contrast, when you sustain a successful endeavor or enterprise, you are likely to experience ennui or depression because you are forced to wonder, "What is the purpose of this work or my life, if all I am doing is amassing money like a mercenary?" This is one of the major reasons success can make a person feel trapped when, to all external appearances, he is sitting on top of the world.

What's lost on those who envy successful professionals is the fact that success marks an ending and, in a very real way, a loss—a loss of challenge, purpose, or inspiration. Most achievement-oriented people will tell you that the pursuit of a goal—the hunt, as many call it—is what puts the passion into any career or business. Once a goal has been reached, many formerly enthusiastic professionals suffer aimlessness or lethargy born of looking for an objective to pursue when none is in sight.

MICHAEL JORDAN'S "CURE"

As most everyone knows, Michael Jordan un-retired from professional basketball eighteen months after he had quit and endured a somewhat embarrassing stint in major league baseball. During his first half season back in the NBA, Jordan was not a dominant player. Yet when the following season arrived, he was back in form, ready to propel the Chicago Bulls again to three consecutive championships. I believe Jordan was able to reenergize himself and, ultimately, once again perform in the manner he and the world had come to expect because of the way he cured his case of Supernova Burnout.

When he returned to professional basketball out of shape and out of practice, Jordan's performance expectations were lowered dramatically. One could say that the rustiness he suffered during his layoff was the condition best suited to protect his self-esteem. You see, all Jordan-handicapped-by-a-layoff had to do was play nearly as well as he once did and judgments of his competence would soar. Good performances were greeted by "Look what he overcame to do that" rather than "That's Michael."

While lowering performance expectations got the proverbial monkey off Jordan's back—he no longer had to live up to his press clippings because they were out-of-date—this addressed only part of what had caused his Supernova Burnout. The other impetus was a need to rekindle the passion that drove him to achieve. How was Jordan able to put the eustress back into a game that, presumably, had become ho-hum? By enacting a drug-free self-handicapping strategy that involved tying a proverbial hand behind his back.

Under the performance-inhibiting influence of a year away from the NBA, Jordan was a mortal slugging it out with other mortals. Handicapped by his lack of physical conditioning, he eliminated the Goliath versus David disparities he previously had with competitors. And rather than his "descent to earth" proving problematic, just the opposite occurred. Basketball was fun again, and he was able to boost his self-esteem when he played because there were impediments to conquer and goals to reach.

In summary, Michael Jordan's initial *strategic* retirement from basketball accomplished two psychological objectives: It lowered performance expectations while raising the personal challenge available to him. It would appear, then, that all anyone needs to do when he feels depressed about a been-there-done-that routine is move on to a new challenge. Would that it were so simple, especially for those of us without the obvious talents of Michael Jordan.

RECLAIMING THE FIRE: THE LEGEND OF PROMETHEUS

In Greek mythology Prometheus was one of the Titans, a race of gods who inhabited the earth before the creation of man. When the Olympians (other gods) fought the Titans, Prometheus sided with Zeus (who wanted to be chief of the gods) to help the residents of Olympus prevail. After the war was won Zeus gave Prometheus and his brother the job of re-creating all the living creatures—animals and man—killed during the war. Providing them with the faculties necessary for their preservation fell upon Prometheus, who wanted to ensure that man would be superior to all the animals. Prometheus determined that if man could have some of the sacred fire from Mount Olympus, his survival and superiority would be guaranteed.

According to legend, Zeus forbade it, claiming, "The fire is for the gods alone." Yet Prometheus could not bear to see his creations shivering in the cold and eating raw meat, so he stole fire from the gods and gave it to man. What made the theft worse than a mere defiance of Zeus's command was that the gift of fire did more than help man reign supreme on earth; it unleashed a flood of creativity, productivity, and, worst of all from Zeus's perspective, the emergence of culture and literacy among mortals.

As punishment for his defiance Prometheus was chained to a crag atop Mount Caucasus where he was helpless against the elements and Zeus's ultimate penalty: an eagle that was sent to tear his flesh and eat his liver every day.

So how do we understand the myth of Prometheus the Fire Bearer? Is it a cautionary tale about how masochistic it is to defy the supreme god? A pessimistic view of the fate that befalls altruists? A warning that the gods can be disdainful? I believe it is a morality tale about an idealistic Greek god who gave human beings the attribute—fire—that has enabled us to achieve self-fulfillment.

I see the fire Prometheus gave man as the energy that fuels psychological development and self-reliance. No wonder Prometheus's largesse angered Zeus; it gave us the passion to be creative. Prometheus's gift of fire transformed man from an automaton to an entity able to transcend Zeus's design for him. Fire made man efficacious. Thus, I would argue, Prometheus is the prototype of the defiant and ambitious individual who refuses to submit to the status quo and, instead, exercises will. Among the Olympians he was the enfant terrible who didn't merely march to the beat of a different drummer but formed an orchestra and gave them the wherewithal to perform however they pleased.

All achievers are like Prometheus when they first dream of success. The soul of Prometheus resides in the entrepreneur tinkering in a laboratory or Silicon Valley garage, convinced that he can build that better mousetrap. The same spirit resided within Wilma Rudolph, who, despite being crippled at birth, dreamed of running faster than any woman alive. Prometheus's gift of fire burned within Chuck Yeager when he broke the sound barrier. Why, then, would the Greek mythologists condemn Prometheus to suffer for his defiance of the status quo and for envisioning a change for the better? Marcus Aurelius cautioned, "Be satisfied with success in even the smallest matter, and think that even such a result is no trifle." Was Prometheus's sin that he didn't settle for the small success? Was he, like Icarus, damned for daring to fly too high? Was it hubris that led to Prometheus's entrapment and torture?

Yes to all of the above, and more. *Reclaiming the Fire* is about the men and women who begin life like Prometheus and find themselves—typically without knowing why—chained to a career crag. Using my laboratory research findings and clinical case studies to illustrate the symptoms of Supernova Burnout, this book will explain why, after Prometheans hit Olympian heights, they can become trapped in psychological chains that sap them of the vital energy—the fire—they need to derive pleasure from their work.

Although I have drawn parallels between Supernova Burnout and the fate suffered by Prometheus, it is important not to confuse the two. People who suffer Supernova Burnout do not necessarily defy the powers that be or consciously expose themselves to punishment. Instead, many modern Prometheans get imprisoned by their stellar careers for all the "right" reasons: social approval, the desire to provide for family, the belief that staying the course is constructive. Others are victims of the consequences of attaining the goals they have set for themselves because success generates incessant demands for more and better successes.

In addition to introducing you to the causes of and cures for Supernova Burnout, *Reclaiming the Fire* will help you understand the Prometheans among us, hold a mirror up to you if you are a Titan, and show you how to escape from, or prevent, the fate of those who achieve heroic successes only to suffer horrendous pain. George Bernard Shaw, the playwright who adroitly escaped a business career that threatened to choke the creative spirit out of him, once remarked, "The people who get on in this world are the people who get up and look for the circumstances they want, and, if they can't find them, make them."

Reclaiming the Fire is designed to help people prevent the achievement of lifelong ambitions, or dream jobs and vocations, from causing debilitating psychological disorders. To this end I will examine a range of problems attributable to success and describe how to prevent or cure them. Yet a precursor to being inoculated against the disease-causing consequences of success is familiarity with the dangers inherent in an uncritical acceptance of the myths surrounding success. *Reclaiming the Fire* was written with that goal as well.

John Steinbeck wrote, "Money's easy to make if it's money you want. But with few exceptions people don't want money. They want luxury and they want love and they want admiration." That's the lesson I learned from those successful people who got drunk, became addicted to Quaaludes, or threw away what appeared to be ideal careers when at the top of their game. Permit me to show you how right Steinbeck was and, in the process, suggest strategies that will enable you to structure your professional life in a manner that will afford you the opportunity to achieve personal and social admiration for as long as you care to.

CHAPTER 2

Success Depression and Encore Anxiety

In the world there are only two tragedies.
One is not getting what one wants, and the
other is getting it.

—OSCAR WILDE

The toughest thing about success is that
you've got to keep on being a success.

—IRVING BERLIN

What is success? Most all of us claim to know success when we see it, but there is little consensus about what the term means. In 1986 I published a book that devoted two chapters to trying to define success, and I doubt that I exhausted the nuances of meaning this cornerstone of the American dream conveys.[1] My primary concern in creating this definition was to differentiate between successful people and those who are merely rich.

Since certain career paths (for instance, academia) pay significantly less than others (for instance, investment banking), it would be inappropriate to suggest, for example, that a world-renowned historian earning $200,000 a year is less successful than a mediocre investment banker earning $1 million. Thus, according to the definition I advanced in 1986, to be considered a success a person must derive both rewards and superior ranking from goal-directed behavior.[2] If you set out to do something, get ranked number 1, and receive public confirmation of that deed, you have succeeded.

An astute observer will instantly note that something is missing from this definition. At the time I constructed it, yuppiedom was sweeping the nation, Masters of the Universe were idolized, and Reaganomics had people believing that there soon would be a Mercedes in every garage and a Rolex on every wrist. And although the economic boom our nation has enjoyed since then seems destined to continue, a change in attitude has swept across America. Today people are amassing more wealth and enjoying it less than ever. Moreover, it is apparent that the commonly held views in America regarding what success is, and what it should do for someone, are in need of a radical overhaul.

In a survey conducted at the University of Michigan, when respondents were asked to indicate what would improve the quality of their lives, the most frequent response was "more money."[3] Yet correlational studies show that although the after-tax personal income of Americans more than doubled between 1960 and 1990, the percentage of people describing themselves as "very happy" remained constant, at 30 percent.[4] Furthermore, a study of some of the wealthiest individuals in the United States found that their level of happiness barely exceeds that of individuals with average incomes.[5]

Unfortunately, these statistics are known to only a handful of academics, and the notion that SUCCESS = MATERIAL WEALTH = HAPPINESS is prevalent throughout our nation. Americans have an unwavering belief that there is inherent worth in beating the competition and becoming number 1. We are a consumer society, so we also share a strong propensity to see correlations between accumulative behavior and self-worth. For some, "whoever has the most toys when he dies, wins" is the preeminent definition of American success. Others must have concrete proof of where they stand in a hierarchy.

Americans are obsessed with lists of "bests" and "worsts," including the Fortune 500, *Forbes*'s 400, even Mr. Blackwell's worst dressed list. But to get to the bottom-line definition of success most Americans carry around, we need to recall the quotation attributed to the football coach Vince Lombardi: "Winning isn't everything, it's the *only* thing." A cornerstone of our collective unconscious is that winners will receive both wealth and all the self-adulation and interpersonal adulation this world can afford.

These definitions of success, however, fail to address the fundamental concern of this book: the linkage—or, more accurately, presumed linkage—between success and subjective well-being. For most Americans success appears to be an end in its own right. It is the only outcome, as Christopher Lasch noted, that in and of itself has the capacity to instill a sense of self-approval.[6] Thus, it would make sense for us to define success in operational terms that include not only rewards and superior ranking but also purported effects on self-image. The key, once again, is the term *purported*. Research has shown that although people anticipate that rankings and rewards will give them the good and happy life, this is not necessarily so. In fact, success often gives rise to a host of feelings that are anything but what achievement-oriented people bargained for.

Sigmund Freud treated several patients who suffered mightily as a consequence of attaining long-sought-after goals. Their disorders shocked him since his psychoanalytic theory was based on the assumption that people "fall ill" with mental disorders as a result of not being able to satisfy their libidinal (sexual, aggressive) drives. He wrote:

> So much the more surprising, indeed bewildering, must it appear when as a physician one makes the discovery that people occasionally fall ill precisely because a deeply-rooted and long-cherished wish has come to fulfillment. It seems as though they could not endure their bliss, for of the causative connection between this fulfillment and the falling-ill there can be no question.[7]

SUCCESS DEPRESSION

Given Lasch's observation that Americans believe success can infuse those who achieve it with feelings of self-esteem and self-approval, it is no wonder that after Mark Lenzi won a gold medal in the three-meter springboard diving competition at the 1992 Barcelona Olympics he thought he had it made. According to press reports, Lenzi believed that winning a gold medal would guarantee him a lifetime of solicitations for product endorsements, motivational speeches, and charity golf tournaments.[8] Instead, he found himself lying in his bed in Ann Arbor, Michigan, sobbing. "It just hit me like a brick wall," he said.[9] The "it" was a form of success-induced depression that athletes call post-Olympic depression.

Post-Olympic depression involves intense disappointment with the experiences that follow what was expected to be a life-altering event. While it can affect any professional, this disorder is particularly prevalent among those who have career tracks with end points, goals, or criteria for advancement that differentiate between those who have made it and those who have not. Why are people whose careers impose structured ranking systems so vulnerable to success depression? Because they follow an internal script that says, "Once I attain X, my life will be set," but when they attain the X, they find out otherwise.

On his ninetieth birthday, Supreme Court Justice Oliver Wendell Holmes, Jr., gave a radio address in which he shared his thoughts about avoiding the type of depression (without using psychiatric nomenclature) Mark Lenzi suffered:

> The riders in a race do not stop short when they reach the goal. There is a little finishing canter before coming to a standstill. There is time to hear the kind voice of friends and to say to one's self: "The work is done." But just as one says that, the answer comes: "The *race* is over,

but the work remains." The canter that brings you to a standstill need not be only coming to rest. It cannot be while you still live. *For to live is to function. That is all there is in living* [emphasis added].

As survey research and Justice Holmes's insight demonstrate, not only is reaching a benchmark no guarantee of psychological satisfaction but it is more likely to be a source of psychological pain. The end point of a quest such as a race or an Olympic competition is just that: an ending. As everyone who has ever aspired to attain a goal will tell you, when you succeed but no longer have a raison d'être, it feels like something inside you has died. To address that feeling, ask one or both of the following questions:

1. What do I do for an encore?
2. What do I do next?

The first question often arouses feelings that I have dubbed *encore anxiety*—the fear of not being able to live up to the performance expectations you have generated. The second question typically induces depression because it can imply that there is nowhere left to go. Let's first examine the pain of some who succeeded without preparing for the future as Justice Holmes counseled.

FROM *WHO'S WHO* TO WHO'S THAT?

Try to imagine a day in the life of Mark Lenzi as the 1992 Olympics drew near. Based upon anecdotes of the professional athletes I have treated for success depression, I am certain that in the months and weeks before the Barcelona games Lenzi engaged in daily workouts to keep the physical conditioning he had worked years to achieve, made scores of practice dives, and endured endless critiques from coaches. At the end of a grueling day of preparation, it is a virtual certainty that Lenzi enjoyed the feeling known as runner's high, the bodily sensations that occur when natural painkillers called endorphins are secreted into the bloodstream. This phenomenon is called a high because it is said to mimic drug-induced states of euphoria, but, since it is natural, an endorphin rush is purportedly much more mellow.

Fast-forward to Lenzi's big day: Epinephrine (the natural version of Adrenalin) is coursing through his veins, causing his heart to pump vigorously. But because he's an incredibly well-conditioned athlete—psychologically as well as physically—he knows to label his accelerated heartbeats as signals of anticipation, not anxiety. Yet, try as he might, there are also butterflies in his stomach. He visualizes himself executing a flawless forward three-and-a-half somersault in a pike position but, for brief moments, he must also drive out fears of belly flopping rather than executing a rip entry—hitting the water with the minimum amount of splash possible. And then the time comes: Lenzi dives "for real" and wins the gold. He has just battled and bested an international field of competitors plus his internal anxieties and has scored a perfect 10. If this achievement can't instill a sense of self-approval, nothing can.

To understand what went wrong in Lenzi's life subsequent to the Olympics we must contrast the intense stimuli he was exposed to en route to his gold medal with the paucity of stimulation he received upon returning home. Training for the Olympics gave Lenzi self-esteem gains (accrued from improving his craft) and purpose (to enhance personal pride and patriotism) as well as those endorphin highs. Back home? No chance to enhance self-esteem (there are no Olympic platinum or diamond-studded medals to pursue), no endorphin rushes since there was no grueling training, and, after having kept an Olympic medal in your sights for over a decade, it is hard to find value in merely recounting the event.

Lenzi's dream that an Olympic gold medal would have favorable consequences was not dashed immediately: He appeared on the talk-show circuit with Jay Leno and Regis and Kathie Lee. But because these appearances forced him to discuss merely what he *had done*, it is easy to understand why Lenzi soon retreated to the protection afforded by his bed.

Try to put yourself inside the head of Mark Lenzi as Kathie Lee gushed, "Wow, Mark; scoring a perfect 'ten'; you were great." "Were great" means back then, not now. Saying, "You *were* great," implies that "has been" is on the horizon. Or, as Walter Wriston once remarked, "When you retire you go from *Who's Who* to who's that?" This depression-generating edge of the double-edged sword known as success is one of the dominant reasons people suffer Supernova Burnout after attaining a goal.

THE ENTREPRENEURIAL EXPERIENCE

Since the early 1990s our culture has become obsessed with entrepreneurs. One indicator of this preoccupation is how the magazine industry has attempted to court these heroes of the new millennium: New ventures such as *Fast Company, Entrepreneur,* and *Business 2.0* have sprung up to compete with the stalwarts *Inc.* and *Success.* The traditional voices of big business, like *Fortune, Forbes,* and *Business Week,* haven't exactly abandoned their long-standing readership, but they have all added sections devoted to the concerns of entrepreneurs. Business schools across the nation are retooling to offer courses that teach aspiring moguls how to build, manage, and ultimately sell the better mousetrap they designed. I now teach a course entitled "Psychology of the Entrepreneurial Spirit" at UCLA's Anderson Graduate School of Management. A decade ago most deans would have laughed me out of their offices if I'd proposed an offering of this sort. Today such courses attract standing-room-only crowds.

Unfortunately for entrepreneurs, being the focus of hero worship comes with a cost: One subset of entrepreneurs, commonly referred to as dot-com millionaires, has spawned an industry of millionaire wanna-bes intent upon finding a shortcut to the lifestyle that Silicon Valley VIPs are alleged to enjoy. Their tactics include vying to appear on Regis Philbin's *Who Wants to Be a Millionaire* or poring over bestsellers like *The Millionaire Next Door,* but rarely have these idolaters looked beneath the surface of life as a dot-com millionaire to get a clear picture of what such a life is all about. Had they bothered, they would have discovered that among those who have reaped untold profits from the information technology revolution, things are not always peaches and cream.

For example, a group of enterprising mental health professionals in San Francisco have set up a clinic to treat patients suffering the psychiatric disorder du jour, *sudden wealth syndrome,* which, in truth, is not new at all.[10] Yet every time our nation comes face to face with a flood of nouveau riche twenty-year-olds who are discontented despite their money (remember the yuppies?), a psychotherapeutic market niche gets carved out. The only thing new about the wave of baby boomers and their kids who have money to burn is how many of them are voicing displeasure with their lot in life despite having seized what is allegedly the American dream.

Long before the term "sudden wealth syndrome" was coined, Mitch Kapor discovered that taking a business from the drawing board to stellar success at warp speed is not necessarily a fairy tale with a happy ending. As founder and former CEO of Lotus Development Corp., Kapor earned his way to the top of the information technology hierarchy by building a business with a market value of more than $275 million in less than five years. Yet, to the bewilderment of many, he left Lotus soon after completing that feat; as he told *Inc.* magazine, "My ultimate departure was part of a conscious plan . . . aimed at extricating myself from my own success."[11]

More specifically, Kapor acknowledged that the aspect of his success most closely associated with his departure was suffering from promotions to a level of management that deprived him of the activities he loved: "[During the start-up phase] at Lotus, I was really good at working one-to-one with people . . . but in the intermediate stage, where you're attempting to run an organization that consists of a mass of people . . . I'm just not very good at that. I don't have the patience for it. I'm too proactive to just let other people work stuff out for themselves and just give a little nudge here and a little shove there."[12]

There should be no mystery as to why the conclusion of Mitch Kapor's meteoric rise to success had a negative impact on his psychological well-being. Psychologists have demonstrated that when a person is deprived of eustress, the "good stress" derived from stimulating circumstances or challenges, he or she will either find alternative routes for generating eustress or suffer intense psychological pain.

Another closely related cause of what (most likely) ailed Kapor is the malaise brought about when success makes a person feel *too safe*. Psychologists and economists have explored the notion that attempting to mandate safeguards in people's lives has a profound psychological boomerang effect. The paradoxical yet empirically validated theory of *risk homeostasis* maintains that the more government creates safety nets for businesses and individuals—the more regulators and court rulings remove threats to our personal and professional safety—the more likely people will seek out the exhilarating feelings of risky activities, enterprises, or investments.[13] Believe it or not, positive levels of risk homeostasis (adding danger) or opportunities for eustress seeking are a need so universally felt it can even affect the health of animals!

In the early 1990s a polar bear from the Central Park Zoo in Manhattan made national headlines because he was starving himself to death. Veterinarians couldn't find dietary solutions for his condition, so animal psychologists were hired to diagnose what ailed him. Their formulation and intervention took a page directly out of the eustress generator's primer: It seems that the polar bear, a notoriously crafty hunter, was bored to death. The most profound source of his angst, according to the animal shrinks, was the fact that his meals were readily available. The psychologists told the zookeepers to hide the bear's food, make him struggle for his reward, feel some threat that he had to surmount. The theory was that if the bear feared for his life and had to be a successful hunter, his passions would be rekindled. The food was hidden and the polar bear thrived.

Could the eustress model and risk homeostasis doctrines explain why founders of billion-dollar businesses like Malcolm Forbes, who raced motorcycles, and Richard Branson, who attempted to set or break hot-air ballooning records, acted as though they were bullet-proof? As Americans amass huge cushions of wealth and safety from economic want, there is an unprecedented increase in so-called extreme sports, such as skydiving, bungee jumping, off-road motorcycle racing, and mountain climbing. This trend suggests that the toll of being denied a healthy level of eustress is a drastic increase in attempts to quash feelings of ennui with daredevil endeavors or worse.

WHEN YOUR WORK IS DONE

The preceding discussion is in no way an indictment of the pursuit of success. On the contrary. Myriad health benefits can be derived from achieving CEO status and exploiting that accomplishment to the fullest extent. Yet this fact poses a profound risk: Many Americans are caught up in the myth that steering a business through its developmental stages is health-threatening and fail to grasp that owning a business that virtually runs itself is typically detrimental to one's health. The prevailing wisdom still holds that too much work endangers health and that retirement is the proper end to an arduous career.

Don't tell that to the family of George Eastman, cofounder of the photographic products giant Eastman Kodak. On the verge of his opportunity to live a life of ease away from the demands of the billion-dollar company he built, Eastman committed suicide. The note he left on his desk, where he lay after putting a bullet in his head, read, "My work is done, why wait?" In 1997, after writing an *Inc.* column that described Eastman's suicide in the lead paragraph, I received dozens of letters from entrepreneurs who could identify with the pain of knowing that the work that drove them toward a goal day and night for years was over.[14] Several of these letters came from entrepreneurs who had built businesses that reached Inc. 500 status only to discover that the fun, joy, or eustress of their professional life had vanished. One writer said that the pain he endured after taking his company public, assuming the chairman's role, and leaving day-to-day operations to his chief operating officer (while he tooled around in a new Porsche) was "divine retribution for my haughtiness."

One entrepreneur I treated for success depression likened building a business from the ground up to a cattle drive. From his perspective, rounding up the resources he needed, dealing with staff defections (strays), and battling the hostile terrain of the marketplace was equivalent to the travails depicted in the rain-soaked pilgrimage for cows that Billy Crystal engineered as trail boss in the movie *City Slickers*. By contrast, the daily routine of J. R. Ewing of *Dallas*, whose character must have been drawn by writers familiar with the pathologies born of excess wealth and no eustress, more closely resembled watching dairy cows amble from the barn to the pasture and back. Absent market turmoil or natural disaster, a Texas oil baron's day typically poses few threats, few challenges, and, as a consequence, few opportunities for self-esteem gain. J.R. may have been only a TV character, but in my clinical experience turmoil generation is a preferred mode of coping with ennui among once powerful entrepreneurial executives sent out to pasture well before they felt their time had come.

ENTREPRENEURIAL ARSONISTS

Most patients of mine who've suffered success depression tell me that in contrast to the starts of their careers, when both elation and dejection were regular occurrences, life at the top was like being trapped in a sensory deprivation chamber. Recall that the mind needs to be stimulated with inputs from the external world or it will create stimulation of its own. A series of experiments that involved placing subjects in a stimulus-proof chamber after dressing them in eyeshades, earplugs, and body swaddling showed that within hours their minds were racing and, in some cases, generating hallucinatory images comparable to those induced by LSD.[15]

I have no data on how many CEOs use mind-altering drugs as an antidote to the sensory deprivation caused by success, but I am quite familiar with some who, rather than popping pills to jump-start their minds, created turmoil in their businesses. While this may sound implausible, I have coached over two dozen entrepreneurs turned CEOs for a syndrome that I call *entrepreneurial arson*.[16] Bored-witless CEOs intentionally created problems (metaphorically, set fires) at their smooth-running businesses so they would be called into the thick of things to help douse the "flames."

With no offense intended to the brave men and women who choose police work or firefighting as their vocation, it is not uncommon to find individuals among these public servants who commit crimes such as arson. Somewhere in the consciousness of these people lies the hope that they can be first on the scene of the disaster they create, positioned to save the day and, they imagine, be treated like the heroes they long to be.

The widespread recognition of this disordered pattern of behavior led the FBI, using a methodology called criminal profiling, to focus on Richard Jewell as the prime suspect in the July 27, 1996, bombing that took place in Centennial Olympic Park in Atlanta, Georgia, during the Olympic Games.[17] Although the bureau routinely investigates the person who reports a crime, there were additional reasons for considering Jewell a suspect: He demonstrated a propensity for being a "police groupie" chronically looking for action and recognition. Although Jewell was ultimately cleared of wrongdoing, the psychological basis for this profiling technique has validity. For example, at the 1984 Olympic Games in Los Angeles, the police officer who found a bomb on a bus carrying Turkish athletes turned out to be the person who had planted it.

The fires that entrepreneurial arsonists set almost always involve generating interpersonal conflicts, as J. R. Ewing did on *Dallas*. The reason entrepreneurial arsonists ignite interpersonal controversies rather than, say, gumming up the works of their businesses is that overt acts of sabotage are fairly transparent, the functional equivalents of hurling Molotov cocktails in broad daylight. Planting seeds of conflict in an organization, family, or industry is another story. A criticism (attributed to a third party) here, a bit of slander (again, merely being passed along from another source) there, and before you know it a well-knit, smooth-running workplace is divided into armed camps that need a peacekeeper—the entrepreneur-founder—to quell civil unrest.

In fairness, most entrepreneurial arsonists I've worked with harbored no malevolent feelings; all they wanted was to cause (and cure) as much disruption to the businesses they built as possible. Some were so tragic in the roles of outsiders yearning to be needed that I nicknamed a subtype of vulnerable entrepreneurial arsonists Wizards of Oz.

As you know from the screen version of this story, the myth was that the Wizard of Oz was omnipotent. Only when he was revealed as a flawed mortal was the Wizard able to help Dorothy and her friends. Scratch the surface of most eustress-deprived entrepreneurial arsonists and you will find vulnerable people intent upon intimidating others rather than allowing their feelings of impotence to be exposed. Ben Franklin perceptively noted, "The empty barrel makes the most noise." What lock far too many competent people in positions of status from which they derive no satisfaction are societal expectations of what "the good life" consists of. Yet despite all the myths about how grand it is at the top, entrepreneurial arsonists create turmoil, and Wizards of Oz bully, all for want of a face-saving way to segue back into the fray.

There are also people who find the expectations born of success so intimidating that rather than engage in so-called action defenses, as entrepreneurial arsonists do, they leave the field of battle. These people are not immobilized by depression; they get stopped in their tracks because they fear that they cannot continue making the grade.

During the week of July 24, 2000, two entrepreneurial CEOs of noteworthy dot-com companies, Kim Polese of Marimba and Candice Carpenter of iVillage, relinquished control of their companies to professional managers and kicked themselves "upstairs" to chair the companies they had founded.[18] Each CEO turned chairperson noted that her move would allow her to work on strategic initiatives and plan for the company's future—exactly the sorts of things she did when she founded her business. While it is unclear what, if any, anxieties derailed Polese or Carpenter, it is certain that their success kept them from one crucial reward most people presume is the right of those who have succeeded: freedom, the flexibility to do what one wants.

SUCCESS: MORE ACCLAIM, MORE MONEY, FEWER OPTIONS

According to M. Scott Peck, author of the bestselling *Road Less Traveled,* "Success eliminates as many options as does failure." In my experience Peck is correct, but he understates the case. Actually, he understates it twice, once culturally and once psychologically. Let's look first at what our society has done to make achieving success harder than ever before.

Although cross-cultural comparisons are speculative at best, historians maintain that other civilizations afforded a much broader range of options for feeling successful than ours.[19] Recall that in twenty-first-century America being successful entails securing both rewards and superior ranking. Yet in other, particularly ancient Asian cultures, an individual could be considered a success because he was exceptionally altruistic, a wise person, a brave patriot, or a stellar citizen. As the renowned psychologist Mihaly Csikszentmihalyi noted:

> Nowadays the logic of reducing everything to quantifiable measures has made the dollar the common metric by which to evaluate every aspect of human action. The worth of a person and of a person's accomplishments are determined by the price they fetch in the marketplace. It is useless to claim that a painting is good art unless it gets high bids at Sotheby's, nor can we claim that someone is wise unless he or she can charge five figures for a consultation. Given the hegemony of material rewards in our culture's restricted repertoire, it is not surprising that so many people feel that their only hope for a happy life is to amass all the earthly goods they can lay their hands on.[20]

In addition to feeling pressured to accumulate material rewards, people seeking psychological satisfaction from success face a number of stressful demands after demonstrating competence. In particular, to satisfy the ranking component of the definition of success we have employed—the sense that one is number 1 or has been declared the victor in a winner-take-all contest—humans are psychologically hardwired to use what is called a *social comparison process* that imposes a naturally escalating standard of acceptability on achievement.[21] Simply stated, if you are the editor in chief of your high school newspaper, you will not be satisfied with that level of accomplishment for very long because you know that someone holds the title of editor in chief at Harvard College's *Crimson*. Should you attain that level of achievement, you would naturally pursue the editor in chief position at a variety of newspapers and magazines. According to social comparison theory, your climb up the editorial ladder would continue until either you failed or all that was left to achieve was the top spot at *The New York Times*.

Social comparison theory maintains that all of us have a basic need for self-evaluation (to know if we perform well or poorly) but that it is impossible to make that determination in a vacuum. The best way of satisfying this need is comparing one's performances with those of similar individuals. You know that you are a fast runner, for example, if you win a race; you know you are smart by getting the highest score on a test; and so on. The problem caused by this drive, however, is the problem suffered by "the fastest gun in the West": People are always striving to outdraw you so they can measure their success against the best.

Even for those who are not targets of aspiring champions, the theory of relative deprivation poses an impediment to feeling successful. We cannot engage in comparisons with people at our level of competence or below to feel we have succeeded; we must compare ourselves with those above us to derive a full sense of self-worth. The problem today, as Csikszentmihalyi noted, is that because success is wedded to wealth, an otherwise successful person is likely to suffer constant states of relative deprivation if he is not also affluent. Consider how many billionaires feel the need to become public figures or, like Donald Trump, flaunt their wealth in order to attain celebrity status. Relative deprivation is, it seems, a drive that cannot be satiated.

The most harmful consequence of being motivated by social comparison needs directly is the number of alternative rewards lost by striving to remain king of the hill. Sustaining success can become a full-time occupation, leaving little time for pursuits that enhance the social and emotional quality of our lives.[22] Part of the psychology that buttresses a decision to invest all one's psychic energy in an ongoing attempt to be, rather than become, successful is economic. As income and therefore the value of one's time increases, spending time on anything other than making money or spending it conspicuously makes less "business" sense.[23] Once you are successful enough to command top dollar for professional services, the so-called opportunity costs of devoting time to family, friends, or hobbies become too high; an hour with the kids can cost an opportunity to land a new client. Using this equation, how can you rationalize stopping to smell the roses?

It has long been a uniquely American fact of life that attempting to broaden the spectrum of eustress-generating opportunities available from a career is, for lack of a better term, self-destructive. The ultimate payoff lies in doing what you do best, over and over, better and better. Capitalism is built upon Benjamin Franklin's notion that "time is money," and from this perspective careers must be shaped by norms and values that place a premium on maximizing the return obtained from every hour invested in work.

Now commonly referred to as ROI—return on investment—this concept has dominated attitudes toward career paths for over fifty years. A direct consequence is that once you achieve a modicum of success, the demand for encores becomes overwhelming because they yield the greatest ROI. Adding insult to psychological injury is the fact that the organizations we work for and the audiences we perform before attempt to bar successful people from experiencing novel sources of eustress when they have the capacity to contribute ever-increasing ROIs. This inextricable link between succeeding and suffering restricted behavioral options is one of the more obvious causes of Supernova Burnout.

ENCORE! = MORE OF THE SAME

> My mind rebels at stagnation. Give me problems, give me work, give me the most abstruse cryptogram, or the most intricate analysis, and I am in my own proper atmosphere. I can dispense then with artificial stimulants. But I abhor the dull routine of existence. I crave for mental exaltation.
>
> —ARTHUR CONAN DOYLE, "THE SIGN OF FOUR"

If Luciano Pavarotti were to respond to shouts of "encore, encore" by sitting down at the piano and playing a fugue, the audience would be anything but pleased. The crowd that pays a thousand dollars or more for a seat to see the great tenor's face undoubtedly expects that every one of his encores will be a vocal rendition of "Nessun dorma" or a comparably complex aria. The bottom line is that you get tons of kudos and money when you're one of the world's top operatic tenors but not a lot of room to experiment or behave in unexpected ways.

Professionals who are not in the performing arts also find themselves coping with the constrictive effects of honing a skill to razor sharpness. What do you think Sherlock Holmes was complaining about in "The Sign of Four," the mystery solved without effort? Nothing is as boring as a sure thing. Holmes felt alive when trying to outthink the "gifted" criminal mind. As he and every superachiever know, it is hard to find challenging competition and people who can sympathize with your dilemma.

Even activities that appear to be anything but shooting fish in a barrel can be sources of irritation and angst if one is extraordinarily talented at them. Consider a lawyer, for example, known for an encyclopedic grasp of contract law and a facility for structuring corporate transactions in a way that attracts clients willing to pay five hundred dollars an hour for his services. Imagine the shock that would ripple through his firm if he announced his intention to try his hand at criminal defense work. Granted, Johnnie Cochran makes a fortune working on behalf of alleged miscreants, but he doesn't make more than a guy who can save millions for Fortune 500 companies day after day.

But therein lies the rub: After twenty or more years of practicing transactional law and being good enough to command top dollar, any once-innovative attorney is vulnerable to a severe case of the been-there-done-that blues as clients and partners yell "encore" for that highly valued yet specific form of legal service. If a person feels she can execute a complex behavior with one hand tied behind her back because she has done so for decades, any specialized skill from brain surgery to rocket science can become as dull as widget making.

The anxiety part of encore anxiety comes from another aspect of more of the same demands: the baseline performance expectations that are set by every accomplishment. "What have you done for me lately?" is not merely a derogatory hint that bottom-line-oriented managers use to prod workers; it is part of the self-talk that all goal-oriented people use to drive themselves to ever-improving levels of performance. Psychologists refer to this as *level of aspiration,* the standard by which a person evaluates his or her performances and what he or she would like to accomplish in subsequent performances.[24]

The poet Robert Browning maintained, "A man's reach should exceed his grasp, / Or what's a heaven for?" Well and good. It is often healthy to reach for the stars; to do otherwise would keep you mired in the mud. But if you follow what Browning advocates without condition, you can become the victim of self-imposed levels of aspiration that rise too rapidly or spiral out of control.

A person's reach, which depends solely on the imagination or the urgings of others, is limitless, while grasp, depending as it does upon physical strength, is finite. If there is never a point at which enough is enough in one's career, it is logical to believe that sooner or later one's grasp will fail to keep one poised to snatch the next brass ring. In those circumstances, where one's level of aspiration is influenced by others, such as a loved one or a devaluing boss, one cannot help but fear letting those people down.

THE JOY OF FAILING

If we reexamine M. Scott Peck's contention that success eliminates as many options as does failure in light of what I've just said, we could make a strong case that those who experience failure are in the cat-bird seat. Ever since Franklin Roosevelt's New Deal initiative, our nation has demonstrated an increasing receptivity to social policies and programs that grant people the right to compensation or assistance should they lose a job. Government-sponsored unemployment insurance is available for most blue- and some white-collar workers who are out of work, and so-called outplacement packages (including lump-sum cash payments, limited health insurance, and job-hunting assistance) are the rule for mid- to upper-level white-collar workers. Some people claim that golden parachutes, the multimillion-dollar severance packages given to Bijan-collared CEOs who get the ax, are supportive, but in truth their primary function is to induce ex-CEOs to tell *The Wall Street Journal* that their exits were voluntary and thus safeguard the value of their companies' stock.

I don't mean to sound hardhearted, but if you consider the plight of a CEO suffering success depression, the loss of a job is not as bad as it seems. Granted, money is an issue, but being terminated from a job naturally thrusts challenge in your face: Find work or suffer. This type of challenge is, for some, overwhelming, but it does stimulate the creative juices and, with a psychological parachute created by caring family members, sympathetic colleagues, and dedicated outplacement counselors, there is often a paradoxical relief at being afforded all the latitude you need to climb the ladder with no expectations of success burdening your ascent.

About ten years ago the popularity enjoyed by management theorists who advocated corporate downsizing (cut the workforce to enhance profits), most notably Michael Hammer and James Champy (*Reengineering the Corporation*), was paradoxically responsible for the heightening of long-standing sympathies for workers who lost their jobs as a result of such programs. Not that sympathy is inappropriate: When Ford Motor Company (one of Hammer and Champy's premier case studies) reduced its accounts payable organization by 80 percent, hundreds of hardworking, competent people suffered legitimate distress. Likewise thousands of executives, managers, and line workers who were ousted from jobs by the organizational decimation engineered by "Chainsaw" Al Dunlap suffered distress that justified emotional and material support. Yet the paradox of reflexively offering sympathy to outplaced workers lies in the fact that they are not necessarily victimized by corporate downsizing. What is systematically ignored in reports of the cruelty of mass layoffs is the fact that people who keep their jobs suffer as much as, if not more than, those who get laid off.

In the late 1980s I was hired by a number of Fortune 1000 businesses to help buttress the morale of workers about to get pink slips. On one such assignment I talked with a senior manager of an advertising agency who not only was spared the ax but, because his direct supervisor was a target of the downsizing campaign, found himself promoted to an executive position that he neither expected nor, it turned out, wanted. "A.J."[25] was the kind of adman who thrived when handling creative processes. He started his career writing copy because he was enamored of the slogans and jingles that became part of our culture. I recall him telling me that had he "invented" the marionette that pitched Speedy Alka-Seltzer or Kellogg's Tony the Tiger, he would have died a happy man.

Of even greater relevance is the fact that A.J. began working in ad agencies because he felt he could "get inside the heads" of product development teams looking for the right pitch to turn their brands into market leaders. For fifteen years A.J. honed that skill to a level that garnered him several industry awards and a faithful following of high-paying clients. Never once, under the tremendous pressure to satisfy the demands of this aspect of the business, did he buckle or bend.

Unfortunately, in the wake of his firm's downsizing, A.J.'s stim-

ulating career came to an abrupt halt. While the CEO of his agency
was shedding deadwood, A.J. was saddled with the responsibility of
overseeing the operation. A handsome bonus and a raise accompanied his promotion, but his new administrative responsibilities deprived him of the time he wanted to devote to servicing his clients.
Despite the fact that A.J.'s empathic skills can be key to effective
management, he wanted no part of the responsibilities inherent in
that role.

What A.J. endured—and what ultimately drove him to retirement—was the expectation that success at one form of professional
activity prepared him for, and made him capable of, executing the
requirements of any and every professional activity in his business.
Some may claim that A.J.'s experience was merely an instance of the
Peter Principle in operation, but I disagree.[26] I believe that the way
our society construes, labels, and reacts to successful people makes
it impossible for them to stop striving for greater levels of success
without incurring recrimination or censure.

Professionals trapped in golden handcuffs are particularly vulnerable to derision if they elect to jump off the fast track. Even if
they are thrown off with all sorts of perks and benefits, the expectation is that they will pursue comparable executive roles as soon as
their noncompete clauses expire. In most large organizations the
suggestion that a golden parachute might include vocational counseling, career-retooling services, the sympathy of colleagues, or pre-
paid psychotherapy would make eyes roll. Few people see the need
for supports for the successful. What could be a better preparation
for an encore than climbing the ladder to the top or occupying the
corner office? The answer, in the short term, is "probably nothing."
Thus, the logic goes, "Stop bellyaching and do it again!"

The bottom line, however, is that not one in one hundred people
who strive for top-of-the-pyramid grandeur doubts the wisdom of
trading psychological stimulation for financial security until severe
damage is done. Money shapes our behavior—and narrows our behavioral options—without creating perceptible discord; the snare
set by golden handcuffs constricts slowly. Yet, typically, progress

along a linear career track ultimately dooms a person to feel like a bear treed by baying hounds. Why? Because the cry "encore" means "do it again," "it" being what you just did. It does not mean "That was great, Pavarotti, what else can you do?"

THE FACE IN THE MIRROR

George Eastman, Mark Lenzi, Mitch Kapor. Extremes on the success continuum you cannot identify with, or images you stare at in the mirror each morning? A fundamental step in understanding, treating, or preventing Supernova Burnout is the "mirror work" or self-assessment that will enable you to change the course of your career in midstream should you detect a need to do so. But this isn't psychoanalysis or some search for a Jungian archetype—it's simply stop, look, and question.

You've never done this and want some help? Use the following checklist. How many of these adjectives apply to you?

- ❑ Single-minded
- ❑ Persevering
- ❑ Self-reliant
- ❑ Assiduous
- ❑ Unremitting
- ❑ Monomaniacal
- ❑ Zealous
- ❑ Indefatigable

If you're not yet thirty years old and swear that four or more of these adjectives apply to you, you can work for any company I am affiliated with, no questions asked. If you're over forty and make the same claim, don't put this book down until you've read the last page: You're a slam-dunk, guaranteed case of Supernova Burnout in the making.

Why the flip-flop? Because the attributes involved in building a business or a professional career are antithetical to those involved in sustaining one. Typically, someone younger than thirty has no need to be oriented to people or causes other than him- or herself. The same cannot be said for the typical fifty-year-old. Someone who is past midlife and suffers egocentric tunnel vision or operates in a workaholic trance needs to recognize that striving to succeed is only appropriate when you haven't done so. Once you have, it is crucial to look beyond the self and see both the rewards and expectations that lie around you.

To understand what is right about being indefatigable, single-minded, zealous, and the like in your twenties and wrong about having those traits after midlife, consider why so many of the metaphors used to describe participation in a vocation invoke travel: People follow a career path, climb the ladder, or, according to Andy Grove, navigate a career.[27] The concepts path, climbing, and navigation connote a course of action that has a predetermined destination, as well as linearity and singleness of focus. To be 100 percent reflective of the American ideal of vocational pursuits, these terms should include references to the rate of travel as well. Since winning is the only thing, you ought not dawdle on that career path; traverse it now. Climb that ladder? Sure, but don't hesitate to skip a rung. And so on. So who is best equipped to make the trek to the top? Most likely the twentysomething, indefatigable, monomaniacal careerist who will persevere in the face of adversity.

The problem, of course, is that because the American dream of success is so obsessed with getting "there" from someplace else, it ignores the fact that no one can know what life "there" will be like for anyone else. Even if you are given reliable descriptions of your destination by someone who has been there, you run the risk that, by the time you arrive, both you and the world at large will have changed. This is precisely what happened to Ken Olsen, founder of Digital Equipment Corporation (DEC), who was once named "entrepreneur of the decade" by *Fortune* magazine.

Olsen would likely have scored eight out of eight on our adjective-matching quiz throughout his career. A brilliant MIT-educated engineer, he made DEC an industry leader by developing the best minicomputers on earth. But because he stayed the course, kept his eye on the prize, and was monomaniacal in his efforts to achieve one encore after another, he refused to consider that there might be an alternative to the minicomputer. Thus Olsen is better remembered today for his ill-conceived rejection of the personal computer than for helping to found the computer industry.[28]

Despite being offered an opportunity to develop Apple Computer's technology long before Steve Jobs and Steve Wozniak formed their own company, Olsen stuck strictly to his minicomputer knitting. Worse yet, he misjudged the direction of the entire industry. At a conference for information technology professionals in 1974, he proclaimed, "There is no reason for any individual to have a computer in their home."[29] In 1998 DEC was absorbed by Compaq Computer Corporation, a firm yet to be founded when Olsen made one of the worst calls in recent business history.

RERUM NOVARUM CUPIDUS

Before I had enough money to take a vacation that involved air travel, I remember how intrigued I was with what I call *the travel agent's maxim:* "Getting there is half the fun." The British philosopher and sexologist Havelock Ellis echoed this sentiment when he said, "It is not the attainment of the goal that matters, it is the things that are met with by the way." But what do travel agents and a philosopher know about sustaining a psychologically healthy career? As it turns out, plenty.

Ken Olsen and others who stayed the linear success course far too long seem to have been obsessed with the fear that they would be denied more money and more acclaim if they pursued side trips on the path to success. In a word, they were greedy. So, let me propose that we fight the greed that regularly undermines the ability to derive satisfaction from success with . . . greed. If it's true that to truly succeed you have to be greedy for things, have it your way. However, be greedy for the things prescribed in the saying *Rerum novarum cupidus:* Be greedy—or, more accurately, avaricious—for new things. If this statement becomes your mantra and you reconceptualize your vocation in accordance with it, you will inoculate yourself against both success depression and encore anxiety.

The way I propose you begin becoming avaricious for new things is to remove any and all travel metaphors from your vocabulary after you turn thirty. As I said earlier, I love the young guy who is hell-bent on making a name . . . up to a point. But if, like Olsen, that hard charger doesn't have the sense to back off and reflect upon what he has been doing, he should prepare to get his lunch eaten. My advice for everyone over thirty: Reframe your career path into something to invest in, as one would invest in a portfolio of money-making holdings. As any money manager will tell you, if you have some investment vehicles that are presumed to be safe, some that are speculative, and some that are downright risky, you will naturally adjust the balance of your holdings should you become aware that any sector of your account fails to deliver a favorable ROI.

This advice is not new: Grandmothers since the dawn of time have advised against putting all your eggs in one basket, but people who strive for success are given all sorts of reasons to ignore this guidance. The knowledge that diversification will offend those who depend upon their continued success for monetary or personal gains, plus the knowledge that not maximizing a proven talent is economically unsound, instills in almost everyone a bottom-line view of careers. Unfortunately, unless the concept of opportunity costs is expanded to include opportunity for psychological satisfaction, success will become an affliction rather than an advantage.

One word of caution: A profitable career portfolio is typically not built on advice from others. You must first get in touch with what psychoanalysts call your *ego ideal*: the totality of your wishes, dreams, goals, and, of course, ideals. Had Mark Lenzi done this, he would have known that a gold medal in diving would be an inadequate springboard to all the social engagements he envisioned for his future. To be a charismatic speaker you need two parts natural pizzazz, one part self-confidence, and one part language skills. Something in Lenzi didn't enable him to get to the grand total of four, but he should have known what parts he was missing well before he made the leap of faith that earned him a 10 and cost him years of his life.

Once you become aware of the components of your ego ideal, you can adjust your career pursuits the way a battlefield medic does triage. For those of you unfamiliar with military parlance, triage uses the ROI model to determine which casualties to treat. With limited medical resources, there are two groups who should not receive attention: those too wounded to save, and those who can walk off the battlefield on their own with a virtual guarantee of survival. Those who warrant attention are the borderline cases; they may die if left unattended but should live if they get first aid.

If you view career success as a means of improving your interpersonal relationships and find yourself needing fourteen hours a day to keep your career afloat, your behaviors and your goals will be at variance with each other, and adjustments will be in order. Likewise, if you covet admiration for achievement and are a bon vivant networking from one opportunity to another, your stock portfolio will be flush but your career portfolio will be sorely lacking in the respect of peers. Let some aspects of your career investments tend to themselves, and let others die. Direct your surplus energies to the goals you anticipate and desire but have not accrued from your hard-won successes.

CHAPTER 3

Why So Many Baby Boomers Suffer Supernova Burnout

Need and struggle are what excite and inspire us; our hour of triumph is what brings the void. Not the Jews of captivity, but those of the days of Solomon's glory are those from whom the pessimistic utterances in our Bible come.

—WILLIAM JAMES

We now understand the psychological reasons a person trapped in golden handcuffs will become infuriated, depressed, or an entrepreneurial arsonist. But is it reasonable to proceed from this knowledge to James's characterization of an entire generation? Are we to believe that mass eustress deprivation deflated the passions of the Jews who lived at the time of King Solomon? Or, of more immediate concern, can the same dynamic happen today?

Yes to all the above, particularly the last. At present the roughly 85 million members of the baby boom generation, raised in America in uniquely prosperous times that afforded unprecedented opportunities, are suffering a higher incidence of Supernova Burnout than any generation before them. Despite the fact that their generation took self-indulgence and self-approval to staggering heights, countless baby boomers are reacting to midlife and enormous (relative to past generations) amounts of disposable income with a shocked "Is that all there is?" A surprising number of the "me generation" teens who became the wealth-obsessed yuppies of the 1980s are feeling emotionally bankrupt after having invested all their psychological currency in the pursuit of material success.

This is not hyperbole; survey data prove that materialism is a false god. In a Gallup Organization survey over one third of employed, college-educated adults said that if given a chance they would opt for a new line of work.[1] Annual surveys by the Higher Education Research Institute at UCLA have found that from 1968 (when the first wave of boomers were in college) to the present, the proportion of college freshmen who said it was essential to be very well off financially grew from 41 to 74 percent. At the same time the percentage who said "developing a meaningful philosophy of life" was a top priority fell from 83 to 41 percent. Derek Bok, former president of Harvard University, said about these trends, "When those numbers crossed paths in the 1970s, that was a huge sign that personal satisfaction was taking precedence over a person's willingness to deal with other people. . . . Along with that came the explosion in divorce, the rise of crime and other antisocial behaviors."[2]

While I am less comfortable linking crime rates with the hedonism and greed of the baby boom generation than Bok is, I am in total agreement with his observation that boomers have an extraordinarily difficult time dealing with other people and with the personal sacrifices essential to functioning in groups. Boomers' failure to internalize the message "to get along you have to go along" has led to a most unusual problem: Despite the fact that our economy has been growing and generating nearly full employment for over a decade, middle-age careerists are retooling themselves out of corporate America and "going solo" as never before. Everyone from corporate recruiters to CEOs is wondering what's ailing these former "flower children" and laments the lack of economic solutions for the problem.[3]

This makes sense since career dissatisfaction is almost always a function of psychological issues. When you see a wealthy executive stepping off a career path that has for years afforded him increasing material comforts, you know the reason must be the existential angst of Supernova Burnout.[4] But is the baby boom generation's widespread career dissatisfaction simply a function of having been reared by parents awash in the spoils of triumph, or is it symptomatic of deep-seated psychological damage?

YEARNING TO FIGHT THE GOOD FIGHT

A number of analyses that appeared just before the end of the twentieth century noted that the baby boom generation was suffering "great crusade envy." The most significant precipitant of this wave of invidious comparison with their parents was the concurrent release of two blockbusters: Tom Brokaw's book *The Greatest Generation* and the box-office-smash movie *Saving Private Ryan*. These sagas of how the "silent generation" vanquished the Nazis and made the world free for democracy left boomers facing the simple question: How do you compare being merely wealthy with winning a war? You don't. Nor do you easily escape the pain of wondering, Is that all I have to show for my time on earth?

When the GIs came marching home, all they wanted to do was marry the gals who had waited faithfully for their return, use their government benefits to buy a little piece of suburbia, and raise a few kids in Ozzie & Harriet–like tranquillity. How could a generation of parents so willing to sacrifice for their children be so unable to produce optimistic offspring? Is it as simple as risk homeostasis at work again? Only in part. It took the convergence of several potent psychological forces to give rise to the unique attitudes and orientations that have made the baby boom generation so vulnerable to Supernova Burnout.

A GENERATION OF RAGING INDIVIDUALISTS

The baby boom generation is commonly defined as children born between 1946 and 1964 to parents brimming with self-confidence and optimism after surviving the hardships of war and being rewarded with economic prosperity. Boomers were raised by stay-at-home moms willing to indulge their every need. And when these moms were not indulging their broods, they were reading a best-selling book that advocated a radical shift in the psychology of child rearing.

Dr. Benjamin Spock's *Baby and Child Care* shifted attitudes 180 degrees away from the children should be seen but not heard school of thought that had guided the upbringing of the silent generation. Not only were little girl and boy boomers raised to believe that what they had to say should be aired but many were so thoroughly catered to that they thought they were the center of the universe. As a patient of mine once said, "I grew up assuming that my role in the nuclear family was spelled S-U-N." The joint influence of a booming economy and Dr. Spock produced a generation of *raging* individualists.

One offshoot of this raging individualism was an unprecedented level of *professed* self-approval. This attitude can be traced to a basic tenet of Spock's: Parents should teach children to be independent in every way possible. Members of the baby boom generation were free to dictate the terms of their existence like never before: Patterns of feeding, access to activities, even socialization were no longer predetermined or parent-dictated. The child's temperament was to be respected, and her pace of development was to favor her individuality, not normative data.

At the same time the most dramatic wave of education enhancement in history was transforming the schools of postwar America. Rote learning, "regurgitation," and even rules governing dress and decorum were out; critical thinking was in. Thus, boomers were led to believe that they were unique individuals in their homes, in the classroom, and, years later, in the workplace.

The repercussions of an upbringing that indulged, educated, and gave a sense of omnipotence to little children were manifold, but none was so great as hubris and disdain for authority. Never before have so many young people behaved as though they knew all the answers and had a right to limitless pleasure. The seed for the 1960s student protests and catchphrases such as "Don't trust anyone over thirty" and "Question authority" was planted on the boomers' changing tables. Likewise, draft card burning, bra burning, and public promiscuity were symptomatic of a central tenet of Spock's perspective: "If it feels good, do it." The corollary—"If it feels bad, I *won't* do it"—had profound effects on how boomers came to view life in groups and, by extension, businesses.

While the fathers of baby boomers, depicted in William Whyte's *Organization Man,* never had the temerity to ask "Why?" of authority figures, their sons and daughters never learned how not to. Boomers retired the Organization Man and in his place introduced Me, Inc. They entered the workforce expecting from employers the treatment they had received at home and on university campuses. They felt it was an injustice if their work wasn't emotionally gratifying *and* economically rewarding, and if things weren't made right, they left.

While there are a number of sound economic and technological explanations for the proliferation of entrepreneurism and solo careers in the 1990s, a psychological explanation is that boomers could not tolerate the limitations required to be a member in good standing of an organization. None of the training the "me generation" received taught them to appreciate what organizational psychologists call process, the arduous, complex effort it takes to work through conflict. As Prometheus learned, the good fight often ends in disaster when those in power disagree with you.

Challenging the status quo, thinking you know what's correct in all contexts, and demanding to know why is neither preparation for, nor the equivalent of, striving for success. At best these stances are forms of opposition to authority or justifications for inaction; at worst they serve as rationales for passive-aggressive behavior. Regardless of how these resistances manifest, they heighten the likelihood of Supernova Burnout because they prevent one from feeling united with, and supported by, others. The child-rearing philosophy that shaped the egos of the baby boom generation put them at risk for lives riddled by dissatisfaction with friends, colleagues, and careers.

THE BURDEN OF BOUNDLESS POSSIBILITIES

> Oh don't the days seem lank and long
> When all goes right and nothing goes wrong.
> And isn't your life extremely flat
> With nothing whatever to grumble at!
> —WILLIAM S. GILBERT, PRINCESS IDA

No less an expert on the human condition than Sigmund Freud asserted, "A man who has been the indisputable favorite of his mother keeps for life the feeling of a conqueror, that confidence of success that often induces real success." Was this the feeling that baby boomers experienced when they left the nest? Unfortunately not. The sense of being the indisputable favorite is obtained from receiving feedback that you, not your brother or your sister, have pleased her most. While certain boomers came to feel that they were the pick of the litter, most were sent an ostensibly uplifting but ultimately upsetting message: You have limitless possibilities and infinite opportunity; you can achieve anything you want.

There are several things wrong with this sort of message. To begin with, a message sent to an entire generation ("You children have been born at a time that affords you limitless possibilities") lacks what psychologists call *personalism*, the sense that it is particular to an individual. Just as "all you teenagers are sex-crazed hedonists" can be dismissed as an irrelevant prejudice, a favorable message presented with too broad a brush comes across as both insincere and manipulative.

One of the major drawbacks of encouragement without personalism is that it deprives a person of knowing why someone felt he deserved the compliment. Furthermore, when presented without a clear-cut implementation strategy, feedback such as "you're the greatest" raises anxiety-provoking questions, not the confidence of success that, according to Freud, induces real success. At a minimum the child shouldering the burden of you're the greatest feedback wants to know how the hell you know that. For example, the child sent off to be a world beater would like to know that your criterion for judging his potential is unbiased, not merely a function of your love for him. Similarly, your competence to judge the opportunities out there is a critical concern.

Everybody who receives a stellar evaluation takes it with a grain of salt unless or until she can be certain of the evaluator's motives: "Are Mom and Dad telling me this so I'll go out and fulfill *their* dreams, or do they have my best interests at heart?" "You're the greatest" conveys as much bad news as good news if it exposes a person to unbearable performance pressures. In fact, such directives are among the most conspicuous causes of Supernova Burnout.

BACKBREAKING EXPECTATIONS

William James created a simple formula that demonstrates how ambiguous and exceedingly high expectations can cripple self-esteem. According to James, who used the term *pretensions* for what I refer to as *expectations*:

$$\text{SELF-ESTEEM} = \frac{\text{SUCCESS}}{\text{PRETENSIONS}}$$

This formula illustrates how you can increase self-esteem by lowering performance expectations. In James's words, "To give up pretensions is as blessed a relief as to get them gratified."[5] Unfortunately, you cannot just give up pretensions; they stay with you for life.

The psychoanalyst Harry Stack Sullivan noted that our sense of self is formed by internalizing attitudes and beliefs derived from how we feel about what we do *and* from the assessments of society. Sullivan called the way we shape our sense of what is valuable or desirable *consensual validation*. The sad fact of life for many people shouldering expectations imposed by accidents of birth—extreme beauty, silver spoons in their mouths—is that although they may feel that these pretensions are malarkey, the consensual feedback they receive thwarts their efforts to shed the expectations.

According to a biography of the Kennedys, the matriarch, Rose Kennedy, would allude to a homily from the Gospel of Luke at every confirmation, commencement, and graduation ceremony her grandchildren were part of: "To whom much is given, much will be required."[6] Following the assassination of President John Kennedy, his brother Bobby assumed leadership of the family and updated Luke's maxim: "America has been very good to the Kennedys. We all owe the country a debt of gratitude and public service."[7] How do you think these messages affect a preteen boy or girl? From my vantage point, they are incapacitating. Here's why:

Message 1: "To whom much is given . . ." This comment taps into the psychological well of discontent that maddened the model I met while at Columbia University. When you are given something without either struggling to achieve it or necessarily desiring it, what you have been given is not psychologically rewarding. Rose's husband, Joseph Kennedy, had amassed enough legitimate self-esteem to cope with St. Luke's maxim because he had endured the process of securing wealth. His offspring had not. Their success-generating expectations came by default.

Message 2: "Much will be required" or "You owe the country a debt." How do you thank a grandparent for sending you into the world with a proverbial monkey on your back? By striving to shake it off, of course. The pressure for a Kennedy to make a mark in the world is infinitely higher than that for a child not raised in the shadow of American royalty. When you are a Kennedy kid the nagging question is "How do I fulfill my obligations?" In time, the answer is often "You cannot," and Supernova Burnout sets in. It is of course unfair to assert that St. Luke's maxim had a uniformly negative effect on the Kennedys. Many have fulfilled the directives Rose and Bobby

Kennedy conveyed, but others met untimely deaths from daredevil behavior.

The assurance "You've got what it takes, the sky's the limit" sets a baseline of acceptable behavior that makes modest success feel like abject failure. By contrast, those given nothing and aspiring to achieve little or nothing can—in a sense—be said to have it easy. While no panacea, freedom from onerous performance expectations precludes worry about the quality of one's achievements. Because the level of expectations set for the boomers by their parents was astronomically high, in order to earn self-esteem, according to James's formulation, they would need to achieve extraordinarily great success.

ACCIDIE

Before *The Greatest Generation* and *Saving Private Ryan, Five Easy Pieces,* starring Jack Nicholson as Robert "Bobby" Dupea, captivated boomers. This character study portrayed a talented man crippled by burdensome performance expectations. Bobby Dupea was born to a family of gifted musicians, whom he was expected to emulate. Despite, or because of, his destiny Bobby lives as a redneck oil rigger who guzzles beer, delights in country music, and carouses with easy women. Although firmly entrenched in this lifestyle, Bobby returns to the family's Puget Sound estate when he learns that his father is near death. Trying to explain why he abandoned his early career as a classical pianist, he says, "I guess you're wondering what happened to me after my auspicious beginnings." He then collapses into sobs.

Five Easy Pieces provided baby boomers a poignant catharsis. While Bobby felt he couldn't reach the heights to which his family legacy destined him, he was neither inherently selfish nor so coldhearted as to dismiss his obligations entirely. Although he succumbed to a lifetime of escapism, Bobby Dupea was a sympathetic character baby boomers could identify with.

I mentioned at the outset of this chapter that never before have so many who were given so much been so dissatisfied with their lot. Nevertheless, the pain of failing to actualize one's potential has long been a subject of philosophers, theologians, and psychologists. The ancient Greeks called this condition *akedeia,* which translates roughly into *accidie,* an indifference to life, a paralysis of the soul, or a permanent noncaring state.

Accidie was the original fourth deadly sin, sloth, but modern connotations of this term fall short of the encompassing spiritual torpor that those who fail to live up to their potential suffer. Was accidie the pain that Bobby Dupea tried constantly to escape? Undoubtedly. And many boomers find themselves running from an identical sense of disengagement from the struggle to make life worthwhile.

The first person I treated for accidie was a man I'll call Jeff. Although Jeff's family paid a lawyer and a PR agent to keep the family name from appearing on *Forbes*'s list of four hundred richest Americans, all of Jeff's self-presentation was designed to tell the world, "I'm from money." He wore alligator shoes every time I saw him, sported at least five luxury watches, and accentuated his wardrobe with ties, jackets, and attaché cases that bore every designer logo imaginable. Yet Jeff never held a job. He earned a law degree, but every opportunity he had to engage in gainful employment was deemed "beneath" him.

Jeff's reason for seeking therapy was his desire to "take control of the family business"—made up of real estate, natural resources, and entertainment franchises. The key, he felt, to assuming the chairmanship of this conglomerate was "proving to Mom [his father was deceased] that I have settled down." Jeff's mother would not cede control of the conglomerate his dad had built until Jeff fit her image of the ideal man—Jeff's staid, conservative father.

What did Jeff do? He got several women pregnant, then sought help from his mother's brother—"the only physician I can trust." He gambled with bookies who knew to contact the family accountant when it came time to settle the debts, and he hosted parties at the family's summer cottage that invariably resulted in thousands of dollars' worth of damage. In short, he spent his energy ensuring that he would remain a self-indulgent narcissist.

After about three months of familiarizing myself with Jeff's modus operandi, I determined it was time for a confrontation: I presented him with a series of increasingly intense interpretations that branded him a failure, and an intractable one at that. Although he could never counter my arguments, he never found them reason enough to change. In one discussion, after I explained that he did not need to tell his uncle about the consequences of his unwillingness to use condoms, Jeff leaned forward in his chair and said to me smugly, "But you don't understand, Doctor; where I come from it is far better to be a success at being a failure, as I am, than to be a failure at trying to be a success. I'm celebrated in and around Boston; do you think I would dare risk losing that status by attempting to do something worthwhile?"

I never was able to help Jeff extricate himself from this pattern of self-defeat, but my association with him taught me a crucial distinction between success depression and accidie. When people, like those who shocked Freud by being "wrecked by success," fall victim to success depression, they are overwhelmed by a sense of loss, helplessness, and hopelessness. All depressions are characterized by feelings that psychiatrists call *anhedonia*—without pleasure—for the truly depressed person can neither respond to nor take advantage of pleasurable stimuli even if they are set before her. Parenthetically, it may be of interest to note a bit of gossip told to me by a number of psychiatrists about Woody Allen's classic *Annie Hall:* The original title was *Anhedonia,* reportedly because Mr. Allen suffered from this condition.

Accidie is not depression. In fact, the person afflicted by this condition mulls over bitter, self-centered "what-ifs" and "should-haves" that fuel his sense of narcissistic entitlement. Although, like the depressive, the person experiencing accidie is disengaged from the real world, accidie results more from a conscious decision to run away from problems that must be overcome than from a sense of helplessness to bring about desired outcomes. Jeff ran away from his problems by keeping in constant contact with his mother, the person he resented for placing the weight of the world on his shoulders, while behaving in ways guaranteed to drive a wedge between them. Most people who suffer accidie are more direct about fleeing personal responsibility.

The great thinkers of antiquity attributed the onset of accidie to causes ranging from fasting to the knowledge that we are all going to die, thus, why bother with anything? But we can offer several psychodynamic explanations.

The primary cause is what psychologists call a *paradoxical incentive effect,* which results when the incentives to perform in a particular way lead to the opposite of the desired behavior.[8] The second explanation is the interpersonal advantages of dropping out of the race when it appears as though you're destined to lose. This strategic, self-protective form of self-handicapping should be familiar to you by now.

PARADOXICAL INCENTIVE EFFECTS

In April 1996, at Augusta National golf course, Greg Norman, a.k.a. the Shark, had a daunting six-stroke lead over his closest competitor on the final day of play of the Masters Tournament. As Norman teed off for what oddsmakers viewed as an all-but-sure victory, he choked. The psychological weight of his lead, and the expectations born of how well he had played up to that point, were too much to bear. By the end of that round, several golfers who had begun the day trailing Norman had surpassed him.

Choking under pressure can be defined as failing to perform up to your ability when it is important and you feel pressured to do your best.[9] This pressure is defined wholly in the eye of the beholder: If you feel that much is riding on a given performance, pressure is high; if not, it's low. And while this phenomenon is related to accidie, it refers to an acute rather than a chronic problem.

Choking involves becoming self-conscious at key moments; self-conscious awareness disrupts overlearned, automatic behaviors. In other words, we become aware of what we're doing while we're doing it and as a consequence don't do it as well as we can.

As I type I normally do not think that the index finger of my right hand is responsible for hitting the *m* and the *y* keys to type the word *my*. If I stopped to consider the process of typing or, worse yet, focused on every keystroke I was making, this book would never get composed. Carrying this example to an extreme, even if I were merely keeping the humiliating consequences of not finishing foremost in my mind, the pressure generated would all but end my ability to write. Some would call this reaction writer's block. But since what disrupted my writing was conscious overattention to the pressures that could be upon me, my hypothetical failure is best described as choking under pressure.

Psychologists who have studied paradoxical incentive effects claim that certain personality types are more prone than others to choke under pressure. Choke-prone personalities typically pay minimal attention to themselves but do, occasionally, feel very self-conscious. They are thought not to focus on the consequences of their actions, show concern for how they appear to others (care about consensual validation), or spend a great deal of time in self-reflective assessment. However, when the stakes are high these people become overly self-conscious. It is this fluctuation between a baseline of low self-consciousness and extraordinarily high self-awareness that makes people most prone to choke under pressure.[10]

This type of person might be deemed a narcissist, or someone who is extremely "entitled" in addition to being choke-prone. Not caring how other people judge your actions can be characteristic of, say, a university student who indignantly challenges a professor because the student says, "from what I know of life your data sound ridiculous."

I was the target of that comment in a course I taught. The student who made the remark, "Ashley," had enrolled in an advanced-level psychology course, although she had never studied psychology (her major was literature). Her lack of familiarity with the subject matter never impeded her from telling me that I (after more than ten years in the field) was all wet.

Ashley's antagonistic objections continued past the midterm exam (which she failed), and I asked her to meet with me to discuss her performance and her dissension. At our meeting she was charming yet so filled with conceit that she evinced no concern about my reaction to her claim that she hadn't purchased, let alone read, any of the materials assigned for class. I warned her that this attitude was not serving her well, but she replied, "There's plenty of time until the final," and left.

Ashley called me at home three days before the end of the quarter and begged for a second appointment. When we met she told me that she had one day either to withdraw from class without penalty (the university permitted this until right before final exams) or to stay, provided I would guarantee her a grade of C. She confessed that she had recently been to her father's psychiatrist for antidepressant medication and again begged my forbearance. But she never offered an explanation of why she deserved a passing grade. I said, "I'm sorry, I cannot give you a grade without merit," and she dropped the course. Two weeks later she dropped out of the class.

While this woman, born in the last year of the baby boom, displayed an extreme form of arrogance, it was both prototypical of the choke-prone personality and reminiscent of how I remember my peers reacting to authority when I was in college and graduate school (from 1968 to 1976). Ashley cared not a bit about my judgments until the performance pressure of finals nearly crippled her. Cajoling didn't alert her to the error of her ways; only a threat could do that. Yet in the end she crumbled without remorse. Not once did this woman stop to work through the conflicts that, I later learned, perennially entangled her in confrontations with authority figures.

Is it fair to say that all boomers are choke-prone? Obviously not. Are many? I believe they are. As William James noted, the struggle gives strength. Boomers were reared in ways that left them with atrophied coping "muscles" and no knowledge of how to persevere in the face of adversity.

THE OTHER FACE OF SELF-HANDICAPPING

Woody Allen once remarked, "Ninety percent of success in life is showing up." I have no idea how he arrived at that number, but I do know that not showing up leads to failure. Yet hard as it may be to believe, there are occasions when failure attributable to not showing up can be a highly desirable outcome.

The classic form of self-handicapping behavior involves using a performance-inhibiting agent to deflect responsibility for failure. If the attribute *charmer* is central to my self-image, and I am going to a cocktail party where I expect to be intimidated by the caliber of the guests, it may be to my advantage to get drunk before the party and be certain that my inebriation is apparent to all. By so doing, I protect the widely held belief that (if not disabled by alcohol) I can schmooze with the best of them.

In general, if you once demonstrated that you were capable of stellar performances and subsequently bomb while under the influence, audiences will suspend judgment on whether you have lost your ability until you show up for evaluation clean and sober. Performing under the influence can protect a threatened sense of self-esteem by temporarily lowering what is expected.

A related tactic involves not showing up for evaluation. This complete withdrawal of effort awards an incomplete to someone who doubts his ability to make the grade. Someone who has been led since childhood to believe that he can have it all can forestall a determination of his true capability for as long as he refuses to get into the game. This type of self-protective tactic has been called a Faustian bargain.[11] Like Faust and my former patient Jeff, many boomers have made a bargain with the devil: In exchange for the right to live immaturely, they've forfeited their claim to the psychological rewards that would be theirs if they could actualize their potential. Yet underneath the bravado of this lifestyle is anguish. All around us boomers are being forced by midlife crises and is-that-all-there-is? ennui to confront their mortality. They are being forced to become more self-aware than they care to, and the disparity between what they have accomplished and what was expected of them sets the stage for a full-blown bout of Supernova Burnout.

TOWARD A PSYCHOLOGY OF BEING: SELF-ACTUALIZATION

My misgiving about the Faustian bargains many baby boomers have made comes from firsthand knowledge of what happens when such self-delusional bubbles burst. It is relatively easy to help a person who suffers success depression. If someone sees that having made it once she has the capacity to make it again, the letdown that follows achievement can be readily overcome. But how do you ease the pain of someone who has played Peter Pan for so long that he has lost the opportunity to star in adult roles? How do you persuade a lifelong dilettante or promiscuous job hopper that what psychologists call *the geographic cure*—moving to a new setting to get a fresh start— is doomed to failure because every fresh start is undertaken with the stale you intact?

THE TAO AND GEOGRAPHIC CURES

In contrast to most spiritual teachings, which are based on doctrine or divine revelation, the ancient Chinese philosophy of Taoism is based on thousands of years of observing nature. According to Taoist philosophy, there is a universal creative energy or spirit—the Tao—which is ever-changing, like the currents in the air or the ocean. To understand the Tao and harness this universal energy, you must be flexible.

How hard is that, you ask? Just look at boomers seeking desperately the "right environment" in which to flourish. The defenses and preconceptions that restrict our thinking are too numerous to mention, but they are so much a part of our daily interaction patterns that we rarely notice them. William James said it bluntly: "A great many people think they are thinking when they are merely rearranging their prejudices." The same holds true for our ability to be open-minded.

A self-actualized person never acts like a bad carpenter who blames his tools for the poor quality of a project. First of all, the judgment of whether he crafted a piece of furniture worthy of comparison to an Eames chair is irrelevant. Second, being in a "good" or a "bad" workshop would not intrude upon the self-actualized carpenter's consciousness. Actually, a person engrossed in the *process of carpentry,* not the products he generates, could care less about the context he was in when he cut, carved, sanded, and stained wood.

If any example could dissuade people from putting their faith in a geographic cure for psychological problems, *Five Easy Pieces* is it. The moment Bobby Dupea returned to his family compound in Puget Sound from his wanderings in the Southwest, he was transformed from an ostensibly carefree Lothario into an intense, competitive, conservative scion of a proud but flawed family. He was overprotective of his sister's good name and became embarrassed by the simple lower-class woman he had been living with. It is obvious that the time Bobby spent as a wildcatter did little to soften the intensity he brought to all aspects of life. All his geographic cure accomplished was to get him thousands of land miles from unresolved psychological pain that reemerged within moments of returning to the scene of the trauma.

The baby boomers who throughout their school years were encouraged to question authority have extended that notion to the world of work and have become reliant on geographic cures for the problems their attitudes cause. Many of the boomers I coach come to our initial meeting with the complaint "If only I were able to find the right job or the right boss, I'm certain my career would take off." While it is easy to understand why boomers put their faith in geographic cures rather than accept responsibility for personal success and, more important, potential failure, helping them let go of that misplaced faith is an altogether different matter. The best way I have found to help people in search of geographic cures understand that they are on a fool's errand is to expose them to the rewards inherent in the process of becoming self-actualized.

The man most responsible for bringing the concept of self-actualization to the forefront of American psychology was Abraham Maslow.[12] His core conviction was that we all have an innate propensity to strive to reach the highest levels of our capabilities; he was a true believer in the ascendancy of human potential. Maslow further assumed that everyone would naturally seek to engage in creative pursuits, a psychologically rewarding vocation, or what many refer to as a calling, unless they either (1) were not certain of their psychological safety (which is based upon the knowledge that you can provide for your fundamental needs), or (2) feared self-knowledge (confronting their authentic feelings, attitudes, and beliefs). People not impeded by these two conditions would be able, according to Maslow, to enjoy discrete moments of self-actualization—what he called peak experiences—during which they would appear to be in a state of blissful concentration, totally immersed in what they were doing and oblivious to their surroundings or the passage of time.

THE HIERARCHY OF NEEDS

Maslow's model of self-actualization describes two sets of needs thought to motivate all people. This hierarchy includes four levels of D or deficiency needs, and one B need, to achieve a self-actualized sense of being. Levels 1 through 4 are physiological needs (oxygen, food, water, and so on); safety needs (protection from harm); belongingness needs (love, affection, oneness with others); and esteem needs (self-respect and self-confidence from authentic achievement).

Once the deficiency needs are met, the theory goes, people can proceed to level 5, the attainment of self-actualization: an ongoing process of realizing inherent potentials, capacities, and talents. It is important to note that people do not give conscious thought to moving from level 1 to 5 on the hierarchy of needs, as they would if they were striving to attain Scout merit badges. Self-actualization is much like following the Tao, becoming seamlessly enmeshed with the ebb and flow of nature.

Maslow gave tremendous weight to this point by taking a page from Taoism that explains how and why *desiring* or *choosing* to be in a state of self-actualization is a contradiction in terms. He repeatedly emphasized that *striving* to achieve self-actualization paradoxically thwarts the process. Taking actions aimed at becoming actualized is like forcing yourself to be calm: The more you pressure yourself, the more anxious you become. Or, in the language of paradoxical incentive effects, bringing conscious attention to bear on an activity that should flow naturally as a consequence of learning and practice interferes with its execution.

By contrast, doing something for the sheer joy of doing it, without regard to reward, audience approval, or obligation—in a manner akin to a child mindlessly playing with a new object of interest—will make self-actualization immediate. When an infant gets a gift, she is often captivated more by the wrapping and the box it came in than by the gift itself. An infant has no self-consciousness to her merrymaking; she plays without reference to what form appropriate play with a gift from a parent should take. Likewise, according to Maslow, a musician makes music because it is his calling; a writer writes for the same reason; people who find parenting a calling need no incentive to love and engage in raising children.

IMPEDIMENTS TO SELF-ACTUALIZATION

If we examine the two impediments to the natural process of moving through Maslow's hierarchy of needs—lack of safety and fear of self-knowledge—it becomes clear why so many boomers, and others daunted by auspicious beginnings, experience Supernova Burnout at the pinnacles of their careers. Looking first at psychological safety, it may be hard to believe that being indulged by parents can lead to anxiety about the ability to provide for your own needs, but it typically does. A person will also lack a sense of psychological safety if his parents impose rigidly defined performance expectations.

Many of the patients I have treated for Supernova Burnout could have claimed that the seed of their disorder was a gift. Possessing some valued asset, or acquiring prized property by dint of another person's labor or an accident of birth, cannot lead to self-respect or confidence in one's ability to cope effectively. Social comparison theory demonstrates that the only way we know we are able, intelligent, or strong is by comparing what we do with what peers do. It makes no difference to a boy's self-image if his daddy can whip everyone else's daddy. What matters is that that boy measure up against the kids *he* fights or competes with.

In a similar way, giving a person direction in life, charting a course for her, or conveying expectations of what she should accomplish always interferes with self-actualization. Consider what Mary Catherine Bateson had to say about defining goals for others:

> The model of an ordinary successful life that is held up for young people is one of early decision and commitment…a single rising trajectory. Ambition, we imply, should be focused.…These assumptions have not been valid for many of history's most creative people and they are increasingly inappropriate today. *Goals too clearly defined become blinders* [emphasis added].

If you know who Bateson's parents were, you might understand why she is so concerned about children who have goals imposed upon them. Her parents were two of the world's most renowned anthropologists: Margaret Mead and Gregory Bateson. While their daughter has clearly made her own way in the world (she is a professor of anthropology and the author of several well-regarded books), there is no doubt that young Mary Catherine received at least implicit direction to immerse herself in anthropology.

Being heir to an ocean of expert DNA generates the expectation that you should actualize the potential in your genes. This directive, in turn, may prevent you from keeping the open mind that Taoists and psychologists who study self-actualization say is critical to growing as a human being and deriving pleasure from your pursuits.

People who are given advantageous starts in life often seem incapable of pursuing career goals appropriate to their abilities for one fundamental reason: Our drive to experience freedom, or exercise free will, supersedes whatever drives may exist in us to achieve ranking and rewards. In fact, the innate drive not to have behavioral freedoms denied us—what psychologists call *psychological reactance*—has been the subject of intense experimental scrutiny for decades.[13]

Here's a simple example of psychological reactance. Assume that a mother who is asking a child to "play like a good girl while Mommy is in the kitchen" says before leaving the room: "You can play with any toy in the toy box other than Barney." The reactance experienced by that little girl as a result of the constraint imposed upon her behavioral freedom will send her running for the purple dinosaur in a New York second.

A child's refusal to follow parental directives is the tip of the psychological reactance iceberg. Advantage-induced reactance works in two ways: By removing obstacles to attaining success, and thereby making that success seem unchallenging, advantageous beginnings can make living up to one's potential a depressing form of conscription. Conversely, when messages conveyed about one's genetic endowment make the fulfillment of potential seem like a directive from above ("Do you know how lucky you are to have such a high IQ? It would be a sin for you to not apply yourself in school"), the pressure can interfere with the capacity to experience academic or professional pursuits as resulting from the expression of one's own free will.

I've worked with people who have actually destroyed their alleged advantages rather than endure the feelings of psychological reactance these advantages imposed on them. Just as the maudlin model on mood-altering drugs harbored fantasies of slashing her face to free herself from the "constraints" of her beauty, one patient of mine whose parents were both musicians sought to ruin her beautiful singing voice by adopting a two-pack-a-day cigarette habit.

Another patient I worked with, a mild-mannered man whose father and grandfather were both two-star generals, assaulted an ROTC officer on his first day of training. When calls from his father to the ROTC commander smoothed things over, the young man spit in the commander's face for "meddling in my affairs." This fellow was intent upon being all that he could be, just not in a manner preordained by his forebears.

Perceiving ourselves to be free agents is a central component of all forms of favorable self-regard, particularly self-esteem. While as adults we are not typically free to play like children do, we are supposed to be free to open ourselves to a range of experiences and pursue those that are most psychologically rewarding. Early decision and commitment to a goal may heighten the likelihood that you will attain that goal more readily than others if you devote yourself to your calling while others are engaged in unfocused play. But the advantage you gain by being more proficient than peers often exacts a terrible toll. Aims too clearly defined and goals too readily attained become blinders to a number of things, including the range of activities needed to enjoy a fulfilling life. One of the more painful paradoxes of success is that highly competent people can be prevented from discovering their true calling because an early commitment was imposed upon them rather than emerging from within.

What Bateson called early decision and commitment can also impede what Maslow saw as the key to self-actualization: self-knowledge. If you've ever dealt with a Type A personality who must be the top of whatever hierarchy he values, you know how the pursuit of a goal can block a person from understanding what he is trying to attain—or escape from. As an old German proverb cautions, "What's the use of running when you may not be on the right road?"

"Sean" was the most driven person I ever worked with in psychotherapy. He had an impressive history of success in refurbishing business wrecks ("Call me the king of the bottom fishers," he would say) by providing what he called new wrinkles to old washups. To his credit, Sean had a stream of good ideas, including the mass-market pairing of espresso bars and booksellers long before Barnes & Noble teamed with Starbucks. But Sean himself was a wreck when weekends rolled around. Although he owned three foreign cars, two vacation homes, and enough suits to shame John Gotti, Sean's evenings were empty. For the most part, he spent them alone. On those rare instances when he stopped to reflect, he sensed that his devotion to work kept him from developing interpersonal attachments. But since achieving success was so central to Sean's identity, he dismissed his musings about building relationships with "I'll cross that bridge when I come to it."

The problem I had forming what is commonly called a therapeutic bond with Sean was a function of how he entered therapy: as a favor to a cousin who believed "a forty-eight-year-old man should not be living with his mother," which Sean was. Unfortunately, whenever I urged Sean to examine either his devotion to business or his devotion to his mother, he brushed me off with a sarcastic "You know how Irish guys are about their Sainted Mothers, Irish whiskey, and fighting fires. Well, the fires I fight are salvage missions to stop valuable enterprises from being consumed by the flames of self-immolation, and the other two are no concern to me now."

Given his capacity for denial, I was shocked when, after roughly three months, Sean immersed himself in therapy as though his psyche was another turnaround project. In particular, he took extraordinary pleasure from uncovering the issues he saw as contributing to his obsession with business. On several occasions he recounted how his mother would tell him that "we're shanty Irish, son, not the lace-curtain types who live on Beacon Hill [an exclusive section of Boston]. Be sure you do us proud and build something that will get you out of the neighborhood."

Sean was also able to discuss the pain he experienced when his mother fell victim to Alzheimer's disease before acknowledging his worth. Yet only once, at the very beginning of our work, did Sean mention anything about his long-deceased father having shown a preference for his older brothers, who played hockey and got into brawls rather than study or read books as he did.

For all the cleverness and intellectual appeal of Sean's therapeutic insights, after we'd been working together for over six months I began to feel that helping him gain a full-fledged awareness of what fueled his drive to succeed might be impossible. I decided it was time to push him to discuss the rage he felt toward his father. My working hypothesis was that if Sean refused to discuss how his father made him feel impotent relative to his brothers, he would never see what was driving him to amass one fortune after another rather than follow his true calling, literature. To counteract the self-loathing he had formed as a result of his father's negative attitude toward his "bookworm behavior," Sean had spent nearly thirty years trying to prove that he wasn't a wimp.

Sean spent another eighteen difficult months in psychotherapy only because a bleeding ulcer convinced him it was time for a change. But for that wake-up call I would undoubtedly have lost him. Today, I'm happy to say, he has retired from the salvage business to live in one of his vacation homes and attempt, as he put it, "to become the next Frank McCourt."

According to Maslow, "The great cause of much psychological illness is the fear of knowledge of oneself—one's emotions, impulses, memories, capacities, potentialities, of one's destiny." He went on to note, "This kind of fear is defensive . . . a protection of our self-esteem, of our love and respect for ourselves. We tend to be afraid of any knowledge that could cause us to despise ourselves or to make us feel inferior."[14] Sean suppressed the rage he felt toward his father for fear it would overwhelm him. Consequently, for most of his adult life he ignored the fact that he was not being true to his calling. Only through a strenuous course of psychotherapy did he become able to feel safe with his emotions and begin to pursue self-actualizing goals.

In closing this discussion of self-actualization, it is important to draw a sharp distinction between level 5 of Maslow's hierarchy of needs—peak experiences—and career success. Quite often, as with Sean, success blocks self-actualization. On other occasions, as Freud noted, becoming self-aware about success can undermine our capacity to realize inherent potentials, capacities, and talents. According to Maslow, when someone either achieves success or is judged to have the potential for success, the resulting self-awareness can be terrifying: "To discover in oneself a great talent can certainly bring exhilaration but it also brings fear of the dangers and responsibilities and duties of . . . being all alone. Responsibility can be seen as a heavy burden [to be] evaded as long as possible."[15]

A FIRST STEP TOWARD RECOVERY

Is there a way not to become tormented by the burdens and responsibilities of success and, simultaneously, to begin the process of self-actualization? Of course, but the prescription is infinitely less complex than the cure. Maslow described the self-actualized person as living, not preparing to live. The healthy person grows when each next step in her or his life is natural and more subjectively gratifying than the previous level of satisfaction. In the language of Taoism, this is the natural way—integrating yourself with the flow of nature and not disturbing the balance of energy in the world. While this is something that people who are comfortable with others never think about, it is daunting when you were raised without understanding that you are part of a system, not a master of the universe, to achieve this insight.

In working with those who suffer Supernova Burnout, it is helpful once again to call upon Freud. According to the father of psychiatry, "To be completely honest with oneself is the very best effort a human being can make." Most careerists—particularly baby boomers—need to admit that their early decisions and commitments to achieve success at all costs were drastic mistakes. After that, the process that will move them toward self-actualization begins by acknowledging the psychological burdens of remaining atop a performance hierarchy that is materially rewarding yet devoid of psychological gratification. The difficulty with this cure is that it is antithetical to "If it feels good, do it."

I am suggesting as a first step toward inoculating yourself

against, or curing, Supernova Burnout abandonment of the mythologies that have shielded your soft psychological underbelly from self-reproach. Only when people who have been driven by agendas not of their own making accept that goal attainment cannot alter their lives, will they be free to enjoy peak experiences.

> Ambition is so powerful a passion in the human breast, that however high we reach we are never satisfied.
>
> —NICCOLÒ MACHIAVELLI

A WORD ABOUT AMBITION

The preceding discussion may have created the impression that ambitious achievement strivings are unhealthy. Nothing could be further from the truth. Setting one's sights on goals is crucial for mental health. What muddies the waters between adaptive and maladaptive ambition is an ends-versus-means distinction. If you are ambitious for intrinsic reasons—what you do enhances your sense of self-efficacy and self-esteem—the drive is healthy. If you're in it for the money, your ambition will doom you to an eternity of dissatisfaction, as Machiavelli maintained.

Maslow never addressed this subject directly, but it is likely that, were he alive, he would endorse the expression of ambition that evokes self-satisfaction because it is naïve to assume that, as adults, we can restrict ourselves to attaining nothing more than the sense of abandonment children have en route to peak experiences. As adults we are regularly called upon to integrate our drive for self-actualization with the requirement to help others—most notably, family—actualize their basic needs. Every person who functions in the role of provider is denied the luxury of living devoid of ambition.

Why ambition has so many bad connotations is perplexing; most likely it is too readily confused with both self-aggrandizement and crass materialism. Regardless, it is important to understand that a key to reclaiming the fire is the capacity to be ambitious in a healthy way.

CHAPTER 4

Pyrrhic Revenge: "I Hope This Hurts You More Than It Hurts Me"

Achievement, *n.* the death of endeavor and the birth of disgust.
—AMBROSE BIERCE, *THE DEVIL'S DICTIONARY*

Ambrose Bierce, one of the world's more lovable and incorrigible cynics, was more right than wrong in his indictment of achievement. There is no denying that achievement is the building block upon which self-esteem develops, yet when achievement is an *end* foisted upon them, and not a *process,* many would-be achievers get thrown off—or, more accurately, jump off—the ladder of success. This phenomenon is far more disruptive to emotional well-being than psychological reactance motivated by a perceived denial of behavioral freedom. When people feel that their entire beings are subordinated to the goals of success set by others, highly antagonistic or even violent reactions ensue.

This notion that trying to motivate someone to succeed could prompt aggressive retaliation does not fit well with our beliefs about the Spirit of America. In the minds of many the roots of our capitalist culture can be traced to the self-help ethos of the Puritans. The beau ideal of this perspective is, arguably, Benjamin Franklin's *Poor Richard's Almanack,* a collection of maxims for achieving success and wealth (as always, linked) through the application of industry, perseverance, and personal initiative.

Roughly a century after Franklin established this genre, Horatio Alger began publishing novellas that championed the other cornerstone of the Protestant work ethic: the self-made man. The message in Alger's sagas of boys like Ragged Dick and Tattered Tom climbing from rags to riches was succinct: No matter what your station in life when you're born, you can always improve yourself if you work diligently and live a godly life.

Unfortunately, the bulk of this literature presents an unbalanced picture. Left wholly unaddressed by Franklin and Alger are the psychological problems that can arise for those whose climb to the top occurs under special circumstances. For example, Alger was quite enthusiastic about the chances that Tom and Dick had to attain any station in life they desired, yet it is well known that when boys named Seamus, Mordecai, and Sun-Yung Lee immigrated to America, they were far less emotionally gratified by their attempts to climb the ladder of success. Likewise, people who climb the ladder to the top out of fear of disobeying the dictates of parents who demand success typically do so at the expense of their emotional well-being.

Franklin and Alger doubtless assumed that their writings would inspire people to strive to succeed. Yet their work has often been employed like a cattle prod, not a shepherd's crook. When "grab the brass ring" is not a form of encouragement but rather a form of coercion, anything accomplished to satisfy that mandate will be tainted by resentment or contempt.

The Protestant work ethic has little to say regarding abusive treatment. When people are pushed to extremes they are likely to turn to the principle of retributive justice, more commonly known as "An eye for an eye, a tooth for a tooth." There is no pain more likely to engender a drive to retaliate than being shamed or humiliated. When your ego gets slapped, an eye or a tooth will not satisfy your desire for vengeance. That can only be quelled by humiliation as great as, or greater than, what you endured.

Exhortations to achieve success are infinitely more damaging to children than to adults. A grown-up knows that professional careers are designed, in large measure, to secure an income. But when a school-age child believes that success in his career—education—is being coerced by parents for their emotional gain or psychological satisfaction, the drive to achieve can be devastating.

ACADEMIC UNDERACHIEVEMENT

At the start of my career, one-third of my clinical practice was devoted to the children of highly successful (read, wealthy) parents, who suffered a kiddie version of Supernova Burnout. Their symptomatology—fundamentally a failure to conform to their parents' demands that they "get an A and make Mom and Dad happy"—is also known as academic underachievement. These children are judged to have academic potential that far exceeds their academic performance, yet there are two major reasons why they won't produce top-quality academic work: fear of social censure and anger.

There are few fates worse for a preteen or teenager than to be labeled a nerd or a teacher's pet. Being ostracized for not being cool is a form of exile that, some psychologists have speculated, can provoke psychologically vulnerable teenagers to engage in extreme forms of violence—for example, the murderous rampage by Eric Harris and Dylan Klebold at Columbine High School. To guard against being targeted for the slurs and social isolation that follow a child once he is labeled a "brainiac" or "know-it-all geek," bright children often fail to perform up to their intellectual capacity.

The most common cause of academic underachievement is thought to be the desire to avoid social stigmatization by not slapping one's peers in the face with stellar test scores and favorable attention from teachers.[1] One can also avoid getting singled out as special by being truant, a discipline problem, or class clown. But the bottom-line motivation appears to be constant: to avoid the problems that befall the academically successful.

A less prevalent yet nevertheless well-recognized cause of academic underachievement is anger toward parents who, from the child's perspective, badger him to succeed. If a child senses that he is being urged to excel for the benefit of those who can lay claim to paving his way, showing him the ropes, or being the source of the DNA responsible for his potential, he is likely to feel enraged. Psychologists who have analyzed this subgroup of underachievers note that nothing will drive a child to sabotage his academic potential faster than a parent who responds to his success with "I knew you could do it all along" or "I told you so."[2] This demeaning commentary conveys a variety of messages, all capable of fomenting rage.

At one level, "I told you so" conveys to a child: "It was our effort to hold your feet to the fire that enabled you to succeed." At another level it turns a child's stellar performance into a form of punishment: You're damned if you don't do as expected because it reflects a bad attitude, and you're damned if you do because your success is what you were told to do and thus was ultimately caused by factors other than your ability.

Teaching children to obey parental directives is good and proper, but healthy parents demand obedience while ensuring their children will be positioned psychologically to take credit for their success. To enable a child to save face if he acquiesces to a directive, exemplary parents act as if the child's observance of the rules was a path he elected to follow because of his good judgment, virtue, and intellect. Yet many parents are insensitive to the needs of a child desperately seeking autonomy, identity, and self-esteem. By imposing their will and, when they obtain compliance, reminding their children that they are pawns, tools, or puppets, such parents inadvertently generate intense resentment in children who initially wanted nothing more than approval and affection for doing as they were told.

SELF-EFFICACY

One of the most psychologically gratifying experiences in life is feeling that you have control over significant portions of the world; psychologists call this feeling *self-efficacy*.[3] Feelings of self-efficacy have a variety of psychological, as well as physical, benefits: They can improve academic performance, enhance social skills, and ward off disorders ranging from the common cold to depression. By contrast, not feeling self-efficacious—as though you are under the control of agents who "pull your strings" as though you are a marionette—is known to induce a range of disorders. In fact, it is well known that feeling out of control or "helpless" is the prime antecedent of most nonbiologically based cases of depression.[4]

The child who develops into an academic underachiever is often motivated to perform badly because he believes that performing "appropriately"—in a way that will lead to success—will keep him under the control of parents. Many children who have no concerns about social ostracism are motivated to underachieve merely to feel autonomous. The child who is motivated to gain control with an ostensibly self-defeating set of behaviors soon discovers that hurting oneself can be adaptive and rewarding—if Mom and Dad take notice.

Parents who are extremely overinvested in having their children fulfill their wishes typically respond to the underachievers' bad report cards or low grades with tutors, educational aids, cajoling, bribery, and the like. Once this pattern of reacting or overreacting is entrenched, the underachievers have effected a full role reversal with their parents: The once-victimized child is now the manipulator and the parent the puppet having his or her strings pulled.

The primary reason so many young children can gain control via self-defeating behaviors is that their narcissistic parents are overinvested in obtaining the rewards a successful child can give them:

the "My Child Is an Honor Student" bumper sticker or the Harvard window decal. There are times, however, when a child cannot turn the tables on a narcissistic parent and must acquiesce to demeaning control for decades. When this situation exists severe problems ensue.

LITTLE EINSTEIN'S REVENGE

"Adam" is a former patient of mine from a suburb of Boston, where he and one sister (six years his senior) were raised in a wealthy, extremely Orthodox Jewish home. As a consequence Adam's life was governed by rigid doctrines that included strict observance of the Sabbath, dietary regulations, and prohibitions against consorting with non-Jewish women. Despite his family's intense involvement in Judaic culture and religious observance, in Adam's household there was no orthodoxy more sacrosanct than achievement. Both of Adam's parents were college-educated; his sister was a straight-A student, ultimately graduating with highest honors from Columbia University. This level of academic success had been a baseline for Adam since he entered preschool. He was preordained to be a scholar and, ultimately, a leader in whatever field he chose to pursue.

As a youth Adam spent virtually no time with his workaholic father, who ran a lucrative jewelry business. Despite being worth "millions upon millions" as Adam tells it, his father would spend Sunday through Friday immersed in work-related matters. Saturdays were spent in prayer, contemplation, or discussing the Bible with men in his extended family. According to Adam, the only event capable of disrupting this routine was his son not getting an A. As Adam tells it, "Heaven forbid his scholar failed to perform according to plan. If I didn't achieve like his 'little Einstein,' I could count on two-hour lectures every day for a week. Fortunately, I was a summa cum laude Harvard graduate before getting my MBA there. Anything less was out of the question."

After completing his graduate studies, Adam married an Orthodox girl he had known since high school and went to work in
Switzerland, where he became immersed in international banking.
But something in his soul, he claims, was tied to the jewelry business, and in three years he returned to Massachusetts to work with
his father. As I learned later, Adam's first trip out of the USA may
have been designed to free him from an unhealthy relationship with
his dad. Yet, as is often the case with psychologically disordered relationships, one or both parties come to view the option to leave the
field as less attractive than remaining on the scene and striving to
emerge as dominant.

Immediately upon his return to Boston Adam was installed as
president and chief operating officer of his father's company; among
other duties he supervised the buying, selling, and ultimate reselling of
millions of dollars' worth of gems and semiprecious stones. This vocation afforded Adam a very comfortable lifestyle, but money was
not what he needed most: Using gifts from his parents and in-laws
(who were actually wealthier than his parents), Adam and his wife
paid cash for a luxurious home, began having children, and became
active in the temple his family had been affiliated with for over three
generations. Life looked great until a team of officers from the Boston
Police came to arrest Adam on charges of fencing stolen jewels.

At Adam's arraignment it was revealed that the police had been
observing him for over two years. They had audio- and videotaped
documentation of Adam making huge purchases of both loose dia-
monds and estate pieces that lacked authentic certificates of owner-
ship. While on the advice of counsel he initially pleaded not guilty,
Adam soon agreed to a plea bargain that allowed him to pay a steep
fine and serve a five-year probation but no jail time. Immediately
after he negotiated his way out of his legal quagmire, he began seeing me for psychotherapy.

The most striking aspect of Adam's case is that although he was
able to make close to $1 million from fencing hot diamonds, he
never spent one cent of it; all the money was deposited in an off-
shore account. Moreover, Adam didn't exploit money for personal

satisfaction. He was a modest, religious family man, with only one vice—custom-tailored clothing—that he could easily afford on the $250,000-a-year salary he earned working for his father. If Adam had all the money he needed to live on and then some, what drove him into crime? Why would he jeopardize his future for riches?

I believe that Adam answered these questions at our first therapy session in response to my opening query: "So what brings you here?" He said, "I think I've killed my father. I know I devastated my mother, sister, wife, in-laws, and sons; I've brought shame upon my family name because of what I've done, but that's not the reason I'm so depressed. The biggest issue in my life right now is the fact that I killed my father." Had Adam not repeated the word *killed* twice, and had I not known that his father was alive and paying for Adam's psychotherapy, I might have let his turn of phrase go without comment. But under the circumstances, his repetition told me that the term had greater significance.

In psychiatry it is generally accepted that *parapraxis*—a faulty association, slip of the tongue, or other error involving cognitive recall or expression—can reveal underlying wishes, thoughts, or motives. A man oppressed by guilt over his extramarital affairs might say, when asking his wife for the device he needs to change a lightbulb in their ceiling, "Honey, could you bring me the *lover*" instead of "bring me the *ladder.*" Adam's saying that his criminal activity *killed* his father—not shamed, dishonored, disgraced, humiliated, or mortified the man—may have *sounded* random, but undoubtedly had profound psychological importance.

One other point convinced me that Adam's Freudian slip was rich in meaning: The moment I met Adam I noticed that his demeanor screamed "overcontrolled." You know how some people smile too much, nod too often, are instantly gracious and universally accessible? That was Adam. He virtually shouted, "Shalom, shalom! Hug me!" with gestures and verbal expressions, but his face told me he was really angry.

I had assumed Adam was angry because he had been caught fencing stolen goods. Yet the moment I heard him claim that what depressed him most was the fact that his criminal activity had "killed" his father, I was certain Adam believed he was not responsible for his state. He blamed only his father.

> There is no trap more deadly than the trap you set for yourself.
>
> —RAYMOND CHANDLER

> Another such victory over the Romans, and we are undone.
>
> —PYRRHUS, KING OF EPIRUS

RETALIATION MASQUERADING AS SELF-DESTRUCTIVENESS

Dozens of people I have worked with have sought to destroy their professional success for reasons that ultimately could be understood as having adaptive value. Some people engaged in self-destructive behavior to remove themselves from career tracks they had grown to despise. Others, like Adam, who suffer deeper psychological scarring, resorted to a tactic that I call *Pyrrhic revenge*. Simply stated, Pyrrhic revenge is a behavioral strategy that enables a person to punish someone else by harming himself and/or his career. People who resort to Pyrrhic revenge to retaliate for past abuses have the political genius of Machiavelli's prince: Their behavior doesn't appear to be retaliatory, but it is.

Despite their political savvy and the adaptive value derived from their self-destructive acts, people who engage in Pyrrhic revenge are, at bottom, suffering intense psychological pain. When a revenge seeker goes to the lengths that someone like Adam did to camouflage his intentions, it is safe to say his biggest problem is not his shattered career but rather how he can cope with his anger without being crippled by anxiety.

The ultimate utility of Pyrrhic revenge is that it affords a vehicle for making the ignoble feelings of aggression or hostility known. A primary goal of people who seek Pyrrhic revenge is to harm someone in a way that leaves their own self-image intact. Such people can claim to be good people, simply misguided, blinded, or stressed. This point is critical to an understanding of what motivates Pyrrhic revenge and, ultimately, what can enable people to extricate themselves from a pattern of self-deception that causes Supernova Burnout. As long as people are unable or unwilling to cope with angry or aggressive feelings, it is impossible to achieve psychological satisfaction.

There is no shortage of stories about people who have grabbed life's brass ring and then acted in ways guaranteed to alienate and shame people they allegedly love, while jeopardizing their chances of earning a living. No two cases are exactly alike, and not all the self-defeating professionals I work with view their behavior as tactical or retaliatory, but sometimes, as they say in the law, *res ipsa loquitur.* The facts speak for themselves.

In 1998 *Fortune*'s star investigative reporter, Richard Behar, wrote an award-winning exposé on Dennis Helliwell, a man he called "the Hannibal Lecter of Wall Street: a monetary cannibal who devoured his own loved ones."[5] As Behar describes it, Helliwell ran a Ponzi scheme for eleven years, ten years and four months longer than Charles Ponzi, the master con man for whom this scam was named, ran his. Helliwell raised nearly $5 million by promising some fifty investors lucrative returns from an exclusive fund he managed for Marine Midland Bank—in reality, his checking accounts. Yet what most distinguishes Helliwell from the legions of white-collar criminals who foist get-rich-quick schemes on naïve investors is that he preyed only on his close friends and family. Before Helliwell was through, he had plundered his sister-in-law's savings, taken close to $1 million from his in-laws, and bilked his best friend, godfather to one of his daughters, for $667,000.

When *Fortune*'s Behar asked me if I could account for Helliwell's ostensibly sadistic behavior toward loved ones, I thought I could, despite the fact that I never spoke to the man. While unable to diagnose Helliwell on the basis of Behar's reporting alone, I was confident that the origins of his behavior were similar to those that prompted Adam to behave as he did. The major distinction between Adam's Pyrrhic revenge and Helliwell's Ponzi scheme, as I saw it, was that Helliwell seemed to be driven by a need for compensatory retaliation—feeling he had been judged damaged goods at some point in his life and wanting to make people pay for such a harsh and incorrect assessment.

White-collar criminals frequently use success or con games to mask negative components of their self-conception. A person raised with this sort of feeling will often resort to self-destructive tactics to entice people into his life so he can punish them for wrongs that they, or others, have committed. In the short term, this strategy can work wonders, but ultimately no amount of success can mollify the feeling that, for example, people you loved have always deemed you unworthy.

In a purely greed-driven confidence game, a criminal will set up a storefront, lure people in, and vanish once he has made a financial killing. This con man's goal is money, and once it has been obtained, why stick around? But the self-destructive white-collar criminal soils his own nest as much as possible. He is in it for the denouement: "You've treated me like crap, lied about caring for me, but I knew the truth all along. Now who's the schmuck?" This type of white-collar criminal doesn't seek to randomly rip off strangers; he uses his illicit schemes to trap and punish intimates. "I'm going down, but you're coming with me!"

Again, in fairness, I cannot be certain that Helliwell's motivations were comparable to Adam's or the ones just described. But if Helliwell was not driven by some intention to harm intimates, why didn't he cast a wider net when fishing for suckers? Similarly, why didn't he seek refuge in Bimini once he had amassed enough money to live high on the hog for the rest of his life? His behavior seems to have been directed more at inflicting emotional distress on friends and family than at gratifying materialistic or hedonistic desires.

SISYPHUS OF ACHIEVEMENT?

While a disorder such as Adam's is difficult to explain in terms of one set of conditions, it is well known that the type of abusive parenting he experienced disrupts the formation of healthy self-esteem. Psychologists call major disturbances in self-esteem functioning narcissistic disorders because the people so affected often compensate for feeling inadequate or insufficiently good by acting as if they are entitled to the kudos and deference afforded people of distinction. It's a whistle-a-happy-tune defense: The more you fool the people you fear, the more you fool yourself . . . supposedly.

I concluded that the messages Adam received from his parents generated a narcissistic disorder because there was no way for him to behave in accordance with his father's wishes and not ultimately end up feeling inadequate. On the one hand, his father's assessment of him—"my little Einstein"—could be construed as idealized. Yet, as indicated by the diminutive *little* and the self-centered *my*, what concerned Adam's father were his own narcissistic needs and his son's capacity to satisfy them. Adam was never urged to achieve so he could feel good about himself, he was exhorted for the sake of his father's self-esteem: "Be great for me, prove that our bloodline is superior; that's what I need in order to love you." Adam's albatross was that he could never generate a sense of self-approval because he was never given the sense that his father put his son's needs above his own. With a developmental history like that, it is virtually impossible to derive psychological satisfaction from attaining a goal.

Yet what truly sealed Adam's fate was his father's devaluation of him. At the slightest hint of falling short of his father's demands, Adam was vilified by the very person whose approval he needed to feel valuable. A report card containing an A— would evoke a torrent of condemnation. While some would point out that the demands of his father motivated Adam to get an Ivy League education, I would ask if a galley slave should thank the whip-wielding taskmaster for enabling him to see the world. A child who is constantly subjected to alternatively idealizing and devaluing messages from a parent will spend a lifetime striving to negate the negative feelings this feedback engenders. For people like Adam, blessed with enormous intellect and indefatigable determination, striving to attain the goals set by a selfish parent is a coping strategy that can be sustained for decades.

Unfortunately, the remedy does not cure the problem; it can only afford two forms of symptomatic relief.

On the one hand, the child who internalizes and acquiesces to a parent's narcissistic demands feels relief when he can gratify the parent and serve as the parent's narcissistic extension—the agent providing narcissistic supplies. Adam's father said, in effect, "You achieve and I'll feel good," so that's what Adam did. Did Adam's achievements provide *him* with an intrinsic sense of gratification? How could they when the goal of the achievements was to make his father feel good? Repeat this process often enough, and the narcissistic extension comes to feel used, manipulated, dehumanized.

There is one favorable consequence of being successful in the role of narcissistic extension: Real accomplishments secure praise, awards, rewards, the cheers of one's peers, and other forms of adulation that can provide a transient sense of self-esteem. Over time, however, a person raised to be a narcissistic extension can develop a craving for the relief afforded by kudos that is as problematic as the rage felt toward the person who spurred him to succeed in the first place.

I liken the condition of patients who suffer narcissistic disorders to that of a Ming vase that has had a hole punched in its base. Try as the person might to fill this invaluable object with what it was meant to hold, the vase cannot function properly because of the damage that has been done to it. The water leaks out, and the flowers shrivel up and die.

The other metaphor I use to capture the futility that a narcissistic extension feels after racking up a history of achievement prompted solely by the desires of a needy parent is *Sisyphus of achievement*. A Sisyphus of achievement finds that the moment after he delivers on his requirement to achieve, the part of his self-esteem that screams "failure" reemerges; the limelight dims and the ascent must begin anew. This is so because there is nothing one can do to satisfy the hunger of a narcissistic parent. There is no celebrating, no basking in glory, no kudos following success, just "Give me more," which translates "What you just gave me was inadequate."

PYRRHIC REVENGE STRATEGIES

I was fortunate in my work with Adam: He accepted and explored my interpretation of his turn of phrase. We were soon able to discuss the link between his self-destructiveness and a wish that involved killing his father, and he immediately began to recollect and describe the anger he experienced when his father "unfairly abused" him and treated him in a "rigid, dogmatic, and dehumanizing" manner. Before long Adam admitted that before he started fencing jewels he was "semicognizant" of the fact that if his criminal behavior was discovered it would devastate his father like nothing else could. As he put it toward the end of our therapeutic relationship, "I guess my message to my dad all those days I was dancing with the devil was 'Father, I hope this hurts you more than it does me; I believe that it will since you love the business more than you love me. I'm now freed from my pain; you're still trapped in yours.' "

This is the essential distinction between people Freud viewed as wrecked by success and people who engage in Pyrrhic revenge. Pyrrhic revenge ultimately affords self-destructive people the opportunity to derive a bit of pleasure, perverted though it may be, from otherwise joyless achievements that were sought to satisfy a parent's narcissistic needs.

The behavior of every white-collar criminal I've ever worked with convinced me that they were not in it for the money: To a person, they waited around the scene of the crime, ensuring that they would be caught, and they felt relief upon being arrested. One of the inside traders I treated, a man who gained national attention in the late 1980s, told the FBI agents who came to arrest him, "I've been expecting you." The lack of self-protective flight, lack of concealment, and lack of denial of wrongdoing are the hallmarks of men (they're almost always men) who engage in Pyrrhic revenge. As I see it, being caught in their crimes breaks both the golden handcuffs and the Sisyphean cycle they have been trapped in for decades. Indeed, as some individuals have discovered once their lives as super-achievers driven to prove they were the brightest and the best came to an end, there may be opportunities galore to pursue more grati-fying roles as scholars or heads of charitable trusts.

When success exposes a person to the realization that nothing gained by achievement can heal narcissistic wounds, his rageful feel-ings demand resolution. Often, Pyrrhic revenge appears to be the best available option. No one who achieves success after a self-initiated climb destroys what he attained in order to inflict pain on someone else. Many people who succeed solely to gratify the narcis-sistic needs of others do. Because Pyrrhic revenge can effectively deny narcissistic parents what they have been so ravenously de-manding, and it is not an *obvious* act of aggression, many achievers who feel trapped or demeaned by success use it to cope with their unique symptoms of Supernova Burnout.

CHAPTER 5

If at First You *Do* Succeed, Try Thinking Like a Woman

Why can't a woman be more like a man?
—ALAN JAY LERNER, *MY FAIR LADY*

Because of their age-long training in human relations—for that is what feminine intuition really is—women have a special contribution to make to any group enterprise, and I feel it is up to them to contribute the kinds of awareness that relatively few men...have incorporated throughout their education.
—MARGARET MEAD

Before I became a clinical psychologist I was enamored with social psychology—the study of the development of groups, institutions, and cultures, as well as how these assemblages influence an individual's mental life and interpersonal behavior. The aspect of this field that really intrigued me was how so-called laws of human behavior could be changed simply by altering context or population.

For example, there is no doubt that the behavioral law "Birds of a feather flock together" holds true for humans as well as geese. Demonstrations can be seen in the cafeteria of any high school, where jocks dine with other jocks and geeks congregate with "propeller heads." This phenomenon is even more pronounced among adoptive citizens of America. Neighborhoods that become home to waves of immigrants are soon renamed Little Havana or Little Odessa to reflect how successfully newcomers replicate the essential features of their points of origin. The problem with the birds-of-a-feather-flock-together law is that it is limited to circumscribed settings. The obverse regularly holds true in one important context: intimate relationships. Opposites attract not only because people who are different may seem exotic but because relationships thrive when divergent strengths, passions, and proclivities stimulate growth and development.

Identifying the psychological forces that account for why a law holds true in one context and not in another is relatively simple. In the preceding examples, the contexts (migration, immigration, and high school) in which the law was upheld were rife with physical and emotional threats; any situation that arouses anxiety elicits intragroup support. By contrast, in circumstances that do not arouse anxiety, people experience the psychological safety that enables them to risk affiliating with dissimilar people (yin versus yang) who can add eustress to their lives.

WHAT APPLIES TO THE GANDER OFTEN DOESN'T APPLY TO THE GOOSE

Most people would agree that Americans have no use for quitters. Western culture extols the hero who perseveres in the face of adversity, from the Little Engine That Could to Robert Fulton, inventor of the steamboat, which was once called Fulton's Folly. Given the entrepreneurial origins of our nation, it is hard to imagine a context in which a never-say-die attitude would engender anything other than respect. But there is one: when the resolute and persevering person is a *woman*.

Ironically, when perseverance helps achieve physical conquest or domination, it is applauded and idealized, but when it fuels efforts to sustain or repair intimate relationships, it is denigrated and de-valued. Stated another way, Americans honor the male soldier who, in the heat of battle, kills an enemy or risks his life to help a dying comrade, yet we mock the Tammy Wynette type of woman who en-dures all manner of hardships to stand by her man.

TOWARD A PSYCHOLOGY OF WOMEN

The branch of psychology devoted to answering the question Why is what's good for the gander not good for the goose? is known as gender differences. Traditional approaches to gender focus on dif-ferences that can be attributed to having XY rather than YY chro-mosomes. This perspective will undoubtedly receive an enormous boost from the Human Genome Project. But until scientists pinpoint which of the 3 billion building blocks of genetic code cause mascu-line or feminine traits, I prefer to consider gender differences with-out reference to biological determinism. I believe that gender should be considered a window on human experience, through which psy-chological variables are filtered and according to which people ap-praise complex social situations and interpersonal dynamics.[1]

The scholar most responsible for this enlightened way of mak-ing sense of the gender gap is Jean Baker Miller. Her groundbreak-ing studies on the psychology of women transformed how both sexes view sex-role-appropriate, or gender-specific, behavior.[2] One of the greatest contributions Miller made came from calling atten-tion to the fact that feminine traits have been deemed not only mal-adaptive but unhealthy. We now know that in many instances just the opposite is true.

A core tenet of Miller's perspective is that because of the way they are socialized, women develop a more nurturing nature than men. The process that causes this psychological divide is quite sim-ple: Gender identity for girls comes from experiencing themselves being as much like their mothers as possible, whereas boys must de-velop their gender identity by behaving as differently from their mothers as they can.

The attempt to be autonomous or independent from their mother's behaviors and role in the nuclear family has a number of ramifications for males. They are not as comfortable with intimacy as women are (males often seem threatened by intimacy and seek safeguards against it), and they are far less able than females to strive for what Miller calls connectedness. In simple terms, while males would be more likely to view being king of the hill as a virtuous, gender-consistent outcome, females would typically see it as anathema to their sense of identity. More often than not, females would prefer to be most popular rather than, say, most likely to succeed, if—and this is a crucial *if*—success were defined in terms that connote an isolated position atop a performance or social hierarchy.

While connectedness can be extraordinarily beneficial, the downside of interpersonal connections is that you are vulnerable to the psychological pain that ensues when they are threatened or broken. In Miller's words:

> A central feature [of women's development] is that women stay with, build on, and develop in a context of connections with others. Indeed, women's sense of self becomes very much organized around being able to make and then to maintain affiliations and relationships. Eventually, for many women, the threat of disruption of connections is perceived not as just a loss of a relationship but as something closer to a total loss of self.
>
> Such psychic structuring can lay the groundwork for many problems. Depression, for example, which is related to one's sense of the loss of connection with another(s), is much more common in women.[3]

According to demographic studies of mental health, 20 to 26 percent of women will experience diagnosable depression at some time in their lives, compared with 8 to 12 percent of men.[4] Reasons for this disproportionately high rate of depression among women can be found in both medical and social-psychological models of gender differences, but because of a number of questions surrounding the medical interpretations of this finding, I will not discuss them here.[5]

It is often argued that women suffer more from depression (and, in related ways, stress) because of their roles in society. Now that women have assumed their rightful position in the workplace, a number of studies have examined the hypothesis that employed, married women would, by dint of the increased demands upon them (breadwinner + parent + homemaker), be less mentally healthy than housewives. Yet research has shown a positive association between occupancy of several social roles and mental health. In particular, higher levels of self-esteem have been found among women who were wife, mother, and professional simultaneously than among women who held fewer social roles.[6]

This finding supports a major point about the consequences of achieving success raised in this book: Attaining a specialized skill or vocational pursuit typically affords high levels of material compensation but low levels of diversified activity. Consequently, the specialist suffers a loss of aggregate sources of self-esteem. Janes-of-all-trades experience higher levels of self-esteem than do unidimensional women because the more roles one has, the more social stimulation and sources of psychological reward one is exposed to.

Since it is clear that women are not more prone to suffering depressive symptomatology than men because of work-related burdens, a number of scholars have focused on how women and men experience the implications of broken interpersonal ties to explain why women are more apt to be depressed than men. Whereas a jilted male could be expected to cope with his negative feelings in ways that externalize emotional pain (for instance, by being physically aggressive or seeking distraction by acting out or abusing drugs), women are socialized not to externalize emotional pain. Because women are more nurturing than men, and because of their earliest socialization experiences, adult women fear separateness and broken ties, and they traditionally make greater efforts to sustain or resurrect relationships that have faltered or failed.

The burden of feeling "I should make this relationship work" will, in the short term, lead to stress. If a woman is chronically attempting to improve the quality of her interconnectedness, psychological depression will likely ensue. This is particularly true if she concludes that the failure to keep her relationships thriving is a function of her powerlessness or helplessness.[7]

DOES THINKING LIKE A MAN CAUSE SUPERNOVA BURNOUT?

Among the many factors known to precipitate Supernova Burnout, one of the most pernicious is American attitudes about the person best suited to achieve success. Like it or not, the American archetype of success is synonymous with all things Titanic save the ship. The successful person, like the Titan Prometheus, is thought to be powerful, strong, and independent. Would a minor god who needed the support of a therapy group risk the wrath of Zeus? Hardly. Can we envision industry leaders slinking off for daily visits to a shrink? Doubtful.

In a similar vein, entrepreneurial heroes who are thought to have what it takes to become titans like John D. Rockefeller are described with robust and autonomous images.[8] They are referred to as self-starters or self-made men, not consensus picks to serve as project leaders. Entrepreneurial business builders "think out of the box." These guys do not worry about what the status quo feels; they march to the beat of their own damn drummers. When you think about it, the model leader of any successful business is thought to have independence, a willingness to stand the heat in the kitchen, and the fortitude to mix it up with anyone. Successful CEOs have THE BUCK STOPS HERE, not I'M OK, YOU'RE OK, emblazoned on their desk plaques.

Cultural biases about the prototype of success make it difficult for people to cope with success when they achieve it. The very way we describe success—in hypermasculinized terms—prevents many people who would gladly abandon loathsome career traps from doing so. Doing what George Bernard Shaw did involves admitting failure (of judgment, forethought, or the like). Abandoning a career path that was bearing material fruit also calls into question things like strength of character. One logical conclusion about someone who jumps off a ship sailing at top speed is "The guy can't take the pressure."

The language of success does not readily incorporate constructive concepts of psychological pain. It's anathema to the way we think about success to look at Shaw's midcourse correction as striving for more diversified rewards. This sort of bias is rampant in America today despite ample evidence that staying the course on a psychologically dissatisfying yet materially successful career track typically spells disaster.

But we can learn to talk ourselves out of these biases. Our nation needs to realign its image of success. This can be accomplished in two steps: First and foremost is the need to realize that our masculinized version of what it takes to succeed is unhealthy. The way we form impressions of people with minimal amounts of data must be understood because, as you will see, this process exacerbates the biases we have about what it takes to be a success. The second aspect of our attitude realignment must involve demonstrating that a feminine attitude toward success is the only one that can stand the test of time. Rather than living according to the adage "Nothing succeeds like success," people would be wise to adopt the slogan "Nothing *impedes* like success."

THE STIGMA OF VULNERABILITY

When I began treating people suffering Supernova Burnout, I was struck by how many of them reported that they "would die of shame" if it was discovered that they were in psychotherapy. One of the most unforgettable executives I treated for this disorder, the CEO of a Fortune 1000 corporation based near Boston, went to extraordinary lengths to ensure that no one would see him on the grounds of the psychiatric hospital where I worked. This exposure-phobic CEO would drive to my office in his secretary's car because his own vehicle sported a highly identifiable vanity plate. While he never used wigs and makeup to disguise himself, he did book back-to-back appointments and used twenty minutes of his double session to create two ten-minute buffers between himself and the patients I saw before and after him.

While this man earned nearly $1 million a year, ran a business that employed over three thousand people, and sat on four corporate boards, he couldn't bear the thought of admitting that he was unhappy with his success. In a nutshell, he dreaded having anyone say to him, "What kind of sissy can't take the pressure of a career like yours?"

This patient feared what many men fear: the stigma of vulnerability. As wrongheaded as this attitude is, many people, particularly those who were born before or at the start of the baby boom generation, do not see the virtues in vulnerability that today's men do. To members of the silent generation and many others, being vulnerable connotes being unprotected, unguarded, exposed, or susceptible, like someone who is not disease-resistant. It will be decades before our culture thinks about vulnerability in terms that connote openness to tender feelings, receptivity to the affections of others, and the like. Until that time people will resist any attempt to characterize them as vulnerable.

Society has come a long way in its attitudes toward those who are vulnerable to psychological distress. In 1986, when I treated the exposure-phobic CEO, his shame about all forms of emotional vulnerability was common. Consider the reaction that the Academy Award–winning actor Rod Steiger was forced to contend with when he went public with the news that he suffered from clinical depression: "My agents went berserk. In this town, if people are unsure of you, your career is over. Everybody thinks, 'He won't be salable; he won't be marketable.' "[9] In fact, his agents' fears were groundless: Steiger wasn't blacklisted and in fact made a feature film soon after "outing" himself.

Although most forms of mental illness are gradually losing the stigma that has surrounded "weakness of mind" since the dawn of time, rigid views about the benefits of success, how to achieve it, and how to enjoy it have proven far less amenable to change. One of the reasons this is so is that so few people experience exceptional levels of success. Emily Dickinson once observed, "Success is counted sweetest / By those who ne'er succeed." Unfortunately, those who ne'er succeed envision all sorts of joys awaiting those at the top when, as we know, the opposite is often the case. In large measure this is a function of how we describe successful people. This bias is also fueled by the universal tendency to form impressions of people predicated on minimal evidence.

Sitting in an outdoor café we notice a couple walk by and believe we can tell how well or poorly their relationship is faring and who the dominant partner is. Problems ensue, however, when the targets of our instant analyses are achievers or the well-to-do. Our judgments of successful people are often quite expansive and resistant to change. But do not chastise yourself for partaking in instant interpersonal analysis. It is not only universal but often accurate.

GETTING TO KNOW YOU . . . INSTANTLY

I readily admit it: I fell in love with my wife at first sight. After years of clinical training and competence in every psychological test of personality worth knowing, I appeared to throw my education out the window when I chose a life partner solely on the basis of watching her walk into a room and say hello to me.

I was forty-one years old when I met the woman who would end my confirmed bachelor status. Fate handed me a consulting project for a corporation based in Los Angeles, and after working there for a week, the vice president of marketing who hired me asked if I would volunteer to address a club for female executives she belonged to. I agreed gladly. During the pretalk gathering I looked at the doorway to the lecture hall, saw a stranger walk in, and was smitten. The intensity of this feeling grew stronger after we exchanged introductions and, once my talk was over, chatted about the possibility of staying in contact.

When I flew back to Boston I told my friends about the encounter, and all but one had the same reaction: "Yup, lust at first sight. Those California girls are gorgeous, Berglas, but is it worth a six-thousand-mile round trip to date a beautiful woman?" The lone dissenter from this cynical assessment was a brilliant psychiatrist, Gerald Adler, who said, "Wow, she must have one commanding personality."

Gerald knew I had formed my first impression of my wife using an *implicit theory of personality*—a system of rules that enables us to form opinions of others on the basis of a pattern of brief glances or gestures, physical appearance cues, or a few bits of conversation. These impressions are organized in ways that are highly resistant to disconfirmation. Because we selectively focus on certain characteristics as being central to our judgments, and see others as subordinate, a single piece of salient data often becomes enough to hang our implicit personality theory hats on. My friend Gerald knew that my instantaneous attraction to my wife was based on sensing that she displayed traits of great importance to me.

Each of us forms implicit theories of personality based on personal history, but the lion's share of this process is conditioned by our culture. And the major cultural determinant of implicit personality theories turns out to be language. If a central characteristic of our implicit personality theory (for instance, what type of person achieves success) is rich in culture-dictated connotations, it is highly unlikely that we will be able to alter that assessment without prolonged effort.

Over time, phrases that include the same combinations of words impart connotative meanings. Thus it becomes virtually impossible to pair certain adjectives in a description.[10] For example, it is perfectly appropriate to say, "He's a domineering, aggressive kind of guy," yet totally inappropriate to describe someone as "a domineering, *shy* kind of guy." It just doesn't feel right to link *domineering* and *shy* in one judgment.

The role of traits such as dominance and aggressiveness in the process of forming impressions of people was the subject of intense scrutiny when social psychology was in its infancy. One of the best-known and most cited series of studies of this phenomenon dealt with the consequences of manipulating the adjectives *warm* and *cold* in a thumbnail sketch of a person.[11]

In one experiment student volunteers were asked to rate a fake guest lecturer. Before meeting this person students were informed that he was either "a rather *warm* person, industrious, critical, practical, and determined" or "a rather *cold* person, industrious, critical, practical, and determined." The results of this manipulation were startling: After leading a twenty-minute discussion, the lecturer left the classroom and students were asked to fill out a candid impression rating. Observers noted that students who were told the lecturer was warm initiated far more interactions with him than those who were told he was cold. Consistent with other studies of this phenomenon, the "warm" lecturer was seen as generous, humorous, and humane, while the "cold" lecturer was seen as ungenerous, humorless, and ruthless.

THE CONSTRICTIVE EFFECTS OF BEING BRANDED A "SUCCESS"

Considering the powerful effects of manipulating the benign adjective pair *warm* and *cold,* imagine the effect of *successful* versus *failed* or *strong* versus *weak.* Ask yourself why so many people successful in fields that have no bearing on government are so readily elected to public office. Successful actors, wrestlers, athletes, and astronauts all have an easy time relative to, say, people with Ph.D.'s in government or urban studies convincing voters they can lead. It's the strength of that central trait "successful" at work in a favorable way.

Unfortunately, there is also a downside to the strong influence a trait such as *successful* has on our impressions. Consider the implicit directives contained in a well-known maxim like "When the going gets tough, the tough get going" or "Never say die." If you look beneath the surface of these action-oriented inspirational sayings, you can see why someone who has defined himself as a winner or as tough can have an incredibly difficult time coming up with a creative approach to handling problems, particularly those that call for "thinking out of the box" or adapting to novel circumstances.

If you believe that any sort of quitting or not getting going is a sign of infirmity, how can you be in your right mind when you reformulate an action plan you've been following for years? If you value being deemed successful, you've got major image problems should you appear uncertain, vacillating, or wishy-washy.

A June 21, 1999, cover story in *Fortune* magazine that analyzed why CEOs fail confirms Americans' implicit personality theory about those who succeed. The authors, the management experts Ram Charan and Geoffrey Colvin, answered the question that prompted the article, "So how do CEOs blow it?" with a telling bottom line: "The failure [of CEOs] is one of emotional strength." Specifically, Charan and Colvin maintained that the lack of strength to deal with people problems in a timely manner was the major cause of a CEO's undoing. Furthermore, most failed CEOs were unable to reverse decisions they had made to put people in key positions despite coming to recognize that their decisions were wrong. "What is striking," the authors noted, "is that [CEOs] usually know there's a problem; their inner voice is telling them, but they suppress it." As one CEO told *Fortune,* "It was staring me in the face but I refused to see it."[12]

While Charan and Colvin were correct in their conclusion, they neglected to explore its psychological underpinnings. Why, once they realized that they had given responsibility to people who could not deliver, did dozens of accomplished and intelligent CEOs become impotent to reverse their decisions? To psychologists the answer is quite simple: The CEOs' implicit personality theory of "successful leader" straitjacketed them. They couldn't see themselves as mistaken and so were not psychologically free to act in ways that were adaptive and, ultimately, self-protective.

Most people who cannot modify, or behave contrary to, an implicit personality theory about success come to this posture honestly. Successful people typically have a history of achievement predicated on their willingness to persevere in the face of adversity, to overcome ostensibly insurmountable obstacles, and to stand tall in the face of rejection. You don't climb from rags to riches if every rebuff you receive knocks you on your butt. The problem is, if the attitude "if at first you don't succeed, try, try again" becomes concretized in one's mind—if it is a mantra regardless of circumstances—the consequences can be dire. Just ask the folks Charan and Colvin interviewed.

ESCALATION OF COMMITMENT

Sewell Avery, former CEO of Montgomery Ward & Co., is a classic example of a successful business leader who was incapable of making a midcourse correction.[13] After guiding his company to a position of dominance in the retail industry, Avery blocked all attempts his management team initiated to expand to the suburbs. In fact, from 1941 to 1957 he failed to open one new store. While he was digging in his heels with regard to not rethinking his decision to stick with his exclusively inner-city base of operations, Sears Roebuck was building suburban outlets as fast as they could. The result? Montgomery Ward announced in December 2000 that it was closing its doors forever, and chains like Sears, JCPenney, and Wal-Mart, which flocked to suburban malls, continue to flourish.

Psychologists have a name for this type of management inflexibility: *escalation of commitment*.[14] In the parlance of gamblers, Avery suffered a chronic pattern of throwing good money after bad, following the notion that sunk costs justify continuing effort. Escalation of commitment is easy to understand despite its often devastating consequences. While a host of peripheral issues heighten the tendency to escalate commitment to a flawed course of action, the primary motivation is a reluctance to incur a personally and socially embarrassing outcome.

To avoid what they perceive will be shame and humiliation should they admit a mistake, imperfection, or wrongdoing, successful people get locked into escalating commitments to bad decisions through two mechanisms: ignoring or suppressing contradictory information and psychologically distorting feedback that casts a critical light on their judgment. Simply stated, by either bullying dissenters into silence or donning rose-colored glasses, many successful people do not hear or see warnings that they are on a collision course with disaster.

From an outsider's perspective, two truths make escalation of commitment puzzling: On the one hand, people in the throes of this syndrome cannot perceive that their intransigence affords them only a short-term reprieve from shame. In fact, obstinate refusal to admit a mistake almost always puts people in jeopardy of long-term disgrace and scorn.

On the other hand, paradoxically, evidence supporting the benefits derived from instantly admitting wrongdoing is all around us. When the late CEO of Coca-Cola, Roberto Goizueta, put his career on the line by replacing the soft drink industry leader Coke with "New Coke," he was bombarded with critical feedback. Rather than increase his marketing budget and escalate his commitment to his new recipe and failed business plan, Goizueta immediately reversed himself and touted "Classic Coke"—the company's original formula. Former President John F. Kennedy was also blessed with the strength of character to admit vulnerability and defeat. Following the botched Bay of Pigs invasion, he not only immediately assumed complete responsibility but publicly apologized for whatever harm his decision had caused. Never did Kennedy externalize blame for his failure (which would have been easy to do), nor did he argue that the Cuban Communist menace justified his behavior. As a consequence of their counterintuitive behaviors, both Goizueta and Kennedy saw their popularity and job approval ratings skyrocket.[15]

THE COVERT CAUSE OF ESCALATION OF COMMITMENT: "VULNERABILITY IS A GIRL THING"

In 1991 "Don," the CEO of a multimillion-dollar trucking conglomerate, came to me because he feared job stress would kill him. At our first meeting I saw a severely overweight man who looked fifteen years older than his age. Given Don's ostensible reason for seeking psychotherapy, I was incredulous when he discussed building his business with the pride befitting a self-made man. He never once hinted of suffering while on the job. Hard-pressed to determine why Don would claim the love of his life was threatening his health, I urged him to describe his other love—his wife. Then I knew why he had come to see me.

Don and his wife were childless—by choice, he claimed. Although Don maintained that his wife, a former beauty queen, was a "phenomenal woman," something was missing from his description. When he noted how beautiful she was about a dozen times more, listed all the social service agencies she belonged to, and went on about what a fantastic hostess she was, I felt I needed to ask him about his sex life. He immediately became testy: "I thought I was here to deal with a problem inside this head," he said, gesturing to his skull. "I guess what they say about shrinks is true; all you guys focus on is the *other* head."

Eventually Don confessed that "sex isn't a big part of my marriage," despite the fact that before they married he had been somewhat of a Lothario. Yet for a variety of complex reasons he married a woman who despised sexual contact with him. More important, it was obvious that this fact was taking a severe toll on his health.

After several sessions I learned how bad Don's relationship with his wife was: It took Don and his bride six months to consummate their marriage. Now, over fourteen years later, their only form of sexual contact (less than once a month) was intercourse in a darkened room. In fact, Don was not allowed to see his wife naked.

When I expressed my belief that living as he did could readily cause his symptoms of stress (panic attacks and carbohydrate cravings) Don disagreed: "You're wrong. I cope with my wife's problem quite well by visiting massage parlors on the way home from work each day. I'm sure I get more sex than anyone you know; it's just that I pay for it directly and there are some risks." When I explored what Don meant by "risks," I uncovered the true source of his stress. It turned out his panic attacks had started soon after the

AIDS virus made headlines. At first, when the press assumed the disease was restricted to homosexual men, Don ignored the dangers inherent in his lifestyle. Yet the moment that falsehood was dispelled, he began to fear for his life.

Don was experiencing panic attacks because he was trapped in a no-win situation: He was convinced that there was no possibility of developing normal sexual relations with his wife, and he believed that his continued contact with prostitutes (he refused to wear condoms) would expose him to HIV. But because discontinuing his visits to massage parlors would doom him to a functionally celibate existence, he was battling to suppress his rage toward his wife and his fear of contagion.

Once Don and I agreed that it was impossible for him to make progress in our work unless he brought his wife to a session, in which the three of us could explore the possibility of their beginning sex therapy, I felt his problems could be solved. How wrong I was. When I told Don's wife that I believed his stress stemmed from tension in the marriage rather than at the workplace, she readily agreed with me. Unfortunately, she anticipated my referral to sex therapy and beat me to the punch: "If you're suggesting that I adjust my lifestyle to accommodate Don's lust, forget it. His need for sex is his problem." With that, she left the office.

Don and I had two more sessions, but he didn't see things my way. His rationale for refusing to address the true cause of his problem had nothing to do with love for his wife and everything to do with his fear of being humiliated. "If my wife discovered that I visited massage parlors or thought I would push her to have sex, she'd leave me. And if she did, she'd tell the world about our marriage and I'd be the laughingstock of the community."

Sadly, I learned that five years after he stopped seeing me Don suffered a massive heart attack and died. While I cannot say that his rage at being trapped in a sexless marriage was the cause of his demise, I am certain that had he been able to admit that his wife's contempt for sex was tearing his guts out, and remain in his marriage while addressing the problem, Don would still be alive. But many men like Don are socialized to avoid what they perceive to be the shame of vulnerability. In their minds, admitting a problem of this magnitude would expose them to unbearable emotional pain.

WOMEN AND CONNECTEDNESS

The emotions that led to Don's demise are the reason I counsel men to think like women. Specifically, I advise that men abandon social status concerns, which are typically based solely on power as opposed to affection, and strive to build relationships that stem from being cared for as a person. I give this advice despite the fact that a woman's propensity for interpersonal connectedness is often disrespected by high-achieving men. For them, "arriving" isn't being embraced by a group or being cared for; it involves having, controlling, or owning resources that afford commercial power and command overt respect.

The truth is that the connectedness women are socialized to strive for has nothing in common with the maladaptive forms of staying the course that result in escalations of commitment. Sewell Avery persevered on a misguided course of action while refusing to acknowledge the pain that potential failure was causing him. Similarly, anecdotal reports maintain that executives suffering from escalation of commitment react to negative inputs by projecting painful psychological feelings outward: Anyone who expresses doubt about the wisdom of their policies gets excoriated.

The stereotypical successful person doesn't bend to the needs of others. His mantra is "I'm not the type to get ulcers; I give them." This attitude, embodied by former New York City mayor Ed Koch (who coined that phrase), does much more than assert dominance and control. It conveys an unwillingness to attend to emotions—particularly negative ones—and suggests that those who do are weaker. Most men who adopt this tough-guy stance will readily admit that feeling emotional pain is not manly. But who said that the manly approach to one's career, business, or personal success was adaptive? Chainsaw Al Dunlap has gone the way of the dodo bird; maybe it's time to rethink macho attitudes toward success.

If you're still on the fence about the value of opening yourself to the pain that may ensue from embracing critics or sticking your neck out to preserve a relationship, consider what happened to another client of mine. "David's" unwillingness to acknowledge vulnerability and dependence on others caused the most needless case of professional suicide I've ever seen.

I met David as a result of a lecture I gave for the Young Presidents' Organization (YPO). YPO, like a number of organizations designed to address, among other concerns, the educational and social-emotional needs of superachievers, hosts "universities" that make a variety of resources available to its members. When I addressed the YPO university that David attended, my presentation was on the perils of success, a topic tailor-made for David. He sat in the front row, asked numerous questions, and ran up (business card in hand) to chat with me the moment I concluded the presentation.

David's complaint was "I'm the kind of guy who hates ignorance." Twice in our brief chat he repeated his signature line: "How can a man like me soar like an eagle if he's constantly surrounded by turkeys?" Without confronting his defensiveness directly (my talk had focused on how success makes many people impossible to work with, and David externalized 100 percent of the blame for his less-than-satisfactory career), I told him there was a way for him to "soar higher" *if* he could learn to articulate and resolve conflicts constructively. With that he thanked me, took my business card, and ran off. I assumed I would never hear from him again.

Imagine my surprise when David called three years later and asked me to serve as a consultant to help him manage his accounting firm, which was hemorrhaging talent at an alarming rate. Like so many business builders who suffer founder's disease, David was adamantly opposed to sharing control of the firm's destiny with its top producers. The event that had prompted him to contact me was the departure of a young man he was grooming to be his successor, who took several key clients with him.

From most of David's partners I learned that there was deep-seated enmity toward him. When I shared this with him, David agreed: "They resent my authority." In truth, the majority of the partners maintained that unless David ceded control to another manager, they would leave.

My recommendation was that David form a management troika with the two most senior members of the firm. The hoped-for outcome of this intervention would be both to broaden the decision-making power base and to divide control over budgets, resources, and the like among several specialty groups. Previously the lion's share of the firm's resources went to the associates and principals who handled David's clients, firms that needed "back office" consultative inputs, as opposed to the less senior principals, who worked with the newer, Web-related clients.

David initially accepted this proposal and seemed committed to the work necessary to shore up relations with his partners. Tragically, his goodwill vanished ten months later, when he was humiliated at the firm's Christmas party. As witnesses told it, David and his wife were chatting with the men (and their wives) on the firm's management committee. After someone remarked that the prior year had been surprisingly profitable, the wife of one of David's co-managing principals remarked, "That's what you get when you have [my husband] lend David a hand in running the business. My [husband]'s a genius."

David's wife turned to him and said with venomous sarcasm, "Gee, honey, you're so dogmatic about what the kids and I can or cannot do around the home, and are so incensed when any of your *rules* are challenged, I cannot imagine you seeking out the advice of 'John' and 'Paul' [the comanaging principals] on what's best for *your* business." Obviously, David had never told his wife about the management changes at work.

Roughly two weeks later David called to see if I would help him convince John and Paul to accept his decision to scrap the three-headed management program. I told him if he did this John and Paul would leave the firm. David's comeback was classic: "Look, it's my firm. They don't know how much they need me, and you don't know how little I need them."

When I reminded David that John's and Paul's billings were twice his, he said, "You're not going to get me to kiss ass again. I never bought into your theory that I was being defensive [the term I used was *counterdependent,* a clinical way of saying "afraid of needing others"], because I'm not. I'm the name here, I have the recognition in the field, they don't. You're fired, and those [expletives deleted] will either go back to the way things were, or die without me." Two days after he delivered what I assume was the same ultimatum to his partners, David was dismissed.

What made David's self-destructive behavior so sad is that it seemed preordained. He hated his superstar jock father, who chided him for not "being a man" whenever his attempts to master athletics failed. Because David could never ask his bullying dad for guidance or emotional support, he ended up identifying with the aggressor, a version of "If you can't beat them, join them." David deduced (at an unconscious level) that his feelings would be hurt less if he learned to act like his father, treating the world the way his father treated him. This meant replacing his yearning for connectedness with a tough and cold demeanor. Yet, as is always the case when manliness is reactive as opposed to the result of gaining autonomy through healthy achievements that afford the security and self-assurance to act alone, David's I-am-a-rock-I-am-an-island mask doomed him to failure.

The best way I know to illustrate this self-deceptive ruse is to contrast the demeanor of teenage boys attempting to learn a martial art with that of a martial arts expert. When a teen starts taking karate lessons, he will often leave class dressed in all the accoutrements of the sport: Ninja pants, a jacket or shirt festooned with Oriental symbols and the name of his martial arts academy, and handheld weapons. When the karate master leaves the dojo, he rarely dresses in anything other than what is appropriate to the weather. A martial arts instructor needs no overt sign of power to feel secure in the world; he possesses an inner confidence of strength. As David's posturing proved, when you fake inner strength, you fool yourself much more than you fool other people.

A WORD OF CAUTION

If Don's and David's failed attempts to cope with vulnerability have convinced you to reevaluate the masculine definition of the person best constituted to achieve success, be careful not to overreact. Mental health professionals are virtually unanimous in the opinion that masculine traits are advantageous in many circumstances. More important, any personality trait taken to an extreme is dangerous. That said, it is important to note that when women stand by their men or their management teams, their posture works because they admit feelings of vulnerability. Typically, women acknowledge psychological pain and reach out for help.

This approach—obviously a result of women's "age-long training in human relations," to which Margaret Mead referred—often creates long-term benefit despite the short-term pain it can cause. This is particularly true of the ability to cope with the stresses of career success. If harnessed *appropriately*, women's propensity to stay connected with others can be one of the most effective inoculations against Supernova Burnout there is.

THE BENEFITS OF LOOKING AT SUCCESS THROUGH A "DIFFERENT WINDOW"

One of the most beneficial consequences of women's process of identity formation is that they seem to develop highly refined interpersonal sensitivity, empathy, and cooperation at an early age. To achieve both a gender role identity and a "normal" heterosexual role identity, women must both attach to their mothers and, periodically, detach from them, to shift attention to their fathers. Women must be both autonomous and connected to be psychologically whole, whereas men form an autonomous sense of self simply by separating from their mothers.[16]

FEAR OF SUCCESS OR FEAR OF CAUSING PAIN?

People who have managed groups of diverse personalities recognize that the traits of an effective leader are the ones that account for women's greater vulnerability to depression. Yet because sensitivity, empathy, and cooperation do not conform to our culture's implicit personality theory of a successful leader, many people who attain leadership roles lose them by being inflexible out of a fear of being perceived as feminine or a wimp.

To understand why in one context female characteristics can heighten the likelihood of disease and in another heighten the likelihood of success, we need once again to examine the many connotations of success. Consider how Julie Christie reacted to being awarded an Oscar for her role in *Darling:*

> I didn't feel I merited all that success. I was rather ashamed of it, rather embarrassed. The best way I can describe it is—well, I rather see my success as a sort of scruffy dog, a little mangy dog that's following you around, and you just can't get rid of it! It was a kind of fear that anywhere you went, this little thing was always at your heels. I felt so damned inadequate with almost everybody and everything.[17]

The most widely cited studies of the role of gender differences in determining ambition or orientation toward success were conducted in the late 1960s by the psychologist Matina Horner.[18] She found that, like Julie Christie, women seemed to be anxious about competitive striving, particularly the prospect of winning. Much of the research that followed from Horner's studies assumed the world was divided (almost always by gender) between those who hoped for success and those who feared failure. Back in the 1970s conventional wisdom held that, for women, being ambitious evoked a conflict: Succeeding was not feminine. Horner described women's fear of success this way: "For most women, the anticipation of success in competitive achievement activity, especially against men, produces anticipation of certain negative consequences, for example, the threat of social rejection and loss of femininity."[19]

Modern research into the psychology of women supports a decidedly different interpretation. One reanalysis of Horner's data found that women were "success anxious" only in zero-sum competition: contests in which one person's gain occurs at the expense of another's loss.[20] Stated in terms that make a feminine worldview a virtue, when their success can effect a rising tide that lifts all ships, women are no more avoidant of success than men are.

The bottom line seems to be, as the psychoanalyst Erik Erikson pointed out, that male identity is forged in relationship to mastery of the world at large, and female identity is awakened in a relationship of intimacy with another person.[21] It seems doubtful at best that women's orientation can be adaptive when beginning one's career; so much of early life success depends on self-generated goal seeking in the face of adversity. But given the disorders linked to mastery, autonomy, and rejection of intimacy, it is a wonder that any successful man makes it to the age of forty without suffering a major psychological disturbance. The hallmark of high-achieving males seems to be anticonnectedness. Women, by contrast, work in networks, form webs of inclusion, and readily acknowledge problematic feelings.

Research in developmental psychology indicates that girls are reinforced not for mastery but for expressing their fears. Boys, however, are encouraged to master their fears and negative feelings, which often involves denying them or attempting to escape them by acting out.[22] Could those championship Green Bay Packers teams that Vince Lombardi coached on the frozen tundra of Lambeau Field have survived if they had discussed anxiety before game time? No way. Yet the cost of failing to express these so-called feminine emotions is enormous if allowed to continue throughout one's career.

MISERY LOVES COMPANY, SHOULD YOU?

Publilius Syrus, a former Roman slave who composed hundreds of maxims between 42 and 1 B.C.E., was the first, according to *Bartlett's Familiar Quotations*, to note, "It is a consolation to the wretched to have companions in misery." Never one to skimp on words, he also observed, "Society in shipwreck is a comfort to all." I have to hand it to him, roughly two thousand years before psychiatry gained respectability, this Roman was handing out psychotherapeutic advice that Beverly Hills shrinks now charge three hundred dollars an hour to dispense. Unfortunately, most successful men won't pay attention to Publilius Syrus's wisdom regardless of the price.

Chris Argyris, of the Harvard graduate schools of business and education, has devoted much of his career to analyzing smart people's resistances to being reeducated when they are in positions of authority and leadership. Among other things, Argyris's findings confirm that smart old dogs are adamantly opposed to learning new tricks.[23] He believes that the root of this resistance is a general human tendency to act in accordance with four basic values: (1) to remain in control; (2) to maximize "winning" and minimize "losing"; (3) to suppress negative feelings; and (4) to behave in what appears to be a rational way to the greatest extent possible.

According to Argyris, "The purpose of all these values is to avoid embarrassment or threat, feeling vulnerable or incompetent. In this respect . . . most people [behave in a] profoundly defensive [manner]. Defensive reasoning encourages individuals to keep private the premises, inferences, and conclusions that shape their behavior and to avoid testing them in a truly independent, objective fashion."[24] In other words, Argyris has unearthed the value system that accounts for escalation of commitment and the machismo on which most failed executives hang themselves.

While Argyris didn't discuss gender differences in relation to his four basic values, I have consistently found that men adhere to them more than women do. As a rule the person who experiences Supernova Burnout has a history of success that renders him wholly unfamiliar with the consequences of failure. So his implicit personality theories about "failed" people become caricatures with traits such as unhappy, weak, and stupid.

Because women are trained to process the negative feelings that arise from failure or simple disappointment, they are familiar with two facts of life not well known to successful men: (1) that you rarely die from committing simple mistakes; and (2) that the company you have in misery can be a valuable resource. Even women with histories of success know, at a deep psychological level, that not only the loser suffers from hurt feelings. This empathy, as the reinterpretations of Horner's data demonstrate, does not make women more likely to fail or more likely to self-sabotage, it just gives them a broader base for understanding the complex consequences of being successful and having to confront negative outcomes.

A number of studies prove that social support promotes mental health. One study done to assess the relative benefits of the ways male and female managers cope with stress demonstrated that male patterns of coping, such as involvement in nonwork activities (for instance, wishful thinking), were far less effective than turning to others for help, as women did.[25] Furthermore, when women managers felt that they had the support of supervisors, co-workers, and friends and family, they were far more likely to engage in coping strategies that resolved problems and made them feel better psychologically than were men who operated without a diverse network of social support.

Given the preponderance of support for the notion that psychological connectedness helps people cope with stressful life events, and the obvious fact that women's heightened involvement in intimate relationships facilitates social support, the question arises again: Why can't a man think more like a woman? Or why can't a successful man use information from others to solve his problems?

The answer is not simple, but I think part of it can be found in the data I gathered for my dissertation studies on self-handicapping behavior. The most problematic finding (at the time) was that only men consistently sought to externalize responsibility for potential failure. According to Professor Argyris, this propensity has several long-term, harmful consequences:

> Put simply, because many professionals are almost always successful at what they do, they rarely experience failure. And because they have rarely failed, *they have never learned how to learn from failure*...when their [problem solving] strategies go wrong, they become defensive, screen out criticism, and put the "blame" on anyone and everyone but themselves. In short, their ability to learn shuts down precisely at the moment they need it the most [emphasis added].[26]

I have found that self-handicappers, and others crippled by the burdens of avoiding the humiliation they anticipated would follow from anything other than successful behavior, naturally concluded that negative outcomes could not be coped with, only avoided or overcome through perseverance. As a consequence, they did everything in their power to attribute blame to anything but their core self.

Management experts like Argyris, and most mental health professionals, like Jean Baker Miller, contend that the only way to correct this disordered mode of thinking is education. I concur; professionals need to see that men like John F. Kennedy and Roberto Goizueta *gained* respect after they acknowledged mistakes and amassed social support for their actions by doing so. But it's the school of hard knocks that offers the best curriculum on earth for this body of knowledge.

Yet the greatest impact on our stereotypic views of what it takes to succeed will occur when more women executives outperform male counterparts by soliciting social support and critical inputs. Then the brightest and best males will model these women's behaviors and amend their implicit personality theories about how successful people behave while improving their chances for long-term success by shifting career paths without having to suffer some cataclysmic event.

Another adjunct to educational efforts designed to highlight the value of a feminine management style involves demonstrating how valuable a woman's capacity for nurturance can be. The illustration I use to differentiate the masculine model of slam-bam-thank-you-ma'am success from a woman's nurturing approach involves contrasting the rewards of growing pine trees in different ways.

The first way, familiar to most, is on a tree farm. Weyerhaeuser does this on a scale that has enabled it to achieve Fortune 500 status. Even smaller tree farmers who ship three- to six-year-old specimens to market soon after Thanksgiving rake in tons of cash by tapping into what seems to be a permanent market for once-live Christmas trees. There is, however, a profitable alternative.

This second method involves taking a single pine seedling and crafting it into a replica of a hundred-year-old weather-beaten, majestic timber, then nurturing it in a pot that forces it to remain dwarfed. The result is a single bonsai tree that not only is a work of art countless people can enjoy but may be worth hundreds of thousands of dollars.

Young male business builders typically work according to the tree farm model: Find the best way to get the most high-quality products to market, automate the process where possible, satisfy customer demand, and reap huge profits. Women seem to manifest a preference for bonsais, particularly when they have enough material comforts to sustain themselves. The bonsai grower knows that if she can give life to a product that lives forever and perpetually adds value to the lives of others, she has not only a success but a legacy.

CHAPTER 6

Toward Resolving the Paradox of Supernova Burnout: How the Enchantment with Success Became an Obsession

When you're green, you're growing. When you're ripe, you rot.

—RAY KROC

How dull it is to pause, to make an end,
To rust unburnish'd, not to shine in use!

—ALFRED, LORD TENNYSON, "ULYSSES"

To resolve the tragic paradox of Supernova Burnout—achieving, or being capable of achieving, the professional and material goals you desire but suffering psychological distress as a consequence—it is critical that we understand the historical antecedents of this disorder. Two concerns are crucial to this analysis: (1) What is it about our cultural heritage that makes us uniquely vulnerable to being devastated by success? (2) Why, despite the availability of limitless data to the contrary, do Americans of all ages unshakably believe that professional success can engender wholesale changes for the good in one's life?

ONE DAY IN MAY

Those of you who doubt that most Americans have a success-at-any-cost ethos would have become true believers on May 16, 2000, if you read *The New York Times*. Two stories, a mere eleven pages apart, illustrated just how blinding the spotlight of success can be.

The first story was shocking to many when it made national headlines in 1995: A faculty adviser and a group of students from Steinmetz High School in Cook County, Illinois, conspired to engineer a victory in a statewide academic decathlon by stealing the test for the competition and memorizing the answers. Although the conspirators captured the championship, their fraud was discovered and they were stripped of their ill-gotten glory. The *Times* story in May 2000 described a reunion of those involved to celebrate a preview screening of the HBO film *Cheaters*, based on what they had done.

You would think that a get-together designed to commemorate a deplorable act of deceit would be a somber occasion. Guess again. According to *The New York Times*, the reunion was a celebration without a single drop of authentic remorse. Most appalling was the students' reaction to what they had done. "Apologize for what?" one asked defiantly, "I would do it again." According to another cheater, "It wasn't the first time there was cheating, and it won't be the last."[1]

The second story was the decision to allow Bob Knight, coach of the Indiana University men's varsity basketball team, to retain his job despite an investigation determining that the coach had been involved in a "lengthy pattern of troubling behavior" that included verbal attacks on players, officials, journalists, and office staff; physical assault; and the destruction of university property during fits of rage. According to the university's president, Myles Brand, "No incident by itself rose to the level of termination" of someone he characterized as "a man of integrity."[2]

The *Times* columnist Harvey Araton said of this decision that when a man who has won three national basketball championships is responsible for highly objectionable behavior, "the welfare and safety of the typical student and innocent employee at Big Time U. is less of a priority than [another] potential run to [a championship]."[3] Although his interpretation was accurate, and, it turns out, prescient—Knight was fired from his job in September 2000 for confronting and grabbing a nineteen-year-old freshman who taunted him—Araton's pique at the time could be considered naïve, particularly from a seasoned journalist. How could a man so familiar with the world of sports expect anything other than this bend-over-backward-to-accommodate-a-winner attitude to hold sway in America? Doesn't Araton realize that big-time college athletics is big business? And could he have forgotten that only months earlier the ace relief pitcher for the Atlanta Braves, John Rocker, was exposed as a ranting bigot with little consequence?

Actually, the response of the Braves organization to Rocker may have been more reprehensible than the course of no action taken against Bob Knight for so long. Is it possible that the owners of the Braves were not aware of Rocker's attitudes long before *Sports Illustrated* exposed them? How do you explain the fact that they ignored their star athlete's misconduct until the commissioner of major league baseball condemned it? Is it simply that if you throw a fastball at ninety-two miles per hour with pinpoint accuracy, the rules governing your behavior are not the same as those for less skilled athletes? It seems that Leona Helmsley, felon, hotelier, and self-described queen of a real estate empire, was slightly off the mark when she said, "Only the little people pay taxes." She probably meant to say, "Only the little people pay for their crimes."

The special treatment afforded Bob Knight and John Rocker, as well as the attitudes of the "scholars" from Steinmetz High School, underscore a fundamental fact about life in America: Not only are we obsessed with acquiring riches and fame but we idolize those who have done so. Our fascination with success has such an effect on our national psyche that it can shield those who have become successful from being judged as harshly as comparably devious people who have failed to convert their illicit behavior into wealth, status, or fame. Consider the following examples of how the aura of success affected the operation of allegedly impartial judicial procedure.

> When the film executive Robert Evans was convicted of cocaine use, his sentence was to create a program to deter young people from using drugs. When the Hollywood studio head David Begelman pleaded no contest to charges of embezzling funds from Columbia Pictures, he was ordered to continue his psychiatric care.
>
> Contrast these sentences to the one given William James Rummel for three nonviolent crimes that netted him a total of $230.00—life imprisonment (a judgment upheld by the Supreme Court).[4]

The social historian Barbara Goldsmith has noted that people striving to "make it" in America no longer pursue winning or achieving as precursors to success, they merely seek the spotlight of celebrity. It's as though the accoutrements of success have become the essence of the experience, supplanting self-esteem gains, pride of accomplishment, and satisfaction as the essence of making it. If you can attract hordes of press photographers, have your picture in *People,* and generate buzz, it matters not if your claim to fame involves having sex with a child prostitute who shot and maimed your wife or having sex with the president of the United States. When you're hot, you're hot.

Goldsmith uses the term "synthetic celebrities" to describe people for whom the sizzle of success has substituted for the steak: "Among the worthy now are these synthetic celebrities, famed for their images not their deeds."[5] This observation begs a question: How did Americans come to be blinded by success? The psychological principle that can shed light on this phenomenon is the law of *mere exposure effects.*[6]

As every advertising expert or political campaign manager knows well, people come to like those things they are exposed to repeatedly. This is true even if our exposure is merely passive. Having any logo—Coca-Cola, Nike or its now-famous "swoosh," or a multicolored apple with a bite taken out of its right side—splashed in front of our faces can cause us to see the product as worthy or good for reasons that are not entirely clear.

Worse yet, in today's instant-access culture that bombards people with millions of images a day, it is easy to achieve celebrity through mere exposure. Consequently, we come to respect people for presumed or imputed expertise when what they do to achieve celebrity often does not at all reflect the skills, competencies, or aptitudes we think are responsible for their performances.

HOW SUCCESS SUPPLANTED THE PROTESTANT WORK ETHIC

Our national preoccupation with success and the belief that it has favorably life-altering capabilities is not simply a function of the fact that our founding fathers possessed material wealth, public visibility, stature, and status. The propensity to view those who achieve success as though they sit atop pedestals or have recently descended from Mount Olympus has its roots in a number of potent cultural influences.

Nearly one hundred years ago, in a letter written to H. G. Wells on September 11, 1906, William James observed, "The moral flabbiness born of the exclusive worship of the bitch-goddess SUCCESS. That—with the squalid cash interpretation put on the word success—is our national disease."[7] James was articulating how the religious heritage of the United States is responsible for both "the squalid cash interpretation put on the word success" and the power that success is alleged to have over our sense of psychological well-being. We might say that success has come to fill a role religion once played in our lives. If so, it is possible that this belief system, which imbues success with the power of the Almighty, is the root cause of a host of psychological disturbances.

Among the myriad philosophies that have shaped our culture, the Protestant work ethic is arguably the most influential. This doctrine emphasized hard work and self-sacrifice as a means of achieving spiritual improvement. Puritanism was adamantly opposed to the accumulation of wealth for wealth's sake: "Avarice and happiness never saw each other, how then should they become acquainted?" asked Benjamin Franklin through his alter ego, Poor Richard. Yet avarice *did* meet happiness, or at least people thought it did. As a consequence, both the Protestant work ethic and Puritanism suffered an affliction that bedevils many organized religions: Sacraments became dissociated from what was once held to be sacred. Because the Protestant lifestyle was easier to follow than the deeply rooted ethics of Protestantism, rituals obscured the understanding of what was righteous. A case in point is how the doctrine of valuing work for its own sake, not for extrinsic rewards such as money, was transformed.

According to the Calvinists, most notably Cotton Mather, the only value inherent in money was the indication it gave that the one who acquired it was among the Elect. Actually, Mather was far less concerned with wealth than with the belief that every Christian had two callings: The first, a general calling, was to serve the Lord Jesus Christ. The second, a personal calling, needed to include employment by which a man's usefulness in his neighborhood is distinguished. In his personal calling—what we would call a career—Mather maintained that every good Christian should see to it that his business glorified God by doing good for others. Unless disabled, a man without a job that involved contributing to family, community, and country was deemed unrighteous.[8] Mather formalized his view that God made man a "sociable creature" in his doctrine of social labor: A man might get rich at his calling, but personal aggrandizement is incidental relative to the collective transformation of nature and the progress of useful arts and useful knowledge.[9]

But Mather's and the Puritans' views became distorted by the Calvinists' understanding of predestination. According to this doctrine, God predetermined who would go to heaven and who would go to hell. Logically, people assumed that God would bless the efforts of "the chosen"—the Elect—by affording them material luxury here on earth. From this line of reasoning it is easy to see how material wealth came to be construed as a demonstration of God's favor. And, human nature being what it is, some people were not satisfied just to wait for demonstrations of God's favor.

All human beings since the dawn of time have been concerned about the fate that befalls us when we die. Scholars assume that many Protestants came to an ingenious, if partial, solution to this mystery: If they worked to produce profitable business ventures here on earth, they could learn whether they were recipients of God's grace. Scoff if you will at the concept "whoever has the most toys when he dies, wins," but it appears to be rooted in the Puritan belief system.

In his classic sociological treatise *The Protestant Ethic and the Spirit of Capitalism,* Max Weber examined how Protestant religious orthodoxy was transformed into capitalist philosophy.[10] While I cannot do justice to Weber's analysis, I feel it is not unfair to characterize his work as claiming that the Protestant work ethic devolved to a point where we now have a nearly complete bifurcation between the process of accumulating capital and the goal of achieving salvation.

According to Weber, it appears that rather than remaining true to the *end* of getting closer to God through habits of industry, self-discipline, moderation, and contempt for self-indulgence, our capitalist society became obsessed with the *means* of securing wealth or profit. In operational terms, Americans acquired a preoccupation with reaching for an ever-higher standard of living, which spawned pathologies such as status-driven consumerism. Lost in this juxtaposition of means and ends was the spiritual goal of Puritanism, a sense of fulfillment. Also lost was the capacity of the Protestant religion to provide meaning. In essence, the seeds of disillusionment with society were sown at the same time Puritan religious principles were converted into a secularized code of competitive capitalism.

PERFORMANCE, NOT PRAYER

In fairness to those who let their adherence to Puritanism lapse after being seduced by capitalist philosophy, this attitudinal shift was not hard. Benjamin Franklin's pithy maxims, such as "Remember that time is money" and "God helps those that help themselves," originally intended to emphasize the spiritual significance of work, soon came to be understood as exhortations to do more work. How can Franklin's message "He that lives upon hope will die fasting" be understood as anything other than a call for action as a means of accessing God? This is why many Puritans came to believe that God demonstrated an explicit preference for those passionately committed to career pursuits over everything else. As anyone in his right mind would wonder after attending to Poor Richard's warning "He that riseth late, must trot all day, and shall scarce overtake his business at night," is there no rest for the *worthy?*

In fact, our national obsession with productivity has grown more virulent. Consider the words of Ray Kroc that opened this chapter. Kroc is the man whose philosophy of success—number of burgers served—was posted on every McDonald's sign while he was alive. From Kroc's perspective, "ripe old age" is tantamount to malodorous decomposition! No wonder many Americans become paralyzed when they realize that they hate their jobs despite making good money. If they stopped functioning as producers, would they become fodder for the compost heap?

Long before Ray Kroc became an American icon, Alfred, Lord Tennyson's poem "Ulysses" captured the psychological pain that once-productive conquerors endure when not engaged in some heroic or profitable pursuit. His metaphor, rusting unburnished, as opposed to shining like a finely honed weapon in use, is rich. Who can read of Ulysses' ennui and not think of Bob Dole hawking Viagra because he is no longer regularly rejuvenated by political combat? Even a literal and simplistic interpretation of Tennyson's allusion speaks volumes: If you're not winning battles like Ulysses did at Troy, you just can't cut it anymore. Is it too great a leap to infer that when your "weapon" is no longer in use you might as well be dead?

RUGGED INDIVIDUALISM . . . GONE MAD

Roughly seventy years after William James complained about the "moral flabbiness" born of worshiping the "bitch-goddess SUCCESS,"

Christopher Lasch combined that appraisal with modern psychiatry in his classic *The Culture of Narcissism*. In this often scathing indictment of American attitudes and values, Lasch maintained that the self-made man, archetypal embodiment of the American dream, originally thrived because the Protestant work ethic paved the way for social mobility predicated solely on individual initiative.[11]

The psychological traits the Puritans reinforced—individuality, autonomy, independence, and achievement motivation—propelled people toward finding their identity in self-contained or self-directed careers (Mather's concept of a personal calling). This devotion to career gained so much significance that it became the essence of identity, supplanting lineage, religious affiliation, and all other identifying data that had historically formed the basis for inferring—and projecting—"who we are."

Underlying Lasch's analysis is the recognition that as Puritanism became more of a secular philosophy than a religious ideology, the church lost its power to help people find meaning. As Lasch points out, when we lionize the pioneers who conquered the western wilderness or venerate entrepreneurs for revolutionizing the business world, we should remember that these modern heroes turned away from society (and, more specifically, organized religion) toward individual career development as the one arena in which they could derive spiritual satisfaction. Because people came to believe that their sense of personal achievement was all they could rely upon for psychological well-being—the self-made man turned into the self-contained man—doing things for the good of the community slowly but steadily went the way of the horse-drawn carriage.

THE INADVERTENT ADVOCATE OF THE SELF-CONTAINED MAN

Although Benjamin Franklin was one of the more articulate voices calling for an adherence to Puritan virtues, he did not march in lockstep with the religious wing of this movement. It has been said that if Cotton Mather and Ben Franklin were in the same philosophical boat, Mather was rowing toward the shore of Eternal Blessedness while Franklin set his sights on the leisure that accumulating wealth would afford him.[12] In this regard Franklin reflected the patrician view of his time that virtue was the result of wealth.

According to the British socialist Harold Laski, Franklin was the supreme symbol of the American spirit because he made a success of all his diverse endeavors: "In his shrewdness, his sagacity, his devotion to making this world the thing that a kindly and benevolent soul would wish it to be, Franklin seems to summarize in a remarkable way the American idea of a good citizen."[13] Russel B. Nye, who edited Benjamin Franklin's autobiography, seconded this opinion. Although Franklin did seek to amass wealth, he never made a psychological investment in commercial enterprise because the game of business, with its "little cares and fatigues," neither excited nor interested him. Actually, had he chosen to patent and market only a few of his commercially viable inventions (for example, his stove or bifocals), he could have been one of the world's wealthiest men. Instead, he retired at age forty-two to a modest life with no professional burdens. As Nye notes,

[Franklin] wanted money because it gave him independence and security to live as he wished, in pursuit of those things he found important in life. He wanted, he said, "leisure to read, study, make experiments, and converse at large with such ingenious and worthy men as are pleased to honor me with their friendship or acquaintance, on such points as may produce something for the common benefit of mankind." ... He was more interested in knowledge than in money. He did not wish to have it said of him, as Poor Richard said of another, "He does not possess wealth, wealth possesses him."[14]

Yet Franklin's writings are inextricably linked with America's success ethic. Although Franklin never treated money or status in a cavalier manner, others took his example as license to do so.

When Franklin wrote his *Autobiography*, which in effect is a manual for implementing the moneymaking procedures set forth in *The Way to Wealth*, his compilation of Poor Richard's maxims, he recounted how he emerged from poverty and obscurity to affluence and reputation.[15] Benjamin Franklin was the Horatio Alger hero that Alger's novellas never truly described. In each of Alger's stories the hero doesn't so much climb from rags to riches as he falls into the lap of luxury through divine intervention. In one story the protagonist, Phil the Fiddler, quite literally falls into money: After dropping from exhaustion into a snowdrift on a frigid Christmas Eve, he is rescued by a wealthy physician who lost his only child on Christmas Eve four years earlier. Phil is adopted and set up for life.[16]

Not Franklin. When he began his career he was a hard-driving businessman who invented a number of still-respected devices and founded a college, and he later was a framer of our nation's Constitution and served as ambassador to France. He was a cultivated patrician who used his money for the luxuries and leisure that mattered to him. Franklin adhered to the ancient conception of the good life—*summum bonum*—and was true to the definition of happiness articulated in Aristotle's *Nicomachean Ethics:* the active exercise of the mind in accordance with perfect virtue.[17]

Isn't it strange now that in just over a century the principles of the person who once embodied the American success ethic, who craved the opportunity to exercise his mind, could be supplanted by those of synthetic celebrities? Franklin's using wealth to avail himself of intellectual joys did reflect some disdain for commerce, but his avowed goal was always to be free to exercise his mind. While there is no way to be entirely certain how Americans substituted celebrity and narcissistic indulgence for Franklin's definition of the good life, it seems that a major step in this direction took place when the love of money began to replace the love of achievement.

According to Christopher Lasch, in the years prior to the Gilded Age, the Puritan ideal of self-improvement through diligent behavior was transformed into an ethos of compulsive industriousness: Value, which was originally separated from spirituality, was now separated from work. Since what you did became far less important than how profitably you did it, money became entrenched as the epitome of "making it" in America. From that time forward our nation would be unable to adhere to the self-effacing homilies in *Poor Richard's Almanack*. Instead, lectures like P. T. Barnum's "The Art of Money-Getting" provided the maxims for turn-of-the-century America. Soon thereafter works like Napoleon Hill's *Think and Grow Rich* ushered in an era of unbridled self-indulgence. Among the many problems born of this attitudinal shift, Lasch highlighted the following:

> Formerly the Protestant virtues appeared to have an independent value of their own. Even when they became purely instrumental, in the second half of the nineteenth century, success itself retained moral and social overtones, by virtue of its contribution to the sum of human comfort and progress. Now success appeared as an end in its own right, the victory over your competitors that alone retained the capacity to instill a sense of self-approval.[18]

Left unarticulated in this observation is the fact that the man who views success as an end in its own right would never be satisfied with victory in and of itself as a source of self-approval. The person Lasch described as a narcissist depends on others to validate his self-esteem; victory in a vacuum does not suffice. In fact, the hallmark of the narcissist is how far he will go to overcome personal insecurities and anxieties by finding audiences willing to confirm his grandiose self-image.

Whereas the rugged individualist fulfilled America's "manifest destiny" by carving opportunity from uncharted lands to forge a life of his own design, the narcissist often designs his accomplishments in the confines of his mind. The American dream that began as endless possibilities has been replaced by incessant self-absorption augmented by public acclaim.

CHAPTER 7

The Goldilocks Dilemma: Embracing Challenge, Innovation, and Change

The flourishing life is not achieved by techniques. You can't trick yourself into a life well-lived. Neither is it achieved by following five easy steps or some charismatic figure's dogma. A flourishing life depends on our responding, as best we can, to those things uniquely incumbent upon us.

—Epictetus

You don't concentrate on risks. You concentrate on results. No risk is too great to prevent the necessary job from getting done.

—Chuck Yeager

Ever since Epictetus was an authority on the human condition, heroic leaders like Brigadier General Chuck Yeager and those who studied their deeds have held that overcoming risk and threat are the fundamental costs of pursuing success. According to the Greek historian Herodotus, "Great deeds are usually wrought at great risk." Jawaharlal Nehru observed, "The policy of being too cautious is the greatest risk of all."

Epictetus had a very personal reason for his interest in the attributes that enabled people to experience a "flourishing life." He was born a Roman slave yet ultimately achieved high political office and great renown as a teacher of Stoic philosophy. His path to success could easily have served as a primer for Benjamin Franklin: Once granted his freedom, Epictetus devoted himself to a lifelong process of rigorous self-instruction. Above all, having never sought refuge from demanding circumstances, Epictetus gave no quarter to those not willing to tackle life's obstacles head-on.

The quotation that introduced me to Epictetus's writings captured both the spirit of his philosophy and the essence of cognitive behavior therapy, the branch of psychiatry that believes in treating psychiatric disorders by helping patients adjust their assessments of, and reactions to, stressful stimuli. Consider a person who develops a fear of public speaking because he believes that any reaction to his oral presentations short of a standing ovation indicates failure. The cognitive behavior therapy approach to treating this person would adjust his views of adequate speaking to better fit with reality. Epictetus was more direct. His position was "Men are disturbed not by things, but by the views they take of them."

RISK AVERSION

It is not surprising that Epictetus would develop a philosophical system predicated on the notion that what you think and say to yourself has a direct, causal influence over your emotional reactions and your behaviors. It is also not surprising that he believed that all people should step up to any and all challenges that come their way. Unfortunately, in this regard Epictetus was shortsighted.

One of the more disruptive consequences of success is that it radically alters the way people view performance demands. Underlying almost every symptom of Supernova Burnout is the feeling that the material, self-esteem, and interpersonal rewards accrued from success will be jeopardized by ongoing assessments of one's capabilities. Consequently, in what should be a sublime afterglow following achievement, many careerists discover that they are blocked from initiating constructive changes by what psychologists call *risk aversion.*

The risk aversion precipitated by achieving success has little in common with the age- or life-stage-determined risk aversion we all suffer as we mature. One of the paradoxes that intrigue social psychologists is the disjunction between young and old concerning sticking one's neck out. In youth we typically greet challenges with a he-who-hesitates-is-lost attitude. But among graybeards, beliefs like "only fools rush in" or "look before you leap" are typical.

The success-induced variety of risk aversion, which gives rise to symptoms of Supernova Burnout such as self-handicapping, encore anxiety, and entrepreneurial arson, evokes far more intense feelings. Success-induced risk aversion is often described as frozen fright—not merely fear of trying new things but an inability to take any initiative whatsoever because of fear of emotional decompensation.

"Jim," a thirty-nine-year-old executive vice president of sales for a major manufacturer of electronic games, was referred to me for executive coaching by his director of human resources. According to the human resources executive, ever since the chairman and CEO of the company Jim worked for had thrust him into a leadership role, Jim had become impossible to work with. For the three months that Jim had been in his new role he had been sabotaging the perceived status of his direct reports by "undermining their capacity to contribute to new initiatives." Allegedly, several vice presidents complained that Jim had been hoarding information about company strategy, market indicators, sales forecasts, and the like. The theory circulating through the grapevine was that Jim aimed to weaken his junior executives' ability to make informed contributions during interdivisional strategic planning sessions.

During my first meeting with Jim I learned that nothing could have been further from the truth. What accounted for Jim's failure to share information was his anxiety and unwillingness to risk actions that would expose him as unfit for his job: Jim was neither dealing with nor disseminating information relevant to strategic planning strategies because he felt inadequate to participate in this process. When I presented Jim with the concerns about him, he laughed. "Hoarding information! They can have every report and spreadsheet in my office. I'd gladly ride someone's coattails given how terrified I am in this job."

As I got to know Jim better I came to understand the reasons for his frozen fright. Both Jim and the CEO of his company were first-generation Italian Americans, and—strange as it sounds—it was widely assumed that Jim had been promoted to senior management because the founder was grooming him to be his successor solely because of their shared ethnic heritage. This widely held opinion was entrenched soon after I began coaching Jim: At a group strategy session during which Jim was literally unable to speak, rather than "ream" Jim, as he was wont to do with other executives, the CEO assigned the COO to "show Jim the ropes of his new position" for as long as needed. Not only did Jim get an executive coach but the man he allegedly reported to was assigned to be his mentor until Jim grew into his new position!

I was able to help Jim master a set of techniques for dealing with his risk aversion because, as it turned out, he actually coveted leadership responsibility: He had an MBA from the Stern School of Management at New York University, and his father and sister were both CEOs of major businesses in his home state. As Jim saw things, he had spent his life preparing to become a leader. Thus, taking a page from Epictetus's book, I reminded him that what was blocking him was his interpretation of what it meant to attain success under false pretenses. Once I convinced Jim that his CEO might have promoted him because he recognized his intellect, and that regardless of how he became positioned to succeed the chance was his to forfeit or embrace, Jim began to reframe his fears of being exposed as a fraud and behave like a man confronting a challenge even if it was a long shot.

The second—and ultimately key—reason I was able to help Jim was that he had a secret ambition. Since he was a young boy Jim had harbored a yearning to make his family's name as prominent in the wine industry as the name Gallo. Jim and his wife were both oenophiles who spent their vacations in the Napa or Sonoma Valley, and they agreed that if they ever struck it rich they would retire to that part of the country and buy a winery.

Knowing Jim's fallback position, I could relatively easily help him cope with his anxieties about failing to live up to the implications of a role he feared he did not deserve. Rather than attempting to convince him of why he could succeed, much of my work focused on how fortunate he would be if he failed. This technique, called *paradoxical intention,* worked wonders. In less than five months Jim was fully committed to his new role and had scrapped his plan of moving to Northern California.

As Christopher Lasch and other social scientists have demonstrated, Jim is not typical of American careerists. Because we have always overvalued professional achievement or its appearance, convincing someone who had attained success that failure was an attractive option would be an extraordinarily hard sell. For most Americans career success is an all-encompassing component of how they view themselves and others, and it is typically the case that their sense of psychological well-being is tied to their ability to sustain stellar levels of achievement. Even careerists who are certain that their success is not a function of luck or fraudulence may come to fear that their status cannot be sustained unless it is vigilantly safeguarded.

Sooner or later everyone who believes "my career = my self" develops a profound feeling of vulnerability: The consequences of career failure acquire a significance well beyond what they deserve if what you are psychologically is equivalent to what you do. Metaphorically, this orientation forces you to put all your self-esteem eggs in one career-defined basket. One slip or fall can lead to the conclusion that you are fated to spend the balance of your days like Humpty-Dumpty on life support. Consequently, a person trapped in a "my career = my self" predicament will likely come to construe challenges, innovations, and change to his career as threats to his existence.

THE CHALLENGE CONTINUUM: FROM EUSTRESS TO THREAT

The process of relieving symptoms of Supernova Burnout derived from the experience of risk aversion involves introducing novel performance demands into a professional's life. This is a complex process, fraught with innumerable resistances, but it is the only one that can be effective.

Challenge, innovation, and change operate according to a fundamental law of nature: Too much of anything is no good. Oxygen consumption is a classic case in point. We are all instinctively programmed to consume oxygen, yet if we do not breathe naturally, horrible consequences may ensue. Too much oxygen can cause intoxication or death, and not enough oxygen will surely prove fatal.

Sensory stimulation is also acutely sensitive to precise apportioning. As noted in the earlier discussion of stress and eustress, humankind has a need for stimulation from the external world, but this need is not constant. After we adapt to one level of arousal, we often require progressively greater levels of arousal, or novel stimuli, to feel comfortable or satisfied. Remember that TV commercial for Lay's potato chips, "Bet you can't eat just one"? It was on point; we tend to want more and more of a rewarding stimulus . . . but only for a limited time. If the only snack we ate for a year was Lay's chips, we would likely grow nauseated at the sight of one.

Challenge, innovation, and change affect one's career in much the same manner: We need a certain amount of all three stimuli, but too much of any one can kill the drive to succeed. Yet novel performance demands can never be subjected to precise control. Not only do the interpretations of these stimuli depend upon the eye of the beholder but, when the beholder is a professional, perceptions are often in constant flux.

Most careers have gradually increasing levels of stimulation built into them. Nearly every professional starts in an apprentice mode, where autonomous responsibilities are limited. The next step affords greater opportunities for initiative. As time goes on the successful careerist usually becomes creative and self-directed. Ultimately, every careerist reaches a point where the need for eustress and the predilection to feel in control and protected from the embarrassment or shame of failure achieve a perfect balance. At this point a choice must be made, because life in business can never be static.

I call this choice point *the Goldilocks dilemma:* Endure an already mastered task whose challenges are too cold (understimulating and likely to precipitate frustration and ennui), take on challenges that are too hot and threaten to disrupt self-esteem, or find a mechanism that will free you from remaining between two undesirable alternatives.

Directing people to resolve the Goldilocks dilemma by adjusting the challenge in their careers to a level that is *juuuuuuusssst* right is equivalent to telling them to climb Mount Everest by putting one foot in front of the other, planting a few pitons, and moving upward. People cannot transition from a point of optimal satisfaction and reward to one that introduces invigorating challenge unless they are forewarned about, fully understand, and take steps to cope with the way challenges can become threats to self-esteem. Figure 1, adapted from a model of the relationship between motivation and performance developed by R. M. Yerkes and J. D. Dodson in 1908, illustrates this phenomenon.[1]

According to what has come to be known as the Yerkes-Dodson law, increasing the extrinsic motivation to succeed—through incentives, pressure, demands, and the like—will improve performance up to a point commonly called an optimum level of arousal. Beyond that point, however, increasing the motivation or incentive to perform will interfere with skilled task execution and result in deteriorating levels of accomplishment.

The challenge-threat curve in Figure 1 details a related phenomenon. When the intrinsically rewarding attributes of tasks motivate

The Challenge/Threat Continuum

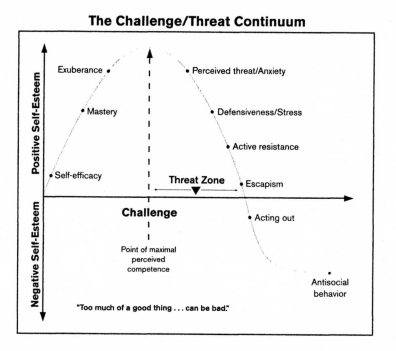

people to engage in them, as the challenges grow more demanding, the psychological satisfaction derived from successful completion rises in tandem. But if the intrinsic challenges rise beyond an optimal point, or if extrinsic incentives are added, exuberance soon turns into anxiety. When performance is demanded as opposed to being elicited by the prospect of feeling good about oneself, psychological satisfaction falls in direct proportion to the level of perceived extortion.

This, then, is the key to what ultimately motivates a person to approach or avoid a task: his beliefs about how performing that task will make him feel in terms of self-esteem. If a person assumes that engaging in a task will enable him to feel competent and self-determining, he will approach it; if not, he won't. But since humans do not function as simplistically as lab rats, a number of qualitative considerations affect whether a person will continue to strive for success after attaining a goal.

Research has shown that a person will be highly motivated to perform in contexts that possess three characteristics: (1) they allow him to feel responsible for a successful outcome; (2) they provide him with feedback from the performance; and (3) the performance settings include some risk of either not succeeding or actually failing.[2] As T. E. Lawrence observed, "There could be no honor in a sure success." This is why performance settings that provide insufficient challenge can be as disruptive to psychological well-being as those that impose threats.

THE PROBLEM WITH LINEAR ACHIEVEMENT

The simplest example of achievement motivation can be seen in the career of a skier. Initially, the end or goal of skiing may be to traverse the bunny hill without breaking a limb. Once personal injury is no longer a threat, a novice skier will typically attempt to add eustress to his life by skiing on a more demanding hill. The skier could proceed from the bunny hill to an intermediate level slope, then the advanced, followed by the expert black diamond and beyond. Once a slope is mastered it becomes a sure success unless daredevil challenge enhancers such as skiing without poles or on one ski are introduced.

If we assume that our hypothetical skier can find a point of maximal perceived competence somewhere in the Swiss Alps—a ski run that poses multiple threats to cause him to spill but is not so steep, icy, or covered with boulders that he fears death—what does he do after mastering *that*? A skier who can traverse virgin snows of the Alps finds that the threat posed by the next greater level of challenge is not merely physical harm; more often it's a worse fate, humiliation or shame. The same is true for all who achieve stellar levels of success.

The three most common problems resulting from a linear model of career success, paralleling a skier's climb from bunny hill to Bern, Switzerland, are (1) choking under pressure; (2) seeking external excuses for failure via self-handicapping; and (3) fleeing performance expectations. In each instance the naturally arising threats to self-esteem increase perceived threats to successful performance.

While it is easy to understand the psychological danger inherent in trying to resolve the Goldilocks dilemma by backing away from performance demands that push one into the "threat zone," the dangers that arise from failing to venture beyond the point of maximal perceived competence are less obvious. Even in our more-is-better culture, people understand that it is adaptive not to take on challenges that can cause embarrassment or shame. Yet precisely because opting for the too cold component of the Goldilocks dilemma looks sane relative to embracing esteem-threatening struggle, a surprising number of successful people get trapped in ostensibly safe but ultimately destructive career slots.

This realization is particularly troubling considering that in the twenty-first century people will be capable of working well into their seventies. As a consequence, those trapped in understimulating career slots are likely to spend thirty or more years being bored to death unless they develop a strategy for moving beyond their point of maximal perceived competence every time they achieve it.

So how does Goldilocks find a career that's just right? By understanding what makes Goldilocks anxious. The question is not "What do I do to add eustress to my life?" but rather "What is making me incapable of moving out of this position where all I am suffering is ennui?" The following three techniques are designed to assist this assessment.

TECHNIQUES FOR INTRODUCING INNOVATION AND CHANGE WITHOUT THREAT

1. Know What You Are Afraid Of

Nothing is more seemingly benign yet ultimately disruptive than fear of the unknown. The imagination runs wild when the human mind contemplates a void. Consider what happened to me several years ago: On my forty-fifth birthday I decided it was time to start scheduling regular visits with a physician. Dr. John Godine, of Massachusetts General Hospital, gave me a head-to-toe exam that included what felt like the removal of a quart of my blood, allegedly for use in a variety of tests.

Roughly a week later, on Friday afternoon, Dr. Godine left me this message: "Hello; this is Dr. Godine. Please give me a call; I'd like to talk to you about your blood work." That was it; period. I received the message after the doctor had left for a three-day weekend. Until I reached Dr. Godine the following Tuesday, I suffered every form of disease I could imagine. Dr. Godine was quite amused by my reaction, because he had called me to share his surprise over how good my test results were. Not knowing him well at the time, I had failed to realize that he was an anachronism: a gentleman who gave hands-on attention to his patients. A "no problems" voice mail was not his style.

Many symptoms of Supernova Burnout produce the rewarding consequence of wresting people from the grip of intolerable ambiguity. This is one reason people cling to their disorders and resist treatment despite the fact that their symptoms are ultimately detrimental to their health. I have worked with dozens of children who repeatedly provoke their parents to rage with, say, underachieving behavior, and as many philandering men who habitually endure vilifying tirades from scorned spouses. But when these people recount the "punishments" they endure over and over again they possess a Zen-like calm. Without question Pyrrhic revenge is the particular type of *secondary gain*—the psychological term for rewards that accrue from symptoms—this strategy affords: It gives people trapped in highly conflictual relationships the ability to bring those causing them pain under some degree of personal control.

So, from a purely functional perspective, the ostensibly self-defeating people who engage in Pyrrhic revenge can be seen as behaving in a highly adaptive manner. When one knows that a dreaded outcome is bound to occur, getting it over with on one's own terms and according to one's own timetable lessens the amount of suffering he will endure. Psychiatry is peppered with theories that claim to explain how, if punishing outcomes are expected, the pain of anticipating a noxious event is typically greater than the outcome itself. In other words, by precipitating a painful experience and controlling when it occurs, a person can paradoxically feel better than he would have had he waited to see what the fates had in store for him.[3]

When we analyze all aspects of risk aversion, it becomes clear that people suffering the Goldilocks dilemma presume many things about the consequences of failure in part because they have no first-hand knowledge of how it feels to fail. Most anxiety about the consequences of failure is derived from secondhand information—the type I used when imagining the disorders Dr. Godine was prepared to tell me I was suffering—rather than from, say, recalling how painful your first, second, or third failure actually was.

If all successful careerists decided to experimentally precipitate the need to sell themselves anew or seek a novel career early in life as though they had endured a failure—not wait until age forty-five or fifty, when most people first reach a point of maximal perceived competence—the perceived cost of failing would not be cataclysmic, and the potential downside risk of being a rookie would approach zero. They would face the "unknown" when it is likely to be surmountable, even if a worst-case scenario ensues.

Employing this strategy immediately need not be an all-or-nothing occasion in today's job market. With businesses desperate for talent and unemployment rates near all-time lows, many careerists can devote 75 percent of their energy to a dominant career, invest 25 percent of their professional activity in a parallel career, and retain the safety net of organizational affiliation. In the twenty-first century more and more people are being given the opportunity to experiment with pro bono or "fantasy" career pursuits that serve two functions: They afford novelty and challenge and allow the anxious careerist to test whether he will starve to death if he loses this job.

One individual who achieved stellar success with this strategy is Scott Adams. The wildly successful creator of the comic strip *Dilbert* spent nine years as a cubicle dweller at Pacific Bell under about a dozen bosses. Yet during his final six years there, all the managers

Adams worked for knew that he fantasized about—and experimented with developing—a comic strip.

On June 30, 1995, like tens of thousands of downsizing victims before and since, Adams suffered one of the most feared outcomes known to achievement-oriented people: the ax. But his transition to professional cartooning was remarkably less anxiety provoking than it would have been had he not sustained a parallel career for years.[4]

2. Forget About Breaking Set. Try Expanding Set Instead

People wondering about addressing the symptoms of Supernova Burnout in their career do not have the luxury of creating whole-cloth modifications to the way they construe the world. It's too late for that. Their goal should be control over, or diminution of, symptoms—if those symptoms derive from character issues such as the ones that prompt Pyrrhic revenge or self-handicapping alcohol abuse. You will not be able to abandon old ways of thinking about the value of career, the need for success, or the consequences of failure. You will, however, with effort, be able to bring extreme perspectives about the meaning of success under control. My former patient Peter offers an example of this distinction.

"Peter" was brought to my office as many Type AAA executives are—by his spouse. The son of an extremely prominent, successful, hypercritical man, Peter grew up feeling a constant need to prove that he was not the moron his father assumed he was. Consequently, he strove for one achievement after another but never rid himself of the narcissistic injury that could not be salved by the kudos or material successes he achieved.

After becoming a combat-decorated officer in the Marines, Peter abandoned his plan to be a career soldier and returned to Boston to make a name for himself that would not be confused with his father's. A bright man with a range of entrepreneurial talents, Peter developed a niche in the recreational sporting goods industry and saw the first retail outlet he opened expand to three stores in just over five years.

This rate of growth would doubtless have continued had his wife, a religious woman who met Peter at a church-sponsored social, not filed for divorce. Years of her appeals for family time with his four daughters, two of whom were now in their teens, as well as for her artistic career, had done nothing. Her attorney suggested that couples therapy might be preferable to a court battle—at least it would be a good last-ditch effort—so she and Peter came to see me.

Like so many successful men who have no idea how driven they are by compensatory—"I'll show you!"—needs, Peter assumed that since he had made millions of dollars and did truly love his wife and family, he could sell his business and retire without much effort. That, he said, would satisfy his wife's demands: "She wants me to spend weekends with the family, return to the church that I've ignored since beginning my business, and share in her life. No sweat." I told Peter (in gentle terms) that he was delusional, and his wife seconded the opinion. As expected, Peter demurred: "Trust me; the situation is under control. I'm not sacrificing my family for my business."

I had two more meetings with Peter and his wife, during which I told him that his business wasn't the issue—the burning passion to prove his father's critical commentaries wrong was—but his will prevailed. Peter went back to church and played soccer dad for a year. Then the couple divorced.

What happened, as Peter told me eighteen months later, when he returned to psychotherapy, this time for good, was this: "Without realizing it, once I started going to church again I couldn't stand how they were running things outside the services." In short order Peter worked himself up to the role of deacon and, in effect, became the chief operating officer of a huge organization. Although he didn't realize it at the time, Peter's drive to achieve and contradict his father's harsh judgment of him had won out again.

Peter's return to psychotherapy was prompted by what he humorously called "getting religion" concerning his character traits. He understood what drove his workaholism and was determined not to let it undermine his second marriage (celebrated a month before he recontacted me). My response was "Peter, Freud said, 'Character is fate.' Let's see if we can modify, not re-create, yours."

People like Peter—actually, most of us, for better or worse—are destined to fulfill drives that get fixed in character before we turn five or six years old. In his second, complete course of psychotherapy, Peter accepted his achievement-striving mind-set and learned to temper it by determining how much of it was adaptive and how much "disordered."

In effect, Peter accomplished what Epictetus directed us to do: Take a different view of the things that upset us. According to modern psychiatry, Peter developed an *observing ego*—psychological distance from oneself that enables us to question our interpretations and motives. In the process he learned to accept half a loaf; he remained dissatisfied with "second best," but he learned to accept it as fair compensation for the love and support of his second wife. Peter never "broke set" completely. What he did was expand his perspective on his set and achieve psychological satisfaction for the first time in his life.

3. Employ Psychological Diversity Training

Aeons before the world was formally notified that men are from Mars, women are from Venus, married couples learned through experience that the old cliché about variety being the spice of life is true. Even couples who experienced extraordinary sexual ardor at the start of love relationships had to admit that, over time, the flames would flicker. Typically, this waning of desire is no one's fault: People become accommodated to most stimuli, sex partners and spouses included.

Psychologists who specialize in marital relations describe the trajectory of sexual passion in monogamous unions by *the penny principle:* Put a penny in a jar each time you have sexual relations during the first year of marriage, and you will be able to extract one penny for each time you have sex over the balance of the marriage. Findings such as this are why some anthropologists have argued that monogamy is unnatural.

Fortunately, couples can help keep marriages feeling new by taking exotic vacations, making love in novel settings, and playing bedroom games. Can careerists add excitement to been-there-done-that vocations in a similar way? Absolutely, if they commit to altering their approach to work according to one of two nonlinear models: (1) bonsai horticulture or (2) chronic diversification.

Bonsai Horticulture. Chapter 5 described the advantages of viewing career development as crafting a bonsai tree as opposed to managing a Christmas tree farm. The value in developing one tree that was both beautiful and of great monetary value is an ideal metaphor for the type of career that will inoculate against Supernova Burnout. In order to have the opportunity to craft your career in the manner of a bonsai expert shaping a work of living art, you have to do some basic farming. One aspect of bonsai horticulture—as opposed to bonsai craftsmanship—is a precursor to enabling careerists to find more fulfilling and burnout-proof lives.

Sooner or later every career suffers the fate of a tree put into a small pot by a bonsai gardener: It gets root-bound; the root system has grown too big for its pot and threatens to kill the plant. In order to keep a bonsai tree—say a black pine—from reaching the thirty-foot heights it could ascend to in the wilderness, you must trim its roots and repot it at regular intervals.

Careerists are like bonsai trees: In order to keep a person with talent and aspirations from suffering ennui or depression because she is trapped in golden handcuffs or a version of Sisyphus's repetitive hell, you must periodically remove her from her constraining environment and put her in a new one. Yet just as the bonsai master knows that you do not merely take a root-bound tree and toss it into a larger pot—the pot is central to the aesthetic aspects of the bonsai—addressing a professional's feelings of being root-bound must proceed from a consideration of who you are repotting. To be effective, an intervention to infuse a career with challenge must match needs with opportunity. One of the biggest mistakes people make when they attempt to address the symptoms of Supernova Burnout is to ignore what every haberdasher senses intuitively: One size *never* fits all. Yet time after time, managers fall victim to the delusion that any reward is psychologically gratifying.

Several years ago I was hired by a 650-person New York City law firm to help address their associate turnover problem. For them, as for every law firm in the United States at the time, keeping associates happy and committed to a career path that couldn't come close to rivaling the thrills inherent in joining a dot-com company was a full-time administrative job. Unfortunately, the well-meaning, naïve lawyer whose job it was to enhance associate retention at the firm decided that it was crass to give young professionals cash as a Christmas bonus. Instead, she determined that the law firm would give them each an $8,000 to $15,000 (depending upon seniority) Christmas travel award. The response to this effort to boost morale was more hostile than you could imagine.

Here are some of the realities of the lives of law firm associates that this kindhearted but misguided attorney failed to consider:

- Associates typically have college and law school loans to repay and young children to raise. Their need for cash far exceeds their need for R and R.
- Most of the associates were raising young children without domestic help. Schlepping kids on a vacation struck them as more work than fun.
- Roughly 10 percent of the associates were gay. Since the travel awards had to be cashed in with the firm's travel agency—tickets that named the passengers would be issued by the firm's agent—many of these associates resented the inadvertent outing that would ensue if they ordered a ticket for a same-sex travel companion.

❑ At least 3 percent of the associates were planning to end their marriages or were involved in extramarital affairs. For them too, the problem of outing arose.

❑ All the associates reported being too busy to find the time needed to cash in their awards.

As you consider either establishing a corporate "repotting" program or creating a personal one, bear in mind how often failures to assess your target's personality undermine the psychologically rewarding aspects of material gifts.

Fortunately, many businesses take a well-reasoned approach to repotting, and their examples are beginning to affect human resource departments across corporate America. The management experts Christopher Bartlett and Sumantra Ghoshal cite Unilever as a multinational corporation that has had success exploiting their theories on matrix management in companywide repotting programs. According to Bartlett and Ghoshal, "The most effective companies recognize that the best way to develop new perspectives and thwart parochialism in their managers is through personal experience. By moving selected managers across functions, businesses, and geographic units, a company encourages cross-fertilization of ideas as well as . . . flexibility."[5]

Today many of the best-managed companies in information technology congratulate employees and give kudos and psychological rewards to managers who shepherd a project to fruition in a unique and insightful manner: They remove them from the content area or business unit where they experienced success. As a reward for doing a job particularly well, these careerists are moved to a new venue, where they are asked to replicate their success.

This simple but elegant version of repotting acknowledges that since a person's talent and skill sets are responsible for success, they must be cared for and nurtured. Monetary rewards alone cannot do this. The only thing that stimulates the mind is challenge. If you know that your success will be met with a novel challenge, and you feel that the nature and intensity of that challenge can be adjusted with your input, you're like Goldilocks telling the chef precisely how you like your porridge prepared and served.

This is not to say that money is irrelevant. However, all other things being equal, the career portfolio that includes provisions for periodic repotting will be infinitely more rewarding than one that showers workers with riches and ignores whether they are root-bound.

You do not need to work for a Fortune 500 company in order to engage in periodic repotting. In fact, the bonsai repotting model is much easier to adhere to if you are your own boss. Throughout his career Pablo Picasso "repotted" himself in myriad ways with seemingly successful results. Not only did Picasso shift his style from realism to cubism but he diversified the media with which he worked.

The master was involved in several projects at any given time. It was not at all unusual that oil paintings, line drawings, collages, and sculpture, all in various stages of completeness, would dominate discrete sections of his working space, which Picasso could visit according to his mood.

By shifting from medium to medium, Picasso did more than prevent himself from becoming root-bound; he strategically protected his self-esteem. Say, for example, his *Guernica* had been panned by critics. Picasso could have readily consoled himself by thinking, "I'm more than a painter of oil paintings, I'm a sculptor as well." By diversifying his artistic pursuits, Picasso found a way to inoculate himself against the potential damage when all of one's self-esteem eggs are in one basket. He also broadened his sense of identity, which, over the long term, builds multidimensional, threat-resistant self-esteem.

Chronic Diversification. This career model expands upon the type of diversification Picasso practiced. The principle of chronic diversification is that if a person's self-esteem has multiple infusions of positive feedback it grows more stable and less vulnerable to the emotional consequences of failing at innovation and change. The diversified careerist has his self-esteem supported by a stable tripod, whereas the one with all his self-esteem eggs in one basket is being supported by an unstable monopod.

All successful people can find ways to build tripods of self-esteem if they are willing to reconceptualize their professional identities. One key is new metaphors. No one on a linear career path can help but suffer the frozen fright of the Goldilocks dilemma when more of the same provides no eustress and a radical leap forward is threatening.

Chronic diversification is fueled by one motive: *rerum novarum cupidus,* being greedy for new things. If you are a portrait painter exclusively, it is harder to practice *rerum novarum cupidus* than if you are like Picasso. If you channel your professional energies into building the career version of a portfolio rather than climbing one ladder to the top of one vocational pursuit, your self-esteem base broadens.

The first step toward overcoming the anxiety inherent in reconceptualizing your career this way is to understand that the strengths that give you a professional identity can be reorganized and reallocated just as a broker moves assets among investments. From a psychological perspective, the thing to remember is that you are a gestalt, not an atomistic unit. The medley of factors that form your identity have created something beyond a charm-bracelet model of a person. On a charm bracelet each item is unchanged by its proximity to its neighboring trinket. Following the metaphor, people wrongly assume that their identities are developed according to an equation such as: IQ + Emotional Intelligence or EQ + love of kids + love of dogs + powerful backhand = Kathy. Thus, Kathy's tennis partners see her backhand skills, the people she sells to and manages see IQ + EQ, and her spouse dreams of building a family because Kathy loves kids and dogs. Each attribute or attribute pairing is there to be accessed as needed.

People are more akin to mosaics formed of thousands of pieces of tile that, from a distance, seem to blend together without borders.

While it is possible to view a mosaic from six inches away and see its component parts, this is rarely done. Typically, the whole person—a gestalt—is visible in each setting.

In conceiving of the self as a gestalt it is important to understand that the "living whole" generates something greater than the sum of your component parts. Hence, each time you reconfigure yourself—adding a long-ignored or underused talent here, dropping an ossified behavior pattern (not character trait) there—a new gestalt is born.

Let me demonstrate a fundamental principle of Gestalt psychology: Recall how those message boards in New York City's Times Square create headlines with lightbulbs by writing words that scroll across the display? I've got a bulletin for you! The words don't move; nothing does. What you see as whole words are stationary flashing lightbulbs. Your mind organizes these atomistic units of light into gestalts—wholes—because that's the way minds work. Thus, the effect of thousands of atomistic units of light presented in rapid succession is a purely cognitive interpretation that creates a verbal message. That's a gestalt: $1 + 1 = 3$.

What about you? What is your professional identity? Manager? If so, try altering that image by rearranging the component pieces such as herder of cats, motivator, translator (of executive dictates or corporate philosophy), communicator, et cetera. It may sound trite to engage in this exercise during an era when every business magazine in print these days has one or more stories on how to reinvent yourself, but the truth is, until you can see yourself as more than the sum of the component assets that can trap you on an identity-fostering-but-frustrating career path, you are vulnerable to all-or-nothing thinking about the consequences of introducing challenge, innovation, or change into your job. Reinventing yourself is impossible; that would be breaking set. Reconfiguring your gestalt retains set and expands it.

People who diversify themselves into assets that form a professional investment portfolio proceed this way: They examine their knowledge base (yes, hobbies count), their administrative strengths, communication skills, selling skills, and strategic planning skills, and mix and match like a starving person let loose at a smorgasbord. Every successful careerist can, at a minimum, combine industry knowledge and communication skills into some form of teaching or consulting career. Selling skills + strategic planning skills = talent agent or lobbyist. The list is limitless if you dig deep enough.

The key is to pick up on the theme of an advertising campaign that Coors beer began running in the spring of 2000. To pitch their product as unique, they paired it with a series of innovative individuals. One of the more popular commercials had Ahmad Rashad waxing ecstatic about Gary Fisher, the man who invented the mountain bike. According to the ad, Fisher took the gear system from his ten-speed racing bike and put it on a conventional touring bike so he could ride over rough terrain. Why didn't he just buy a mountain bike? There was no such thing at the time.

That is gestalt logic in action. You can make this sort of transition—and stabilize your self-esteem by resting it on a base with multiple legs—if you commit yourself to the process of repackaging or reorganizing your career from a linear model to an investment portfolio. To begin this process with less anxiety, consider the following suggestions:

1. *Relax. You Are Reapplying Your Strengths, Not Reinventing Yourself.* With all due respect to those who claim that professional reinvention is possible, it is not, even when character issues are not the determining factors. Every human has innate temperamental qualities, such as shyness (or introversion) versus gregariousness (or extroversion). If you are an introvert you may learn to overcome a fear of social gatherings, but it is doubtful you will ever be the life of the party. Similarly, when there are openings for librarians, extroverts need not apply. But if, for example, you are gregarious and dominant, your career exploited your physical prowess, and you fear that your strength may be waning, consider

Jesse Ventura. Governor Ventura seems to have engaged in a lifelong process of reconfiguration: from Navy SEAL (using strength and courage) to professional wrestler (using strength and sociability) to politician (using sociability and emotional intelligence) to XFL TV commentator (using celebrity and chutzpah). By reorganizing and reaccentuating his strengths, while always relying on at least one dominant trait, Ventura made the reconfigurations he needed without attempting a whole-cloth reinvention.

2. *Be an Origin, Not a Pawn.* As noted before, we find enormous comfort in bringing as many life experiences as possible under our control. Moreover, as countless research studies have shown, loss of control or helplessness is the major antecedent of depressions not caused by biochemical imbalances.[6] If you dictate the time and place to begin reorganizing your gestalt, you benefit in several ways: Not only are you more mentally equipped to cope with the stresses inherent in such risk taking but you exude confidence to those who may facilitate your success. The adage "Nothing succeeds like success" was coined because we perform best when not plagued by self-conscious doubts. Anxiety makes us aware of exigencies, real or imagined. Contemplating "what-ifs" in a career move saps your energy and heightens the likelihood of failure. Controlling the terms of your leap into the abyss of professional reconfiguration—as opposed to doing it in response to a pink slip or a substance abuse disorder—makes you infinitely better able to cope with whatever you encounter.

3. *Embrace Bad News.* Never wear rose-colored glasses when readjusting your career. Optimism is not denial, but people who don rose-colored glasses are prone to engage in denial. In the late 1990s, Andy Grove and Lance Armstrong captured the hearts and minds of Americans

for the way they waged their battles against cancer.
Each man knew the odds against success, each refused
to cease the activities that afforded him eustress, and
each prevailed. Most important, as Grove and Armstrong
considered the battles they had to wage, they readily acknowledged a multitude of fears. Yet by preparing for—
neither denying nor diminishing—the problems that
confronted him, each man coped infinitely better than
expected. Embracing bad news does not mean that you
should imagine all possible ramifications of a negative
situation; that is *catastrophizing,* a form of anxious thinking far more debilitating than being a Pollyanna. But
knowing your enemy, rehearsing a battle plan, and anticipating the consequences of your actions makes experiencing a painful outcome manageable.

4. *Don't Forget That Eustress Is a Cousin of Distress.*
When a person is excited about an opportunity, the biochemical reactions in the body are virtually identical to
those when one is anxious about a problematic situation.
Immediately after any instance of reconfiguring a gestalt,
people are anxious about what lies before them. We get
aroused by epinephrine—the chemical that causes our
hearts to race—in anticipation of any event we are heavily invested in and want to succeed at. That goes for
vying for a gold medal, beating the crap out of a mugger,
or going on a first date with a person you have a crush
on. If you prepare yourself for the fact that you will experience epinephrine surges and train yourself to label
them in self-affirming ("I'm excited") rather than self-
defeating ("I'm terrified of failing") ways, you significantly
enhance your likelihood of success. Remember: "Men
are disturbed not by things, but by the views they take of
them." That was true in 135 C.E., when Epictetus said it,
and it is true today.

CHAPTER 8

Generativity: Developing People, Not Building Monuments

The renown which riches or beauty confer is
fleeting and frail; mental excellence is a
splendid and lasting possession.

—SALLUST

It is not the mountain we conquer, but
ourselves.

—SIR EDMUND HILLARY

Most business executives want information in concise units. The information technology revolution has only exacerbated their sense of urgency. For those who live by the mantra "No paralysis by over-analysis," one basic, unpretentious intervention can help alleviate symptoms of Supernova Burnout: Read the message printed on the back of a dollar bill—"In God We Trust." Now why, if the Treasury Department is running public service ads on currency, didn't they post a warning label on the dollar bill to alert consumers to the *inverse correlation* that exists between amassing greenbacks and trusting in God, other people, or anything apart from money?

Since people began recording their observations of the human experience, great thinkers like Sallust have cautioned against investing our hopes for happiness in the renown that riches or beauty confers. The same message appears quite regularly in the Bible; Proverbs (11:28) warns: "He that trusteth in his riches shall fall." Even Sigmund Freud remarked, "It is impossible to escape the impression that people commonly use false standards of measurement—that they seek power, success and wealth for themselves and admire them in others, and they underestimate what is of true value in life."[1]

Sir Edmund Hillary, a man who could easily have been seduced by the lure of great wealth had he let the acclaim generated by his accomplishments go to his head, was the sine qua non of the self-made man who did not put his trust in money. He knew that psychological satisfaction has nothing to do with accumulating riches and everything to do with conquering one's fear of confronting personal vulnerabilities. According to Hillary, psychological growth is possible only after people assume responsibility for their flaws and stop blaming "the mountain" for thwarting their progress. Left unstated in Sir Edmund's aphorism is the fact that nothing is more difficult than authentic self-assessment. Helping a person identify impediments to self-actualization (golden handcuffs) or critique his own character is a Herculean task. If the person narcissistically overvalues the accoutrements of success, the difficulty will be increased immeasurably.

Most people who suffer Supernova Burnout are loath to engage in authentic self-assessment because they fear being humiliated, shamed, or disgraced. Unless a trauma pierces their defenses against experiencing emotional vulnerability, it is doubtful that people who consider "Think and grow rich" Holy Scripture will see the value of engaging in activities that in no way enhance their material wealth or social status. It is even less likely that such people will ever rely upon the largesse of others. Neediness—in a literal or figurative sense—is antithetical to the appearance of success. Self-made men generate feelings of confidence in others because they are wholly independent. People who need people may be the luckiest people in the world, but they are not traditionally thought of as the ones who'll get to the head of the pack.

SELF-LOVE OR SELF-DECEPTION

The association between a narcissistic lifestyle and a mistrust of others is not mere coincidence; there is a causal connection between an exclusive reliance on material wealth for psychological gratification and an inability to form truly intimate relationships. The root cause of this connection is a child's attempt to defend against messages from caregivers that he is all bad. When adults manifest excessive displays of narcissism, flaunting their wealth or touting their prowess, you can be certain that their self-congratulatory remarks are subconsciously or symbolically telling their parents, "See, you were wrong."

Psychiatrists have argued that people can protect themselves against the consequences of internalizing condemnatory feedback through a defense mechanism called *projection*—seeing others as the source of negative feelings they hold toward themselves. Thus, if the person destined to live a narcissistic lifestyle feels devalued, projection allows him to believe, "It's not that I'm all bad, it's that they are." Extending this argument a bit, projective defenses can help you sustain the belief that you would get the special treatment, applause, and recognition befitting a person of your caliber but for the fact that you are envied and resented by those not as great as you. Yet the ultimate psychological fuel for sustaining projective defenses is anger. Virtually all people who warrant a clinical diagnosis of narcissistic personality disorder unconsciously use their symptoms (grandiosity; entitlement; obsession with success, wealth, power, and beauty) to mask the anger born of profound feelings of inadequacy.

While it is nearly impossible for narcissists to rise to power or prominence without keeping their anger in check, once they attain success their long-repressed, underlying self-assessment almost always emerges. As part of their defensive structure narcissists are often devaluing of others; they behave in an arrogant, exploitative manner that lacks the slightest hint of empathy. In extreme cases, when their needs are not gratified immediately, these people are prone to outbursts ranging from righteous indignation to violent tantrums.

As you would expect from people who are the products of devaluing, rage-inducing childhoods, most narcissists are exquisitely sensitive to real or imagined insults or slights. People develop all the external trappings of an active contempt for humanity if the only way they know of to defend against psychic pain is to project their sense of inadequacy. The irony of this defense is that it creates a vicious circle: The narcissist defends against an incapacity to trust others for signs of approval by devaluing them. This behavior, in turn, typically generates hostility from the wrongfully devalued. Then the narcissists have unambiguous justification to engage in more devaluing, distancing, and distrust.

FAUSTIAN BARGAINS

An initially benign yet ultimately quite damaging defense used to shore up an ego battered by negative feedback is compensatory behavior or overcompensating: "Since they do not love me for *who I am*, I will have to make them love me for *what I do, achieve, or accomplish.*" In essence, the slighted person reasons that the best mechanism for coping with what he lacks (lovability) is to compensate for that lack with an attribute he has an abundance of—talent, skill, ability. This defense has a hidden benefit: It will often propel a person to achieve rewarding outcomes. Overcompensation can even shore up a bruised ego in the short term. The problem, however, is that if people evoke love from others by harnessing the energy derived from suppressed anger, the moment they succeed, their buried feelings emerge.

On the one hand, the coping mechanism—"I will secure love, admiration, or acceptance with my prowess or the accoutrements of success"—brings an unsatisfying, immature version (idolatry) of what they want (mature love). On the other hand, once narcissists become sensitized to what idolatry truly represents, they are hurt, and more devaluing behavior ensues. Ultimately those who engineer this trade-off of adulation for love end up in a tortuous Faustian bargain: They develop an overdependence upon tangible rewards as indicators of self-worth while coming to mistrust others and fail to pursue the types of relationships really needed to achieve long-term psychological satisfaction.

THE FAUSTIAN BARGAIN OVER TIME

This Faustian bargain is a tragic version of Groucho Marx's classic observation "I wouldn't want to belong to any club that would accept me as a member." The love you get from displays of power or wealth is love you do not want because it is so superficial. Adding insult to injury, this bargain inevitably creates a doubled-edged problem: the awareness that "they only love me for the things I do to please them" and the awareness that success cannot be sustained indefinitely, and once the performing stops, the love stops as well. When people enter into the Faustian bargain that trades success for love, the dread of "If I'm not succeeding, they'll stop caring" can be addressed by willpower or physical strength. But this is actually a pernicious form of appeasement—a misguided attempt to placate the god of authentic self-assessment. Until people face the truth about themselves—most achievers know what is buried beneath their facades or synthetic status—they are like rats on exercise wheels.

CONNECTIVITY: THE PRECURSOR TO GENERATIVITY

Narcissists are not initially aware of how much pain they will ultimately inflict upon themselves, but once they realize that they cannot sustain a successful career forever, they come face-to-face with the incongruity of their existence: Their pursuit of status and material success has led them to ignore the need to develop social skills.

According to Christopher Lasch, the narcissist's "devaluation of others, together with his lack of curiosity about them, impoverishes his personal life and reinforces [his] 'subjective feeling of emptiness.' . . . His fear of emotional dependence, together with his manipulative, exploitative approach to personal relations, makes these relations bland, superficial, and deeply unsatisfying."[2] This is why people who have spent a lifetime trying to conquer the mountain in pursuit of adulation find it so difficult to shift gears and attempt to conquer themselves. Their greatest fear—when they admit to having one—is that after a lifetime they will be completely unprepared for life when they can no longer generate the image of success and must instead look to others for love.

"Roy" was a fifty-five-year-old management consultant referred to me by his partner (and only friend) because he was concerned that Roy would "suffer a second heart attack and die." The friend's concerns were well-founded: Roy did nothing apart from devote twelve hours a day to his consulting practice and two hours a day to nursing martinis. As Roy's friend put it, "Ever since he lost his Japanese clients I've really feared for his life. At least when he went to Japan he would mess around with JAL and Singapore Air stewardesses or go on sex junkets; now all he does when he's not grinding out hours is punish people for things they are not guilty of."

Roy consented to an initial interview with me to appease his partner. Although he was perfectly comfortable in the role of counselor, adviser, and arbiter of right and wrong, he could not imagine what it would be like to be on the other side. Roy was the only child of immigrants from Poland, who raised him in near poverty in New York City. His father, an alcoholic truck driver, abandoned the family when Roy was five. Following that trauma Roy's mother suffered a schizophrenic breakdown that, when she wasn't hospitalized, left her emotionally unavailable. Roy received the message internalized by all children when parents die, depart, or are emotionally incapacitated—you are unwanted.

Roy's salvation was that he was brilliant. From the first grade he knew he could garner praise for his mental acuity. Thus, although

there was never a time when Roy wasn't receiving kudos, every bit
of positive feedback he received was linked to performance. It
wasn't that Roy got punished for not bringing home A's but that he
could tell that every gain in attention he accrued from the world at
large was attributable to his academic prowess. And while academic
honors and overindulgence from caring teachers are gratifying, they
will always be poor substitutes for a proud father's smile or a loving
mother's hug.

Because he was delicately built and bookish, Roy never partici-
pated in organized athletics. He was also terribly shy, which prevented him from engaging in most of the other extracurricular
activities available in his high school. At City University of New
York, he always made the dean's list, but he made virtually no
friends. Upon graduation he married a girl from his neighborhood
whose interest in accounting paralleled his affection for economics,
and the two formed a bland, functional, childless union.

In all likelihood Roy's life would have proceeded this way had it
not been for the economic boom of the 1980s. Like so many
"eggheads" transformed into powerhouses during that decade, Roy
went from existing in relative anonymity at a Big Six accounting firm
to being a million-dollar-a-year economic strategist at one of New
York's hottest collections of corporate raiders. Although it seems
paradoxical at first glance, the moment Roy experienced social status and wealth, with his high-flying group of new partners, his suppressed anger emerged with a vengeance. Since he was a child Roy
had been first in his class academically and a no-show socially. In his
new role with the corporate raiders, things became much more complex.

Because Roy clearly wasn't a deal maker or a schmoozer, he felt
he was relegated to second-tier status, a role he was no longer willing to tolerate given his presumed intellectual contributions to the
firm. Yet because the spotlight in his firm would never be directed on
someone with "only intellect," Roy started to experience narcissistically fueled rages: He actively resented the partners skilled at client
relations, calling them sociopaths, ass-kissers, and the like. When

that didn't do the trick, Roy began attempting to hoard credit for successful deals by claiming that had it not been for his work, clients who had originally been secured by other partners would have taken their business elsewhere. Roy went so far as to plant seeds of dissension between his partners and their clients by both innuendo and outright lies.

The end of Roy's career with the corporate raiders was precipitated when five of the young partners he had been casting aspersions on for months opted to set up a boutique of their own. While some people close to the scene at the time maintained that these young men would have left even if Roy never existed, the firm's founder didn't care. After a public screaming match that Roy lost, he was dismissed from the business that had converted him from frog to prince. Fortunately, the one friend he had at the company agreed to join forces with him and open a consulting practice. It was advantageous for Roy in a professional sense to have a stable ally to start a business with, but this safety net only exacerbated his psychological problem by dampening the pain that should have been inflicted by the loss of his job. It appears as though his instant rescue allowed him to avoid all discomfort. Rather than being a sobering experience, getting fired from his dream job only fanned the flames of Roy's narcissistic entitlement.

In what seemed to be a compensatory attempt to suppress his shame, Roy's appetite for celebrity status became insatiable. He described to me how, between being fired and forming his consulting practice, he spent "weeks of ecstasy" in Asia with prostitutes who would oblige his wish to hear of his sexual prowess. When he returned to New York, he drank to excess while ignoring his health. The consequence of Roy's narcissistic self-indulgence was that he suffered a heart attack at age fifty-one.

When I began working with Roy, four years after his heart attack, it was apparent that he had again refused to use the implications of a trauma as a wake-up call. He belittled junior members of his consulting practice, denied credit to his peers, and demanded kudos for work that was not his. In what seemed to be an accentuation of his problem brought about by the pressure I was putting on him, Roy even turned against his friend.

Seeing how out of control Roy's narcissistic demands were, I feared that he would terminate our relationship and suffer further decline if I didn't play the one ace I had up my sleeve: I convinced a friend on the faculty of a New York City business school that Roy would make an ideal lecturer in a new program that served older students.

Once I introduced Roy to my professor friend, I abandoned all efforts to coach him and, in effect, encouraged him to indulge his pathological pursuit of the spotlight . . . but in a healthier way. Having an audience of aspiring business executives who found his braggadocio exciting, Roy soon lost the need to engage in self-esteem building by character assassination in his firm. Coincidentally, as he spent more time in self-glorifying pursuits and less time berating others, Roy inadvertently allowed the junior consultants in his firm to develop their skills and clients unimpeded. As a consequence, his firm's profitability improved, which, because he was a principal, gave Roy additional bragging rights.

Under ideal circumstances, one might have persevered to "cure" Roy of his narcissistic preoccupation with glory. But his long-term outcome was quite favorable: He retired early from his consulting practice because he could continue to bask in the spotlight he enjoyed as a popular instructor. Although Roy never got authentic psychological satisfaction, considering his traumatic upbringing, the narcissistic rewards of his students' admiration may have been all the psychological satisfaction he was capable of enjoying.

HOW SELF-HELP PSYCHIATRY UNWITTINGLY EXACERBATED THE FAUSTIAN BARGAIN

One major reason it is so difficult to help narcissists recognize that they are their own worst enemies is the overwhelming social support for their modus operandi. Forget about how Hollywood inundates Americans with movie stars, how the fashion industry generates an ever-changing market for must-have styles, or how Madison Avenue has convinced the world that youth and sex sell every product under the sun. The industry that has kept the narcissistic lifestyle flourishing at record levels since the 1960s is the self-help publishing industry.

While this problem didn't begin with the 1975 publication of *Looking Out for #1* by Mark Monsky, his title captured the trend. In fairness to Monsky and other self-help authors, there is often much useful material in their writings, and much of the damage done by this body of literature is a function of the fact that these books are not read in depth or at all. Many people quote "insights" from the books based upon a cursory reading of the dust jackets and titles. Nevertheless, it seems as though psychiatric self-help gurus have concluded that pandering to the defensive self-love of narcissists sells.

The worldview perpetuated by tomes that advocate a look out for number 1 orientation exacerbates the core pathology underlying all narcissistic disturbances: entitlement, grandiosity, a desperate need for approval, lack of empathy, and obsessions with beauty, youth, power, and riches. Whereas the goal of psychodynamic psychotherapy has always been to help people who suffer disorders of this sort adjust to, and integrate themselves with, the cultures they are part of, the gospel according to the look-out-for-number-1 school is interpreted as an endorsement of the narcissist's view that "I don't need fixing, I need strategies that will enable me to overcome the external entities blocking me from success." This genre focuses on conquering the mountain, not conquering the aspects of the self that are vulnerable or in need of psychotherapy.

These kinds of self-help titles can be particularly problematic when they reinforce attitudes that exacerbate narcissists' difficulties forming healthy intimate relationships. Many take the looking out for number 1 literature as an endorsement of the belief that you may—if you are lucky—find someone good enough and wise enough to give you the love you deserve. As Erich Fromm noted in *The Art of Loving:*

Most people see the problem of love primarily as that of *being loved*, rather than that of *loving*, of one's capacity to love. Hence the problem to them is how to be loved, how to be loveable. In pursuit of this aim they follow several paths. One, which is especially used by men, is to be successful, to be as powerful and rich as the social margin of one's position permits. Another, used especially by women, is to make oneself attractive, by cultivating one's body, dress, etc....People think that to *love* is simple, but that to find the right object to love—or be loved by—is difficult [emphasis in the original].[3]

BREAKING THROUGH THE DEFENSES

According to modern psychiatry, the only impetus capable of motivating someone caught in a narcissistic lifestyle to begin valuing people in anything other than utilitarian terms is a *narcissistic injury:* a loss typically involving, or initiated by, a loved one. I have seen people who have spent decades swindling business associates, claiming credit for outcomes they stole from others, engaging in unambiguous criminal activity—doing whatever it takes to amass the trappings of success—adamantly refuse to heed pleas from loved ones to reconsider how they are living. Nothing works until a child engages in Pyrrhic revenge or a spouse gets caught (often on purpose) with a paramour.

Frequently, narcissistic injuries are inflicted without any subterfuge or amelioration. One bigoted, workaholic patient of mine was moved to sell his multimillion-dollar business after his daughter became pregnant a third time by a member of the minority group he expressed the most overt contempt for. Another man I worked with, who escaped Nazi Germany and nearly attained Forbes 400 status, refused to adjust his abusive behavior until his son had a swastika tattooed on his chest within inches of where a Star of David had once hung.

Such cruel wake-up calls await those who ignore the fact that life involves more than the material rewards of success. Unless narcissists realize that a fulfilling life involves the capacity to enrich the lives of others, a family member is highly likely to lash out at them. Yet to profit from a narcissistic injury people must have a belief in, or devotion to, a transcendent force or spiritual being that supersedes their personal, narcissistic needs.

Even Sigmund Freud, an avowed atheist and critic of organized religion, argued that only those who devote themselves to achieving "[a] feeling of an indissoluble bond, of being one with the external world as a whole"—a "religious" feeling—would be able to avoid the psychological traps inherent in seeking power, success, or wealth.[4] Today, owing to the brilliant work of the psychoanalyst Erik Erikson, Freud would probably have argued that human beings should strive to achieve generativity. Erikson defined *generativity* as follows:

> Evolution has made man a teaching as well as a learning animal, for dependency and maturity are reciprocal: mature man needs to be needed, and maturity is guided by the nature of that which must be cared for. *Generativity,* then, is primarily the concern for establishing and guiding the next generation [emphasis in original].[5]

Erikson took pains to ensure that generativity would not be confused with the tasks inherent in child rearing. And while he allowed that generativity could include nonbiological productivity and creativity, expanding the concept to include contributions to science, social activism, and so on, he was clear that contributing to the welfare of future generations by promoting a connection to the whole of mankind is the goal and essence of generativity:

> The mere fact of having or even wanting children does not "achieve" generativity. Some...parents suffer, it seems, from a retardation in the ability to develop true care. The reasons are often to be found...in faulty identifications with parents; in excessive self-love based on a too strenuously self-made personality; and in the lack of some faith, some "belief in the species," which would make a child appear to be a welcome trust.[6]

STAGNATION AND OVEREXTENSION

According to Erikson, people who did not have a "belief in the species" were fated to endure significant suffering. Specifically, he claimed that those who could not engage in generativity after an adulthood of professional success would regress to a lifestyle characterized by "an obsessive need for pseudo-intimacy [marked by] a pervading *sense of stagnation,* boredom, and interpersonal impoverishment" [emphasis in original],[7] in other words, an is-that-all-there-is? sense of ennui and depression.

People mired in what Erikson called stagnation have often merged their identities with their roles in an organization, for, according to Erikson,

> All institutions by their very nature codify the ethics of generative succession. Generativity is itself a driving power in human organization....The essentials of an organized human community have evolved together as an attempt to establish a set of proven methods and a fund of traditional reassurance which enables each generation to meet the needs of the next in relative independence from personal differences and changing conditions.[8]

While one is at the top of one's professional game, merging one's identity with, say, one's CEO status affords perquisites and power. According to those who have attained stellar success, the highs it provides can be at least as powerful as the high from a psychoactive drug. Yet it is possible to become as dependent on a role as an addict becomes on a narcotic. Social scientists call this identity dependence, a condition that leaves one so obsessed with the zero-sum aspects of professional success that victory is pursued solely to defeat others or sustain a synthetic self-esteem.

Being hooked on power or prestige is tolerable for many until they are forced to dissociate from the roles they've become dependent upon. Few people are as lucky as Roy was to have found an inexhaustible audience. On the contrary, anecdotal evidence reveals that professionals who derived an intoxicating sense of power from their careers typically come to believe that leaving their seats of power is "a kind of mortality."[9] Entrepreneurial arsonists are the clearest example of this phenomenon, while aging "hipsters" seeking to impress young girls with their alleged sexual prowess are the most pathetic. Only generativity prevents such humiliating states of delusion or denial.

At a functional level generativity represents the abandonment of self-interests and sources of self-esteem gain dependent upon audience approval. You will recall from the discussion of self-actualization that there are several ways of achieving psychological rewards not linked to the reactions of others. Children play for the sake of play, not for the sake of cheers or winning. Likewise, a self-actualized parent derives fulfillment and satisfaction from child-rearing activities that may never be witnessed by others. In a comparable manner, the person who engages in generativity substitutes external rewards for an opportunity to actualize unrealized plans in ways that allow others to derive gratification from his accomplishments. People who aim to achieve generativity utilize their wisdom or mental excellence in ways that allow them to realize their dreams while enabling successive generations to prepare to realize theirs.

As you might imagine, some people cannot engage in generativity. Erikson believed that the vast majority of them were blocked by a maladaptive drive he called *overextension*. Simply stated, overextension is an excessive desire to be as giving or "involved" as one can be. Stated another way, overextension arises when an individual pursues generativity as an end, not as a means.

Just as one cannot strive for, or be coached into, self-actualization, Erikson maintained that pushing to be generative, as if one were in a competition, leads inevitably to overextension. This process misses the essence of generativity—ceasing self-absorptive thoughts and actions in order to nurture or give of yourself to others.

"Barbara" was one of the few people I have worked with who was an unadulterated self-referral. She found out about me and my specializations by conducting a Lexis-Nexis search, something that I had never heard of at the time, 1990. According to Barbara, I appeared to be an expert on work-related stress, and that was exactly what she was suffering. Yet the complaint that a patient presents with at her first therapy session is almost never what you end up treating her for.

Barbara was the vice president in charge of event planning for one of the biggest corporations on the East Coast. She served two bosses or, if you will, constituencies. From one perspective, her work fell under the human resources division of her company. Yet from another perspective, every manager who planned an event was Barbara's boss for that effort.

At our first appointment I listened attentively to Barbara's description of the stress that was routinely crippling her. At roughly our seventh meeting I asked her to account for an anomaly: Never had she complained about symptoms manifesting in anticipation of a deadline. "I don't get it," I said. "You've got all the pressure of a restaurateur and a hotelier on your back, and you never get ticked off as the zero hour draws near. You regularly get migraine headaches the day after an event, you develop eczema a week later, and you suffer sleeplessness from the night an event ends until you opt to miss a day of work to catch up on your rest. You're not stressed by your job, you're stressed by the aftermath of a job well done."

Since there was no denying the pattern as I presented it, Barbara became angered. The analysis that appealed to her was that she became stressed by the pressure she felt to do a "perfect job." While I didn't discount this, I reiterated my belief that something in the aftermath of a successful event was what stressed her.

When our failure to see eye to eye reached a flash point, Barbara declared, "When an event is about to go off, I know it's going to be a home run so I relax for a moment and then mentally throw myself into my next project. Don't you understand that I 'catastrophize' about the potential problems that lie ahead each time I plan an event and that's what causes my stress?" She didn't know it, but her use of the term *catastrophize* enabled me to help her. Because *catastrophize* was in 1990 a technical term that had not become part of the vernacular, I sensed that Barbara could only have come across it through exhaustive research. I tested that notion, and she said, "Of course, I research everything to death. *Don't you appreciate me for what I am?*" "Yes, I believe I do," I responded, "but I'll bet the folks in your company don't." With that she thanked me a dozen or more times.

Over the next month the focus of our work shifted to where it belonged: We analyzed how Barbara became the superachiever-perfectionist whom no one thanked sufficiently. First we looked at how her symptoms benefited her. It soon became obvious that Barbara's somatic disorders were a self-generated wake-up call to stop suppressing anger. Her body was alerting her that she could no longer keep a lid on feeling undervalued and continue working in her current role. We agreed that her sleeplessness, headaches, and eczema were attributable to stress, but not the type she'd originally assumed. In reality Barbara's body was "breaking down" from the stress of keeping her fury from emerging and, she feared, ripping someone apart. We were ultimately able to address this problem through a short program of assertiveness training.

Barbara's deeper problem involved the source of her coping style: striving to be perfect in order to deal with fears of being inadequate. One of the most difficult challenges confronting a child is developing a system of controls to handle naturally occurring aggressive impulses. Of particular concern is helping the child block excessive aggression by choice, not as a function of dread—of being severely punished or of seeing her aggression traumatize or destroy someone else. Excessive threats or prohibitions against acting out teach children to acquiesce to authority rather than enable them to learn the benefits of being prosocial. A far knottier problem emerges when children come to fear their own impulses.

Barbara was afraid of every "aggressive" impulse she had. The reason for this is rather classic: She was raised by a powerful, domineering mother and a Milquetoast father, whom she adored. Whenever Barbara was "tomboyish" or "wild," her mother had no trouble spanking her, screaming at her, or punishing her. Barbara quickly became inured to these tirades. Her father reacted quite differently, however, when his "Bobby-Baby" acted up: He would cry. It was as though her dad saw Barbara as his salvation from a loveless marriage, and every time she violated his idealized image of her, he was crushed. The consequences of Barbara's aggressiveness grew worse when her mother began chiding her father for "acting like a pussy."

When Barbara and some friends were caught smoking in the junior high girls' room and she was suspended from school, her dad cried as usual. Her mother, in cruel, mocking tones, asked her husband, "What the hell will you do when your little virgin starts screwing boys in the school parking lot? Cut your heart out?"

Although she never knew for certain that witnessing the aftermath of the smoking-in-the-girls'-room event was the precipitant for her lifelong pattern of perfectionism, Barbara does recall that in junior high she vowed never again to act "like a slut" and began striving for goodness with excessive zeal. This reorientation was altruistic and adaptive in that she spared her father ongoing suffering, but it was self-defeating in terms of the burdens it placed on her. Because she decided to be a "good girl" out of a fear that her aggressive impulses would destroy her nuclear family, it was as though Barbara had an invisible gun against her temple. While she never actually harbored urges to act out sexually, she did have a temper, was opinionated, and wanted control over her destiny. All those propensities were squelched by a desire to maintain her father's vision of her as the best girl on earth.

Over the next two years Barbara worked with me to resolve her remaining ambivalence toward her parents, as well as her propensity to engage in overextension. At last report she was extremely pleased with all aspects of her life.

PASSING THE TORCH

When discussing generativity it is logical to be reminded of passing the torch. If a successful person did not make some sort of handoff or gift to successive generations, how could he transition from a lifestyle of doing, making, achieving, or attaining to one that fostered those behaviors in others? Yet the idiom "pass the torch" implies much more than mentoring or teaching competence. It is, as John F. Kennedy suggested in his inaugural address, an inspirational process that inflames passion and purpose in its recipients. Erikson would likely have agreed with this sentiment, particularly in light of the way his psychoanalytic theory departed from Freud's. From the perspective of Freudian psychoanalysts, there is always dynamic tension between generations. For example, according to Freud's concept of the Oedipus complex, it is assumed that if during the son's pursuit of his mother's affection the boy's father realized his intentions, the father would become enraged and seek vengeance. Hence, the notion (and origin) of *castration anxiety* in young boys.

Conforming with this theory of intergenerational tension is the Freudian notion that while parents influence the development of children, children have no such power over their parents. But in Erikson's view a person's sense of "being" is activated by interactions with the egos of others, even children, in what might now be called a reciprocal feedback loop: If I am generative with my daughter, her laughter, mimicry, and intellectual development foster my self-esteem and ego development, which makes me more likely to spend quality time with her, and so on. Erikson was so convinced of the benefits derived from this intergenerational reciprocal influence—what he called *mutuality*—that he claimed it was "the secret of love."[10]

Yet much of the world does not accept that mutuality—particularly the intergenerational variety—exists. A case in point is the French philosopher Gaston Bachelard, who viewed the world from a rigidly Freudian perspective. Bachelard identified what he called the Promethean complex, a process engaged in by men seeking the power of gods. According to Bachelard, fire is a symbol of intellect, and those with a Promethean complex are driven to steal fire here on earth as Prometheus did from Mount Olympus. Would-be

Prometheans can achieve their goals by acquiring the intellectuality of their fathers or their teachers.[11]

People who narcissistically cling to their career paths find that their attempts to preserve their income and status set them up to feel competitive with, or antagonistic toward, successive generations. How could it be otherwise for a winner-take-all mentality? In contrast, the person who feels generative and looks past the here-and-now can gain the support of successive generations, establish a legacy, and attain professional and spiritual growth. The process of generativity removes the pressure to enhance one's stockpile of beauty and riches and instead glorifies one's cumulative wealth of knowledge. In fact, becoming involved in the development of a younger generation gives those who are generative the feeling of safety and strength that fosters their capacity to review their lives and candidly assess their failures or weaknesses.

THE INABILITY TO ADMIT, LET ALONE CELEBRATE, FAILURE

Most people agree that the American, hypermasculinized idea of what it takes to be considered a success causes disease. The tendency to condemn vulnerability as a sign of weakness is most responsible for the inability to remedy symptoms of Supernova Burnout. One of the ways in which macho successes harm themselves is by adopting a posture vis-à-vis subordinates that blocks generativity. In order to give of oneself and achieve the benefits of helping successive generations, one must first set the stage for mutuality by being approachable.

If successful people could acknowledge that they were not Olympians once Supernova Burnout was detected, that admission alone would have overwhelming benefits. At a minimum, the admittedly flawed former Olympian is in a better position to achieve performance goals because *until you abandon the pretense of perfection, you cannot possibly acquire the new skills or resources needed to sustain success through a career.* As Epictetus observed nearly two thousand years ago,

To do anything well you must have the humility to bumble around a bit, to follow your nose, to get lost, to goof. Have the courage to try an undertaking and possibly do it poorly. *Unremarkable lives are marked by the fear of not looking capable when trying something new* [emphasis added].

Investing energy in appearing successful rather than enhancing the long-term success that comes from being generative and connected brings about the professional demise of a startling number of otherwise capable people. The true cost of believing "winners never quit and quitters never win" is that it ultimately blocks you from establishing generative relationships with others.

The belief that failing to maintain a successful reputation will destroy a career is injurious in other ways too: It blocks people from asking for the help needed to learn techniques that would enable them to compete with those who possess generative interpersonal skills. Worse, the intense intellectual focus that goes into sustaining a reputation blocks people from assessing threats to self-esteem with an open, objective mind. Francis Bacon observed, "He that will not apply new remedies must expect new evils; for time is the greatest innovator." You cannot learn new remedies until you stop applying the old ones.

Far too many people who subscribe to the nothing-succeeds-like-the-*appearance*-of-success school of thought feel that they can avert humiliation or shame by bullying others into supporting their self-image of competence. These people should be pitied, not envied, for whatever material success they inveigle. From a long-term perspective, they are committing slow suicide. As Eleanor Roosevelt noted,

You gain strength, courage and confidence by every experience in which you really stop to look fear in the face. You are able to say to yourself, "I lived through this horror. I can take the next thing that comes along." ... You must do the thing you think you cannot do.[12]

Is there a facade that exacts a heavier psychological toll than sustaining an image of infallibility for fear of risking exposure as a fraud? Probably not. Apart from the effort of remaining ever vigilant, to either mask or externalize blame for the missteps that even the most competent among us must occasionally commit, trying to deny that you are subject to the human propensity to fail actually sabotages your ability to succeed. According to Henry Ford, "Failure is the opportunity to begin again more intelligently." How can you profit from the insight brought by failure if you refuse to accept that you have failed?

George Bernard Shaw recognized that "the more things a man is ashamed of, the more respectable he is." Shaw's understanding of how much can be gained by turning failure into a learning experience is slowly acquiring acceptance in corporate America. According to an article in *The New York Times*, many venture capital firms and headhunters now view those who have failed or suffered a career setback as "sexy hires."[13] A number of psychological truths justify the change of heart that now applauds what was once deemed a sign of weakness. For example, anxiety can be reduced considerably by embracing bad news and preparing your body and mind to cope with it. Similarly, the person willing to acknowledge a history of failure knows well the value of early intervention in minimizing the costs of failure.

TRYING TOO HARD TO BUILD AN OLD-GIRLS NETWORK

When "Sharon" was referred to me in 1991, attitudes toward vulnerability and failure were quite different than they are today. No one could have convinced Sharon that admitting failure or weakness was adaptive; if there was ever a prototype for a female Horatio Alger, Sharon was it. The second of six girls born to a South Carolina high school teacher and his homemaker wife, Sharon climbed the ladder of success because she felt it was a blessing to be able to do so. During our first meeting she remarked offhandedly, "You know, I'm not telling my folks or sisters about my problem because

I would die of shame if they knew. No one in my family bellyaches, and I'm not going to be the first to break *that* tradition."

Had she been of a mind to, Sharon could have "bellyached" quite a bit about a phobia she developed within three months of being promoted to executive vice president of human resources at a Fortune 500 company based an hour from Boston: a morbid fear of driving her car. Although she was unaware of the exact moment her disorder became manifest, she told me that after feeling queasy and lightheaded for weeks before entering her car every day, one morning as she shifted into drive she found herself vomiting and shaking with fright. After changing her clothes and calling her office to say she would be late, Sharon called her ex-husband and got him to drive her to work. The following day she vomited again before beginning her commute, and decided to seek help.

The doctor who first treated Sharon gave her both an antianxiety drug and a medication designed to prevent the symptoms of panic attacks. Sharon's symptoms abated for a while, but the beneficial effects of these pills ultimately wore off. That's when a friend recommended she see me.

First I needed to determine if Sharon's disorder bought her some form of relief. I could find nothing about her relationship to cars that justified the fear-of-driving diagnosis and drew another blank when I asked her about work. She loved the company she worked for, was thrilled that she reported directly to the president, and felt challenged daily. The only area left to explore was her love life. When I broached the subject, Sharon told me I was off base. She was recently divorced but asserted that she had "a burning desire" to remarry one day and raise a family. As luck would have it I was familiar with the isolated town she lived in. I felt I might get some useful information by asking her how living there fit with her intention to remarry. I said, "Sharon, no one lives where you do by accident; I know you actively chose to live there for a very important reason, and it wasn't to have an active social life. What's up?"

My gambit worked. Sharon laughed and said, "You're right; it's odd that I would live there given that I'm looking to raise a family someday." When I pushed her to tell me more, she said something quite revealing: "The town reminds me of South Carolina . . . except for the weather. I know that sounds crazy, but I'm homesick. Here I am, just thirty-three years old and professionally on top of the world, but I'm homesick. It's so bad I dream about South Carolina."

When you attempt to understand the utility of a phobia, you must explore the gains a person can accrue by being blocked from behaving in a particular manner. For instance, you could ask someone afraid of bridges what lies on the opposite side of the bridge. If it's a feared object (school or work), the utility of the bridge phobia is apparent: It prevents the person from encountering a dreaded entity. But Sharon loved driving her BMW, she loved work, yet she was vomiting every time she neared her driver's seat.

Eventually I risked angering Sharon by asking if she was looking to get a disability discharge from her job. She chided me for being overly simplistic and suggested we stop meeting. But I pushed her: "How else do you get back to South Carolina? You're too competent to be fired, your direct reports love you, so how else do you get out of the trap you're in unless you get sent home in an ambulance?"

A week later Sharon confessed that I was partially correct, adding: "But as I said, you were shortsighted. Yes, you're correct insofar as I want off the fast track, but I'm not looking to claim a disability as an excuse. I came to understand over the past week that by being late and missing more days of work over the past three months than I had in the past ten years, I was giving 'Maureen' [Sharon's director of employee benefits and the person she respected most in her department] vital experience filling in for me. I'm not going to leave [the company] high and dry; I'll leave when I'm done grooming my successor."

Once I heard this epiphany, I knew that our work should focus on Sharon's feelings about being blocked from actualizing her generative propensities. Two comments were particularly revelatory: The first came soon after her acceptance of the fact that her fear of driving was a message to stop driving to work in Massachusetts. She was talking about how she was still irked with me for suggesting that she would allow herself to get fired because of how upsetting it would be to her younger sisters. "Those girls are modeling themselves after me, and every career move I make is replayed countless times at our home. How could you assume that anything means more to me than that responsibility?" The second set of comments concerned her ex-husband. Sharon twice alluded that she got divorced in large part because the man she married was too possessive of her time. "If either of us won the lottery," she once told me, "I'm certain he'd demand that we go to a South Seas island and say, 'Screw you, world, we're having fun.' That's not me; I'm a people person and I live for family."

Sharon and I stopped working together before she developed a complete understanding of why it had been impossible for her to announce her desire to step off the fast track, groom a successor, and return home. The good news, however, is that within six months of realizing how she was satisfying her desire to return to South Carolina by inadvertently grooming Maureen to succeed her, she left Massachusetts for her home and a much lower-visibility job that allowed her to engage in the generative pursuits she hungered for.

APPLIED GENERATIVITY: MENTORING

It seems obvious that only those who can acknowledge failure have the temperament needed to be a mentor. From Erikson's perspective, unless a successful person can accept his own vulnerability, he cannot be tolerant of a neophyte mastering the learning curve in fits and starts, and struggling with all the anxieties and doubts inherent in intellectual and emotional growth.

In today's business environment the attribute that should be valued most in a senior executive is generativity. No recruitment technique under the sun can fully satisfy America's need for competent entry-level members of the workforce given the current record levels of employment we enjoy. Yet a person who can mentor a trainee or shape the career of someone with raw talent but little applied expertise is able to help retain employees during this seller's market for talent.

Good mentors believe in the attitude that made Dee Hock, the founder of Visa, so wildly successful: "It is no failure to fall short of all you might dream. The failure is to fall short of dreaming all that you might realize." Recall that Erikson's definition of generativity rests on two fundamental tenets: human beings as teachers and a primary concern for establishing and guiding the next generation. These attributes are an operational definition of good mentoring.

At age eighty Walter Wriston, who ran Citicorp from 1967 to 1984, was "cutting a swath through Corporate America" by serving on seven boards that enabled him to mentor young careerists in, among other specialties, the emerging field of biotechnology. Wriston's view of what he was doing captured the value of generativity for the future of America: "When you've been there and done that, you may have useful experience for companies that are very young."[14]

Yet generativity also benefits the mentor, in ways ranging from improved physical health to psychological satisfaction. For example, research has shown that people who are identity dependent upon their roles in organizations often suffer increased susceptibility to disease, and may even die, shortly after unplanned retirement.[15] By contrast, when the effects of generativity between people not biologically related are assessed—in groups such as academic mentors or Peace Corps volunteers—the results demonstrate that giving affords donors a number of psychological payoffs, ranging from feelings of self-efficacy to enhanced *psychological hardiness,* the capacity to cope with stressful events.

This effect is particularly pronounced among retirees who actively mentor. According to their personal reports, staying involved in generativity is key to their ability to sustain both physical and emotional health. The organization known as SCORE—Service Corps of Retired Executives—demonstrates this truth on a daily basis. The service matches men and women who have attitudes like Walter Wriston's with companies who cannot afford professional consultants. As young careerists learn the tricks of the trade, the SCORE mentors derive enhanced self-esteem from being seen as successful not for what they are achieving but for the mental excellence necessary to impart wisdom to others. In fact, it has been shown that during the mentoring process many retirees inadvertently resume traditional nonteaching roles in businesses as a natural outgrowth of sharing their experiential wealth.[16]

LEGACY

I believe mentoring's greatest benefit is the opportunity to build a living legacy. It is generally accepted that a good teacher can influence the world for eternity because his or her influence never ends. When I try to describe the benefits of teaching and mentoring to high-powered professionals who feel awkward about needing such things as affection, I suggest the following: Think of becoming a mentor as initiating the world's only socially valuable Ponzi scheme. You attract people to invest in your vision or your wisdom, they provide you with psychological wealth (appreciation, admiration, and so on), and when they become successful they recruit others to join the scheme. Your resources expand geometrically, as do the benefits.

The essence, however, to building a living legacy is the attitude realignment that is step one in the process of reclaiming the fire: divesting yourself of worship for success and with it the squalid cash interpretation put on the word. In its place substitute relationships, which have come to be called connectivity or connection.

When used in this context, the word *connection* has nothing to do with the connections that can get you seats for Los Angeles Lakers games adjacent to Jack Nicholson. A connection is what is formed between a mentor and a younger person. Connectivity is the result of taking responsibility for the intellectual and emotional development of others. Here again the hypermasculinized approach toward success is disease causing, and the female attitude about relationships is health-promoting.

Recall the insights offered by Jean Baker Miller on what she refers to as "ties to others": "Women's sense of self becomes very much organized around being able to make and then to maintain affiliations and relationships."[17] This is the essence of generativity, and it is the foundation upon which all living legacies develop. Paradoxically, it is what caused Sharon so much pain until she was able to proclaim that her connections were more valuable to her than her fast-track status. Achievement orientation and the zero-sum attitude to career advancement that so many narcissists exploit to their short-term advantage are antagonistic to developing psychologically rewarding relationships.

Corporate CEOs, stellar attorneys (particularly litigators), athletes, and any professionals who feel they had to claw their way to the top are deprived of the living legacy that comes naturally to those whose lives are devoted to maintaining affiliations and relationships. Because I am confronted by this predicament almost every time I coach a senior (fifty-five or older) executive for Supernova Burnout, I give many of them a plaque with a quotation from the Gospel of Matthew (16:26): "For what is a man profited, if he shall gain the whole world, and lose his own soul?" The only way those who have spent a lifetime striving for achievement with a winner-take-all attitude can find the passion needed to reclaim the fire is to be certain they are behaving in ways that gratify their souls.

CHAPTER 9

True Happiness Is a Verb

It is easy to fly into a passion—anybody can
do that—but to be angry with the right
person and at the right time and with the
right object and in the right way—that is not
easy, and it is not everyone who can do it.

—ARISTOTLE

F. Scott Fitzgerald once said, "There are no second acts in American lives," a remark obviously motivated by deep-seated resentment or disappointment. How else could a man of his genius ignore religious conversions, patients' response to psychotherapy, even the rehabilitation of so-called career criminals? One way to explain Fitzgerald's jaundiced view is to examine what is arguably his finest work, *The Great Gatsby*, a vivid portrayal of how a young, successful man fails in his attempt to use his wealth to obliterate his past and capture the heart of his beloved. The book is a powerful indictment of the American myth that success, in and of itself, can change life for the better.

Jay Gatsby, a charismatic bootlegger and flamboyant entertainer, is murdered before he can reclaim the love of his life, Daisy Buchanan. The novel reveals that, while Gatsby was overseas in the Army, Daisy married a man who held out the promise that his old money could provide her with the lifestyle to which she yearned to become accustomed. Although she was smitten with Gatsby, he had yet to make his way in the world, so Daisy took the sure thing. When they were reunited after the war, both Jay and Daisy met the criteria for synthetic celebrity status. Yet their considerable material wealth did nothing to eradicate their poor-side-of-the-tracks heritage, or purge them of their crass materialism. Fitzgerald understood that character is fate and that, in the end, material success could not remedy the character flaws keeping Jay and Daisy from the intimacy they both longed for.

Fitzgerald did not create characters like Jay Gatsby and Daisy Buchanan in a vacuum. Countless men and women pursue synthetic celebrity status because they believe in the transformational powers of success. If most Americans held the view, after Martin Luther King, Jr., that "the ultimate measure of a man is not where he stands in moments of comfort and convenience, but where he stands at times of challenge and controversy," strength of character, not wealth, would be the quality deemed most capable of transforming a life. But Americans are as unwilling to abandon their belief in the power of success as they are resistant to authentic assessments of their strength of character. We can confirm this fact by examining two recent trends that help people suffering Supernova Burnout to disavow personal responsibility for deriving psychological gratification from their careers: (1) an epidemic of one-size-fits-all employee assistance programs, particularly those designed to address workplace stress, and (2) a dramatic rise in opposition to differential advantages in schools or job settings.

THE TYRANNY OF LEGISLATING JOY

Drug manufacturers advertising their prescription medications on national television caution prospective patients that they must have physicians take detailed medical histories before prescribing any drug. The folks who make, for example, Prilosec and Paxil want us to request their products by name, but not if we are ill-suited to tolerating them or vulnerable to known side effects. Why, then, don't professionals who sell training programs designed to relieve job stress and related disorders take the same precautions?

In a 1999 report on job stress in Silicon Valley, *Newsweek* described a program designed to help workers derive more satisfaction from their lives and, in turn, be more happy and productive in their career pursuits. According to the *Newsweek* article,

> Tech companies are turning to so-called get-a-life consultants—mentors, psychologists, gurus, even yoga instructors...to help the over-worked silicon-collar class maintain some semblance of a personal life while surviving in the pinball world of high tech.... [One] author of [a self-help book] says that tech firms "are going to great lengths to convince their employees that work is not a nightmare."[1]

Given the fact that in Silicon Valley people work an average of sixteen hours a day, it is no surprise that a great deal of energy has gone into developing interventions aimed at unburdening overtaxed talent. The problem is, many of these programs contain components that can actually make matters worse.

Consider what John Gage, chief of research at Sun Microsystems, told *Newsweek*. His company hired get-a-life counselors to coach software engineers and others "*on the joys of the real world—*sunlight, bike riding, children" (emphasis added).[2] But any intervention based on a predetermined notion of what will make people happy is prone to backfire. So, too, what I call the work-is-not-about-making-money-it's-about-doing-something-you-love model of career success.

These programs have incredible surface appeal: "Darling, the seminar leader did make a good point. I have never been as happy at work as I was during those halcyon days in high school when I had all the time in the world to build ships in bottles." Sorry; nobody lives adulthood like that. By the way, when you're being honest with yourself, try to recall *why* you had time to build ships in bottles when you were a teenager. Was it because you couldn't get a date?

Another reason these money-doesn't-matter programs don't work is that there is no way banal activities can fulfill an adult's desire for self-efficacy, self-esteem, and self-fulfillment. The human mind is structured to experience reward by both surmounting challenges and contributing to work that promotes generativity, feelings that cannot be derived from an interminable arts and crafts session at camp Sun-n-Fun. Epictetus was similarly suspicious of any attempts to define or achieve happiness in a self-indulgent manner. For him, *true happiness is a verb:*

> The virtue that leads to enduring happiness is not a *quid pro quo* goodness. (I'll be good "in order to" get something.) Goodness in and of itself *is* practice *and* the reward.... It's a lifelong series of subtle readjustments of our character. We fine-tune our thoughts, words, and deeds in a progressively wholesome direction.... To be good is to be happy; to be tranquil and worry-free. When you actively engage in gradually refining yourself, you retreat from your lazy ways of covering yourself or making excuses. Instead of feeling a persistent current of low-level shame, you move forward by using the creative possibilities of *this* moment, your current situation.... You move *through* life by being thoroughly *in* it.[3]

NEGATIVE PLACEBO EFFECTS

The problems caused by prepackaged therapeutic or morale-building programs are significant and extensive. People who participate in these programs and fail to experience symptomatic relief may suffer a worsening of the problems they sought to remedy. This occurs because people who get forced into one-size-fits-all treatment programs are often victimized by a negative placebo effect.

Traditional, or what should be called positive placebo effects, are obtained when, for example, a person ingests a pill that cannot have a salutary effect on his disorder yet his symptoms diminish. The positive placebo effect works because expectations of favorable outcomes harness forces in a person's mind and body that bring about the desired outcome. We can convince ourselves of many things, even that a physical symptom will be relieved.

The so-called negative placebo effect occurs when the positive placebo effect boomerangs: Your mind prepares to experience a favorable effect, but it doesn't occur; the pill that you expect to relieve a symptom doesn't help. What happens next under these circumstances is that the patient typically infers that his disorder is worse than originally imagined. The reasoning that generates the negative placebo effect goes as follows: "I must be getting worse or be suffering a whopping case since I feel as bad after the doctor gave me the medicine as I did before."

Corporations with the best intentions could avoid negative placebo effects if they would administer one simple assessment tool before prescribing a get-a-life program: the ask-the-person-who-is-distressed-what-will-make-her-happy test. Then, if you must, engage in the Regis Philbin follow-up assessment: "Is that your final answer?" At Sun Microsystems, program administrators could easily have polled participants to determine who would have preferred substituting moonlit strolls, scuba diving, or ringside tickets to World Wrestling Federation spectaculars over the standard joys-of-the-real-world offerings. The problem is, this form of questioning is the first step down a pathway Americans are loath to follow: authentic self-assessment.

Creators of get-a-life programs find it easier to adhere to their one-size-fits-all mentality because confronting people with personal questions about their preferences *or* flaws is not the American way. This may be a derivative of our latent respect for the rugged individualists who founded this nation, a consequence of our admiration for the authentic might of the silent generation, who crushed the Axis powers in World War II, or a vestige of the false pride that locks so many people in golden handcuffs for fear they would be chided for complaining while living on (presumed) easy street. Whatever the reason, if you want to help a group of successful people deal with a work-related problem, asking them to admit to feeling pain is often a fool's errand. Imposing something that everyone is doing makes it appear as though no one has asked for help. Unfortunately, this course is also far less effective.

ARE WE TRULY FREE TO SING, "TAKE THIS JOB AND SHOVE IT"?

Negative placebo effects represent only half the damage that can be done by one-size-fits-all career counseling programs. A second set of problems can be as damaging, if not more so. They advance the deceit that people are free to follow the do-what-you-like, money-doesn't-make-work-meaningful school of thought.

In fairness, the theoretical foundations of this premise are sound: Extrinsic rewards like money are not reinforcing over time, particularly when it comes to sustaining a career. As Samuel Clemens said through his alter ego Mark Twain, "Work consists of whatever a body is *obliged* to do. . . . Play consists of whatever a body is not obliged to do." Yet the obviousness of these points begs a question: Given that people know what is rewarding and cannot be paid to enjoy drudgery, why do they need gurus to advise them to have fun doing work they want to do? Why don't people just ignore what they are obliged to do and seek self-fulfillment in play? Because life doesn't work that way. In essence, there are three fundamental deceptions inherent in the ignore-money, do-what's-fun school of thought.

1. *Too much of anything is no good.* Sooner or later, even the pursuit of a cherished hobby will drive one crazy. To make matters worse, hobbies, like all pursuits with rewarding outcomes, are subject to self-imposed encore effects. If you've built hundreds of schooners in bottles, won't what began as fun become as boring as watching paint dry? Wouldn't you then be motivated to build an armada of ships in one bottle? Where does it end? It doesn't, which is why life as hobby is a lie.

2. *We all have obligations,* and most people develop symptoms of Supernova Burnout because of their drive to ful-

fill obligations to others. The so-called *provider paradox*—"If I leave this job that has me trapped in golden handcuffs, I will be hurting my children"—is frequently an accurate statement. Nevertheless, remaining trapped in golden handcuffs could easily drive a provider to drink or more extreme escapist pursuits. Since remaining trapped in golden handcuffs can be as dangerous as fleeing from them, careerists must recognize their responsibility to conduct regular cost-benefit analyses of their situations and act responsibly—to themselves and others—on the results.

3. *People whose work is an extension of their hobbies don't need a book to tell them this is a brilliant career move.* There are those who have turned what they cherish into a career—Michael Jordan or the syndicated columnist George Will, to name two—and their work products make one certain that it is possible to get paid for doing what you love. Once that is accomplished, achieving psychological fulfillment without guidance is as natural as feeling sleepy after a Thanksgiving feast. But most of us cannot achieve the remarkable synergy between avocation and vocation that Jordan and Will have, even under idyllic circumstances, let alone while being tutored by a how-to manual designed to meet the needs of millions of readers.

YES, BUT I HAVE REWARDS OUTSIDE WORK

Organizations that have attempted to implement do-what-you-consider-play programs as antidotes to work-induced malaise seem to understand that it is impossible to legislate the wholesale abandonment of something as fundamental and appropriate as the drive to make money in order to fulfill responsibilities. As a consequence, they strive for half-a-loaf outcomes. Program administrators sense that it may be possible to achieve some psychological benefits by advocating balance in life: mixing work and play, an approach that approximates Freud's definition of mental health: love and work.

Here again, though, what is well-intended often misses the mark. The majority of these balance programs suffer from what I call *the sundae fallacy*. You can cover a lump of clay with chocolate sauce, whipped cream, chopped nuts, M&M's, and whatever else your sweet tooth craves, but what you have when you're done is still just a high-calorie lump of clay. Regardless of how much the joys of life improve overall psychological well-being, they can never address or remove the need to cope with aspects of careers that are onerous yet unavoidable. Nor can they obliterate the tedium, drudgery, or depression associated with abhorrent tasks that are a crucial component of one's profession.

ANGER: POLITICALLY INCORRECT . . . AND INEVITABLE

Once you are able to penetrate sundae fallacies and similar attempts to distort the reality of careers, you can address the bottom-line prerequisite for reclaiming the fire: *confronting what it is about you, personally, that allows certain aspects of your career to evoke anger.* Apart from the notion that success has uniformly favorable life-altering consequences, the belief most responsible for generating Supernova Burnout is the 100 percent false conviction that success in career pursuits will mitigate anger—both on and off the job.

People who do not learn to cope with anger engage in a deadly game of avoidance that is bound to have severe consequences. If you see a person who is always joyous—a person who appears to be working at his hobby in a blissful re-creation of childhood play—you are watching someone who either is under the influence of hallucinogenic drugs or has learned to cope effectively with anger.

Most Americans encounter seemingly insurmountable obstacles to the expression of intense feelings, anger in particular. Many of these obstacles are reinforced by the pronouncements of splinter groups in the political correctness movement that have warped fundamentally sound social concerns in often ill-considered ways. One case in point is how the well-intentioned campaign to stop mistreatment of workers by abusive bosses unintentionally fostered intolerance of emotions such as anger and moral indignation in the workplace. Many senior executives who seek help from psychologists today can trace their problems to a fear that they will incur social censure if they express intense passions and desires at work, particularly if these feelings involve criticism of subordinates or coworkers.

Setting aside the fact that voicing interpersonal conflicts can actually enhance group cohesiveness and morale if carried out in an appropriate manner, denying outlets for the expression of intense negative emotions is guaranteed to disrupt both the person suppressing those feelings and the organization he would like to contribute to.[4] If only the activists seeking to eradicate anger from all discourse would consider the wisdom of Buddha: "Holding on to anger is like grasping a hot coal with the intent of throwing it at someone else; you are the one who gets burned."

Similar problems arise when advocacy groups seek to eliminate competitiveness and the experience of failure from public institutions. While efforts to level competitive playing fields for the authentically disadvantaged are laudable, many programs designed to achieve this goal have been transformed into attempts to legislate an across-the-board equalization of talents, skills, and abilities. Some designers of social programs appear intent upon outlawing self-actualizing actions by those with extraordinary aptitudes. Attempts to control the behavior of the exceptionally talented are often justified by the erroneous presumption that people who exploit their advantages in life necessarily damage the psychological health of those not similarly blessed.

In May 2000, Reuters reported that Britain's Labour government had published a booklet urging teachers to ban the game of musical chairs on the grounds that it encourages aggression or excessive competition. According to the author of the booklet, Sue Finch, "A little bit of competition is fine, but with musical chairs the competition is not fair because it is always the biggest and strongest children who win." Finch went on, "Musical statues is better because everybody wins."[5]

She is wrong on several counts. First, there are many strategies that can prove successful in musical chairs apart from brute force. For instance, a clever child can discern that by moving slowly, strategically, and out of sync with the music he or she might gain an advantage over those who seek to secure seats by dint of brute strength alone.

Second, Finch assumes that a game of musical statues would be as gratifying to children overflowing with energy as musical chairs. But all children, regardless of strength, are eager to be as active as possible. Posturing like a statue may prove frustrating to many school-age children, and, as all psychologists know, frustration leads to aggression. Finch's third misconception is that there is an inherent benefit to having children grow up in environments where everybody wins or, more accurately, no one wins. This is both incorrect and disruptive to the development of a healthy ego. The world does not ensure that everyone gets an equal set of rewards, blessings, or breaks, and the sooner a child learns this fact—and learns to respond to it in a healthy manner—the better that child's psychological development will be.

THE PERIL OF SUPPRESSED EMOTIONS

The reason Finch's booklet stuck in my mind was a news report that set the wire services buzzing three days after the musical chairs story appeared: It seemed related to the type of aggression that Finch was trying to curb. On May 26, 2000, a thirteen-year-old honor student in Lake Worth, Florida, allegedly shot and killed an exceptionally well-liked thirty-five-year-old English teacher and basketball coach nicknamed Shaggy (because of his hair). According to authorities, the student had been sent home from school by an assistant principal, not Shaggy, because he had been throwing water balloons. He returned two hours later with a semiautomatic pistol and allegedly committed murder.[6]

What prompted the thirteen-year-old to behave as he's accused of behaving may never be known. He could have felt shamed and humiliated because he was sent home from school, or he could have felt emasculated by a cruel administrator. Yet it is hard to imagine that there weren't a number of hostile feelings left unattended to or unresolved tormenting this child for a very long time before he supposedly opted to bring a pistol to school and start shooting.

I wonder how Finch would account for the fact that a thirteen-year-old honor student manifesting none of the *presumably* telltale signs of a troubled teen (such as membership in counterculture groups or identification with rock groups that advocate violence) might commit murder. This boy was so overtly well-socialized. Honor students do their homework, study hard, and act with decorum in class. Yet in one eight-hour period this young man engaged in a minor prank and then allegedly committed homicide. How can that be?

COMPLIANCE VERSUS SELF-CONTROL

Since I never met the alleged murderer, I cannot say for sure what prompted his violent outburst, but there is good reason to assume that this child's exemplary behavior came about at a significant cost: forfeiture of authentic control over his feelings. When a person suppresses a thought or a feeling that he is told is bad or wrong, that thought or feeling does not vanish from the mind. Instead, it is forced out of consciousness but will fester or merely dwell unresolved until such time as an external stimulus evokes awareness of it.

Had every firearm on the planet been melted down long before this unfortunate child learned what a gun was or did, he would still have expressed his hostility in an inappropriate manner—by hurling a rock or throwing a punch—unless steps had been taken long before the shooting to facilitate the appropriate resolution of the pent-up feelings that were inside him.

What strategy could have helped this child resolve the pent-up feelings that drove him to behave as he did? Airing them in psychotherapy, participating in conflict-resolution training sessions, or learning to sublimate them in prosocial ways. In short, anything that would, with appropriate supervision, enable the child to give voice to what was causing him psychological pain.

Authentically healthy behavior is never achieved by prohibiting antisocial acts. The result of forced adherence to rules of appropriate decorum is behavioral compliance with rules. Abstaining from something is not the same thing as not desiring it. Healthy people who want to behave in a prosocial manner become this way by one of two means: resolving antisocial feelings or learning to cope with stressful circumstances.

The ultimate paradox of programs that attempt to rid schools and other public institutions of activities that promote competition and aggression is that many of these so-called aggressive activities actually teach children to control antisocial impulses while building self-esteem.[7] A good example is training in martial arts such as karate, boxing, or wrestling. Unbeknownst to many, martial arts training proceeds from rules that punish acts of inappropriate aggression or violence. Furthermore, contestants who rely exclusively upon brute strength to defeat an opponent (the attribute that Finch feared) or lose their head and behave in a hyperaggressive manner will almost always be outfought by someone who truly understands the art of their technique. Rage is the enemy of a skilled pugilist, which is why the best practitioners of sports like boxing and karate learn to master fury and other feelings that get in the way of good performance. They learn self-control and control over their emotions.

To rid the world of as many undesirable aggression-fueled behaviors as possible, we must meet the challenge implicit in the assertion from Aristotle that opened this chapter: Learn to be angry with the right person, at the right time, in the right way. As Aristotle noted, that is not easy, and not everyone can do it. Those who can have mastered techniques that enable them to control their natural tendency to fly into a fit of passion whenever they experience frustration, disappointment, or sorrow. In the words of the psychiatrist Karl Menninger, "To 'know thyself' must mean to know the malignancy of one's own instincts and to know, as well, one's power to deflect it."

SUPERNOVA BURNOUT: A BY-PRODUCT OF UNEXPRESSED ANGER?

Conquering the mountain does not mean that we have conquered the malignancy of our instincts, and as synthetic celebrities and narcissists illustrate time and time again, success often comes with a hefty psychological price tag. In their circumstance the cost begins with intense feelings of anger evoked by the realization that using success to secure love has led them to detest those who love them only for their success. But this anger is only the start. To assess the real cost of the Faustian bargains many successful people get trapped in, they must determine, following Aristotle's dictum, if they are being angry with the right person, at the right time, and in the right way.

Typically, they are not. The easiest way to resolve such a Faustian bargain is to follow Menninger's advice: "Know the malignancy of [your] own instincts." Since people will only enter into Faustian bargains if they fear they cannot secure a desired outcome without assistance from the devil, their primary responsibility when they become dissatisfied with the deal is to analyze what angers them about their succumbing to temptation rather than striving for authentic success.

Most of the disorders that cause Supernova Burnout arise from anger with yourself. This is so for either of two reasons: (1) awareness that you lack what you believe are the requisite skills or attributes to feel wholly competent in a career, or (2) frustration that you do not know how to negotiate your way out of a situation in which you feel forced to perform according to expectations imposed by others. To instill a career with the healthy passion that will enable you to conquer symptoms of Supernova Burnout, you must remove the major impediment to healthy passion, namely, self-directed anger.

"Doug" was one of the most powerful businessmen in Los Angeles when I met him, but when he walked—I mean, limped—into my office the first time, he appeared to be convalescing from a near-fatal accident. Instead of a $150 Hermès tie that harmonized with his $3,000 Brioni suit, a cervical collar supported his neck; instead of an alligator attaché case, he carried a cane. Doug was referred to me by a neurologist who believed his pains were completely psychosomatic.

The referring physician told me that Doug was likable and brilliant. Both were true. Yet despite his intelligence, Doug adamantly refused to entertain the thought that his ills had a psychological origin. Over the twelve years that he had suffered what he called intolerable pain, this forty-eight-year-old man had visited more than twenty neurologists and read enough about chronic pain to teach a course on it. Nevertheless, he knew that a somatic cause for his agony would one day be discovered.

Knowing that the pain in Doug's leg could not possibly have had a neurological origin given its location—it radiated from his knee through his calf to the ball of his foot—I immediately began to probe for the meaning of this symptom. My assumption that Doug's leg pain contained a message came straight from Freud, who began his career as a neurologist but left that specialty to pursue an understanding of the human mind after treating a number of patients suffering "neurological" disorders that could not have had physiological origins. One of Freud's classic cases involved the analysis of a woman whose many forms of paralysis could not have had neurological origins. Freud determined that this woman's paralysis functioned to block her conscious awareness of sexual impulses that, in Austria during the early 1900s, were both shameful and forbidden.[8]

Once we became acquainted, I elected to tell Doug that I would model my work with him after Freud's; I even gave him the classic case study to read. I also told him that I was assuming that the blocked feelings being expressed in his leg pain were, in all likelihood, unarticulated anger. Although Doug didn't actually embrace my treatment plan, he grudgingly agreed to start talking about anger at our next session.

When he arrived to begin searching for the meaning of his symptoms, Doug looked like a trial lawyer bound for court: He wheeled a documents case filled with memorabilia from his childhood into my office. When I asked him what this was about, he said, "You want to find buried anger, so I thought I'd start from the beginning; these items will help me free-associate." When I told him that most patients resist that type of psychoarchaeology, opting to dwell on current complaints, Doug laughed and addressed me in the manner of an aged rabbi: "Steve, please; what pain is there in my life today? My business generates more than enough profit to support three families in the grandest style; my wife loves me, my children love me, and my community respects me. If your Freudian theory of psychic conflict being expressed through my leg is correct, it must have originated in my youth, right?"

Until that moment I didn't realize that Doug employed relatives in his business, but once he alluded to "three families" supported by his company I knew where something might be amiss. This is not to imply that a family business cannot provide relatives with extraordinary wealth and interfamilial bliss, it's just that such an enterprise is a rare exception to the rule.

As it turned out Doug's business followed the rule: I discovered that Doug despised the two brothers-in-law who worked for him. While it was true that his business generated more than enough money to go around, Doug had been galled by his sisters' pressure to employ men he considered ne'er-do-wells. Unfortunately, Doug did not—or could not—articulate his feelings about his brothers-in-law or succumbing to his sisters' pressure for quite some time.

Then, on the spur of the moment, one of Doug's sisters decided to fly to New York City to see the U.S. Open tennis tournament. Previously, neither of Doug's brothers-in-law had taken a vacation without giving ample justification and notice. But in this instance, since the sister in question and her husband were both self-confessed tennis freaks, and since the seats they would be occupying were given to them by a VIP who could not attend the tournament, his sister's husband called to say that he, too, would be traveling east the next day to take advantage of an opportunity he "could not pass up." With that, Doug flew into a fit of rage.

Doug's appointment with me occurred two hours after their conversation. For the first twenty minutes of our session Doug spewed rage as though the dam that had been holding it back for over a decade had burst. When I sensed that he was calming down, I confronted him: "So, how's the leg feeling right now?" Shocked, he looked at me, rubbed his knee and shin, looked at me again, and said, "It's gone . . . the pain's gone."

Although his pain returned within hours and was intermittent for another two years, from that session forward my work with Doug was divided between helping him craft a strategy to remove his brothers-in-law from his business in a manner that would allow them to save face, and understanding why he couldn't deal directly with anger. Doug's cure was not simple, but it did progress steadily. One key factor accounting for his ability to rid himself of pain was that some months after his epiphany Doug recalled that whenever his father was annoyed with him he would threaten to give him "a swift kick in the ass," and, on more than a few occasions, he delivered on that threat. It also emerged that Doug's father was a critical and judgmental man, who was stingy with money as well as affection.

As Doug became comfortable discussing the contempt he felt for his father and had buried over the years, he became aware that he always feared he would ultimately turn into the sort of person his father was. Consequently, Doug soon realized that whenever he sensed himself displaying attitudes or behaviors reminiscent of his father's—such as the urge to give someone a swift kick—he struggled against them. Yet because Doug loved his father and felt respect for him, he chided himself for "not appreciating my dad and learning to love him while he was alive."

To handle his conflicts over identifying too closely with his father, Doug overcompensated for hints of selfishness or judgmental behavior. Specifically, he became an excessively generous person incapable of condemning behaviors or people that he found objectionable. His initial resistance to dealing with this overcompensatory style came from the fact that he was ashamed to admit how "weak" he had been: "It was cowardly of me not to tell my dad how I felt; he didn't hurt people intentionally." Fortunately, once Doug was able to articulate his excessive shame as well as his ambivalent feelings for his father, he developed the capacity to deal with problematic people in ways that were respectful of both his needs and theirs. He was also able to throw away his cane.

THE MASTER PASSION

Almost all theories of psychological development proceed from the postulate that the feelings of dependency and helplessness we experience during infancy shape our character throughout life. Some models argue that we all initially suffer from feelings of inferiority (relative to masterful adults or older siblings) that are resolved in either healthful or maladaptive ways.[9] Other models maintain that how well or poorly we manage so-called libidinal drives during infancy and early childhood—when, for example, an urge to possess an object or a person can feel overwhelming—will determine what sorts of adults we grow up to be.[10] While no theory of psychosocial development is without flaws, one common truth exists: The struggle to feel favorably disposed toward oneself begins at a time in life when the likelihood of achieving feelings of self-efficacy is relatively low.

Given how easy it is for an infant to feel ashamed or humiliated rather than self-satisfied or proud, it is unquestionable that much of our early development is devoted to shoring up a tenuous sense of self-competence. Every human endures interactions in youth that arouse feelings of self-doubt and shame, just as we all attempt to defend against feelings of anxiety, rage, and depression that get evoked from fearing we will never be able to master the world around us. This is why Mark Twain's observation that "it may be called the

Master Passion, the hunger for self-approval" is both self-evident and profound.

The fact that most of our developing years are spent striving for self-approval can also help explain why so many people become overinvested in achieving success during their adult lives. Arguably, the erroneous belief in the mythic powers of success stems from the hunger to achieve self-approval by erasing memories of inadequacy, ineptitude, and humiliation from our minds. There is nothing abnormal about feeling some degree of this master passion for self-approval; what is abnormal, however, is when that master passion dominates our lives.

THE PASSION TO AVOID SELF-REPROACH

Epictetus, the self-made man turned philosopher, had no patience for people who allowed the hunger for self-approval to dominate their lives. He was wholly intolerant of those who would externalize blame for failure, self-handicap, or be pretenders to status or success. Epictetus was also unsettled by the airs, hubris, and malevolence he saw in ostensibly successful people too cowardly to admit flaws and engage in self-generated efforts to improve themselves. In this regard, Epictetus understood what blocks people from reclaiming the fire: *an inability to drop the facades they erect to compensate for, or mask, a lack of self-approval.* Unless or until they do so, they will be unable to initiate the only process—honest self-assessment—that will allow them to overcome perceived personal inadequacies:

> Let whatever appears to be the best be to you an inviolable law. And if any instance of pain or pleasure, or glory or disgrace, is set before you, remember that now is the combat, now the Olympiad comes on, nor can it be put off. By once being defeated and giving way, proficiency is lost, or by the contrary preserved. Thus Socrates became perfect, improving himself by everything, attending to nothing but reason. And though you are not yet a Socrates, you ought, however, to live as one desirous of becoming a Socrates.[11]

Epictetus also maintained, "Those whom the gods would destroy they first make mad with power." One of the most unsettling paradoxes exhibited by those who actively celebrate and advertise their power is a propensity for throwing fits of impotent rage. These people often actively prevent themselves from examining the feelings that prompt them to behave as they do, arguing that these outbursts represent an unwillingness to suffer fools gladly. A person who occupies a seat of power yet eviscerates others is almost always overwhelmed by feelings of inadequacy or self-reproach. I use this maxim (taken from Ben Franklin) with most angry people I coach: "The empty barrel makes the most noise." If you are supremely confident in your abilities, you will never feel a need to get angry with others. You walk softly because you know you have a big stick at your disposal.

Displays of aggressive rage prevent psychotherapists or executive coaches from working with people to expose and analyze their self-critical feelings. Unfortunately, our culture gives license to these outbursts. The supersuccessful are exempt from the laws of political correctness that quash displays of anger. Adding insult to injury, powerful people are rarely held accountable for creating the smoke screens that block them from examining the origins of their anger, hurt, or pain. As James Baldwin once observed of an emotion akin to anger, "I imagine the reason people cling to their hates so stubbornly is because they sense, once hate is gone, they will be forced to deal with the pain."

"Jane" is the president and CEO of the health food division of a multinational agribusiness worth billions of dollars. When I was hired to coach Jane on how to deal with her managers she was, in the words of the holding company's chief operating officer, who hired me, "quick to cut people down." Her division was barely two years old, but the holding company was willing to make a large investment in Jane and her product line because she had a hot commodity that was ideally positioned to meet the demands of a burgeoning market created by baby boomers shopping for products that would help restore their waning youth and vitality.

Jane's entire career had been spent selling mass-marketed food products, and she was good at her job. A tall, striking woman who bore a faint resemblance to a well-known movie star, Jane would exploit her personality on the job but never her looks. She was proud of her sales skills and believed her career would be successful if she stuck to her strong suit. That was why she was shocked—but flattered and eager to excel—when her company put her in charge of its newest division. Jane's ascension to top management was somewhat cataclysmic: She, along with five other vice presidents and a CEO, were given the responsibility of building a new division of specialty foods conceived of by the chairman of the agribusiness. While the early stages of the division's development went smoothly, things hit a snag when the holding company's only real competitor hired away the CEO, COO, and marketing director of the new business unit. In a panic to reorganize as rapidly as possible, Jane was handed the top spot based on the assumption that it was she who could best "put points on the board" (sell the fledgling product line). Jane rose to the occasion. One of her first executive decisions was to introduce a product with an incredibly catchy name, and within nine months of her becoming president, Jane's business unit showed a profit.

Yet Jane did not respond to her success with equanimity: Before her first year at the helm came to a close, the COO Jane reported to received more than ten complaints from her vice presidents about being belittled in public, cursed, and threatened with termination. Always a heavy smoker who ignored the prohibitions against lighting up in her building, Jane once hurled a full ashtray at a colleague who told her he felt her marketing plan was shortsighted. When the victim of that assault quit, the COO of the agribusiness called me in.

At my first meeting with every client—be it for coaching or psychotherapy—I conduct a complete psychological assessment. When I completed Jane's, I was at a loss for what could be causing her rage. She had bumps and bruises in her life, as we all do, but nothing stood out; no trauma, no loss, no pattern of abusive parenting. I asked Jane if she would allow me to do an in-depth assessment of her direct reports' feelings about her; she consented without hesitation.

Every vice president in Jane's office used the word *bully* to describe her. Beyond that, while all agreed she could sell any product on earth, few saw in her the capacity to manage a team of executives; some felt that the stress of being in over her head was most probably affecting her. Yet I still could not find anything sufficient to account for why, after a commendable first year on the job, Jane grew ever more abusive.

My last hope for gaining insight into the etiology of Jane's problem was a series of interviews with her sales force. One saleswoman had known Jane since college, and I was hoping she could shed some light on what was ailing Jane. She did, although she probably didn't know it. She jokingly remarked that had Jane been a man she would have entered the priesthood, that's how decent a person she was. Her old friend also said, "You know, Jane is truly blessed; everything she touches turns to gold. Like her launch of [the blockbuster product]. I was with Jane in Chicago having drinks with an old friend from [the agribusiness's competitor], when he said, 'You know, given your push into health foods, why not come out with a breakfast food called [the new product]? Boomers will love it.' "

As I explained earlier, few people can endure noncontingent success without some form of psychological damage. When I learned that Jane was not responsible for the product that had made her division profitable—and, some claimed, secured her position as division president—I suspected that either she was struggling with guilt over the belief that she had stolen the idea that accounted for her good fortune or she feared she would ultimately be exposed as a fraud.

I confronted Jane with what I had learned at our next meeting. In response she screamed: "If you dare publicize this I'll ruin you." I swore I wouldn't, but Jane ranted on for what seemed like an hour, tearing me apart for "ruining her career" and jeopardizing her entire division. She insulted me in every imaginable way, then began to cry. My reaction—counterintuitive but effective—was to laugh.

"Have you ever heard the expression 'It ain't what you've got, it's what you do with it that counts'? Do you think a person cannot be an effective senior executive unless every idea that helps her company is her brainchild? How many Fortune 500 CEOs actually founded the companies they run?" With that I rattled off the names of a dozen newly installed CEOs who were darlings of Wall Street for their ability to turn around moribund giants, and Jane's rage began to taper off.

Over the next three months Jane and I worked on sorting out her feelings about having stumbled on a brilliant idea. I learned that Jane was plagued by self-doubt since, in her words, "All I do is hype; I create nothing. I'm pretty and glib, so guys pay attention to me. But real leaders are brainy, and I'm not. That pisses me off."

While I was never able to help Jane uncover the origins of her belief that "real leaders are brainy," this is a very common, albeit entirely untrue, opinion. What followed was a combination of coaching and cognitive therapy that focused on disabusing her of her erroneous beliefs and helping her to identify what events provoked her to attack colleagues. I helped Jane learn that each of her assaults on colleagues was preceded by self-directed anger. The most important insight Jane took from our work was that any intimation that she wasn't "brainy" was a trigger for acting out. Similarly, she became riled when too much credit for success came her way, since it rekindled her belief that she was merely lucky, not good. But the key to our work was to have Jane find ways of accepting the self-description she presented to the world: a great salesperson who would always succeed if she stuck to her strong suit.

I helped Jane see that effective management involves, more than anything else, selling people on the merits of a behavioral strategy. I explained that if she took credit only for her contingent successes—holding her division together when it could have folded, initially uniting a group of anxious executives behind her, and being an effective hands-off manager of salespeople—she would have more than enough credit to sustain her role as president for years to come.

UNLEASHING HEALTHY PASSIONS

Pressures to perform in line with expectations drawn from a history of success, the presumption of limitless potential, or noncontingent success evoke intense feelings of anger and precipitate a variety of psychological disorders. We have yet to address how anger—or, more appropriately, impotent rage used to defend against feelings of inadequacy—prevents people from experiencing *healthy* passions that would enable them to overcome Supernova Burnout. Once again Aristotle's insight hits the mark: To be angry with the right person and in the right way is not easy, and not everyone can do it. Yet the sooner one's anger is articulated and addressed appropriately, the more likely it is that one will be saved from the self-destructive avoidance of psychological pain.

THE LIAR'S PUNISHMENT

A tragic example of anger-induced career self-destruction involved "Patrick," a man of average intelligence and enormous charisma who rose from selling cars to an executive position with a Big Three automaker. Patrick's route to becoming an executive with a Fortune 100 corporation was never intentional. In fact, he began selling cars only after it became obvious he would never succeed at a career that required academic ability. Knowing that his lot in life would rest on his skills as a smooth talker, he took advantage of the fact that his uncle owned one of the largest car dealership chains in America and began hawking cars within days of getting out of school.

During the fifteen years he worked for his uncle, Patrick achieved astounding sales figures. Ultimately, his salesmanship came to the attention of the automaker whose cars he was selling, and he was wooed to Detroit for a career in sales management. Patrick and his uncle saw this as a Horatio Alger tale come true; in fact, it was more akin to an episode of *The Twilight Zone*.

Although Patrick could do sales with the best of them, managing scores of men and women with skills comparable to his demanded attributes Patrick had never developed. To his credit, I believe Patrick knew he was in over his head within weeks of moving to Detroit. Yet to avoid the humiliation of quitting and reconciling himself to what then seemed like a bush-league life of selling cars, he attempted to steel himself to the demands of life in a Fortune 100 corporation. His two most heavily relied upon supports were self-help management books and that popular executive coach Jack Daniel's.

I was called to work with Patrick after he got drunk at his first corporate retreat and challenged a regional manager to a fistfight. The human resources director of the automaker who hired me believed that Patrick was a self-handicapping alcohol abuser. He wasn't. What I discovered after interviewing about two dozen of Patrick's direct reports was that he was abusive not only when drunk but at every available opportunity. Furthermore, his enmity was typically directed at managers who manifested competence or, more important, intelligence. Patrick's modus operandi was to meet with his managers in one-on-one meetings, pick their brains, steal their ideas, and excoriate them in sales team meetings. At first many assumed that Patrick's rages were merely inappropriate manifestations of the passion that drove him to achieve record sales levels. Unfortunately, what was originally deemed a fire in the belly cost the automaker five of its most talented managerial prospects during the first two years of Patrick's tenure in Detroit.

I worked with Patrick for six months or so. Helping him control his drinking was easy; helping him control his rage was not. Although he ultimately developed some cognizance of why he felt threatened by the men and women he called "Ivy League assholes," he was never able to comprehend fully how self-contempt prompted these feelings. The closest we came to what could have been a clinical breakthrough occurred when we were able to discuss his lifelong pattern of misrepresenting his intellectual competencies.

During the moments of candid exchange I enjoyed with Patrick, he allowed that during college he purchased several term papers, cheated on most tests, and regularly paid friends to complete take-home exams for him. To his credit, he also admitted that what threatened him most as an executive was that management—by contrast to selling—forced him to return to a pattern of "intellectual theft" he thought he had put behind him the day he graduated from college. In essence, he felt he had to steal ideas from his direct reports in order to succeed.

The most important thing I learned about Patrick but, regrettably, was unable to fully capitalize on was that he had been faking his way through school as long as he could remember. While Patrick refused to discuss his pattern of deceit at length, he did admit that he always hated school yet longed to get good grades to please his mother, who taught high school calculus. Patrick's earliest—and most significant—memory from his childhood was the aftermath of his failing a grade-school test and having to bring the exam paper home for a parent's signature. When he showed his F to his mother, the tongue-lashing he expected never occurred. In fact, rather than being berated, he ended up comforting his grief-stricken mother, who wept hysterically over "my poor boy."

From that point forward, Patrick vowed never to "devastate her" like that again. Yet rather than seek help with his schoolwork, he used guile and cunning to fake his way up the academic ladder. The result, I am convinced, is that he blamed his mother for pressuring him to excel at something he disliked. Moreover, in order to spare her the devastating pain he witnessed when he was a child, Patrick embarked upon a life of deception that he was never able to extricate himself from.

The interpretation I offered Patrick for his chronic state of embattlement with direct reports was this: He was projecting anger that he felt toward himself and his mother onto those he was jealous of for having authentic intellectual competence. I tried to help him understand that with the amount of self-contempt he carried, coupled with his considerable anger toward a mother he loved, he could never acquire the collaborative support he would need to survive in a major corporation. Quoting from the magic-bullet management guides he read, I told him, would only entrench his lack of skills. Despite my best efforts to warn him that his career in Detroit would go downhill from where it was unless or until he was willing to reveal himself to be a fraud, he would have no part of my interpretation. Patrick terminated our relationship four months after that discussion, and his former wife wrote to me a year later to tell me that he was again using Jack Daniel's to cope with life back at his uncle's car dealership.

TO THINE OWN SELF BE TRUE

While it may seem facile to attribute Patrick's demise to self-contempt and deception, the philosophical support for this contention is overwhelming. The most widely known articulation of the link between healthy success and lack of self-deception comes from Shakespeare's *Hamlet* (Act I, Scene 3):

> This above all: to thine own self be true,
> And it must follow, as the night the day,
> Thou canst not then be false to any man.

People suffering Supernova Burnout are particularly prone to being false to others because the American definition of success is audience dependent. Since part of our ethos is "In order to get along, you've got to go along," those who seek to be successful have two choices: They must acquiesce to normative standards or they must be bold enough to set them.

One of the greatest leaders of all time, Sir Winston Churchill, had no compunction about defying the status quo. He was able to maintain a stubborn independence by rigorous self-assessment. According to an aide of his during World War II, Churchill claimed, "Every night I try myself by Court Martial to see if I have done anything effective during the day. I don't mean just paying the ground, anyone can go through the motions, but something really effective."[12] If you're willing to impose standards like that upon yourself, you'll never fear bucking the status quo for want of social approval.

Unfortunately, most of us are more dependent on the status quo than this and use it as a reference in many ways, ranging from social status to physical competence. This dependence leads to a herd mentality that, in large measure, is responsible for what is judged successful. The influence of normative standards extends well beyond trend-setting and status symbols. It even affects Olympic events. For instance, all forms of ice skating, gymnastics, and diving demand that athletes be sensitized to how judges believe they should perform, so succeeding and failing come to depend on adhering to transient norms.

If, for example, a figure skater is determined to maintain his flamboyance, he puts himself in jeopardy of losing a medal by his nonconformity. Yet if he adjusts his performance to suit the taste of the judges, he will probably have less passion for his career than if he were to say, "Damn the consensual validation; I'll skate as I see fit." Were he to sell out to win a medal, our skater would doubtless earn more money from endorsements and have more invitations to televised events than he would without a gold medal. But selling out would heighten the likelihood that, sooner or later, he would end up feeling like a mercenary. No such fate awaits the person, like Churchill, unwilling to compromise his personal standards. The truth, particularly the truth you unearth through self-assessments like trial by personal court-martial, does set you free.

Arthur Miller, a playwright who, like Shakespeare, has been concerned with the self-respect derived from authentic self-assessment, once observed: "One of the central elements in life is the driving need of people to define themselves, not merely as individuals, but also in terms of a function *they can respect*" (emphasis added).[13] It is clear that Patrick could never fully respect who or what he was. Contrast his failure with the example of Lou Gerstner, who achieved phenomenal success at IBM. Apart from his managerial skills, Gerstner's success was due, in large measure, to a passionate refusal to live a lie. After being touted as the übermanager responsible for RJR Nabisco's profitability, he took the top spot at IBM with none of the defensive bravado that ended Patrick's career in Detroit. He admitted he knew little about the technological underpinnings of the business he was hired to manage . . . and could not have cared less. Gerstner was strong enough to allow skilled IT professionals to do their specialized engineering work while he did what he knew best: creating efficient systems to market, sell, distribute, and service the product.

Managing to one's weakness is the business school version of Shakespeare's "to thine own self be true." To be true to oneself it is essential first to conduct a personal audit and accept what you find. If you are angry about being weak or deficient in an area of expertise or competence you deem necessary for success, you will never compensate for this deficit by denying your problem, bemoaning your fate, or using others as scapegoats. Patrick was filled with hate because of his inadequacies. Gerstner is phenomenally successful because he acknowledged his. Patrick used defensive rage to mask his pain. Gerstner avoided self-inflicted pain by accepting "weakness" and managing to it.

DISCOVERING YOUR PASSION

There are few things harder for professional men and women than pulling up stakes from a successful but dissatisfying career solely because they feel stultified by what they are doing. Victims of Supernova Burnout do not lose passion for a career because they are deadbeat, exploitative users. They are doers—or would-be doers—thwarted from attaining psychological satisfaction because their eyes have been on the wrong prize.

"Connie" seemed to have her eyes firmly focused on the prize she desired when she hired me to help her find a new CEO for her company, help transition the person into the job, and "see if you can find any pitfalls that I may be missing in my new personal business plan." This plan was Connie's decision to leave the dot-com company she founded and become part owner of one of the "incubators" that began springing up around Silicon Valley in the mid- to late 1990s. Her goal, as she initially articulated it, was "to let my money work for me while I enjoy life and help seed new ventures."

Connie was the type of referral every executive coach lives for: an articulate person who is not in a crisis and who wants help with strategic planning and personal development, not "repair" work. When I met her Connie was a thirty-four-year-old graduate of UC Berkeley (BS and MBA) who had a dual undergraduate major in computer sciences and sociology. She blended her academic interests perfectly: She was neither a "propeller head" nor a social reformer. Instead, she was socially responsible and savvy, which was why—after making more than $20 million by the age of thirty-three—she decided to ease her way out of running a business and apply the skills and insights acquired during fifteen years in Silicon Valley to identifying people and products destined to thrive in the future.

My early work with Connie proceeded without a hitch: A friend of mine was willing to work with Connie and me to find her an appropriate replacement. Her plan to fund an incubator also proceeded flawlessly. What gave me pause, however, was my discussion with Connie about her personal life—something I check into with everyone I coach. Connie was reluctant to offer specifics about her social life save to say, in a halfhearted manner, "If you know of any single guys who aren't geeks or over age fifty, send them my way." When I suggested we pay a bit more attention to the nonprofessional aspects of her life she cut me off, although she did promise to call me again, "if I ever run into trouble." Roughly a year later Connie came to Los Angeles to discuss her personal life.

The world seems to be divided between people who believe that age is just a number and those who freak out when they pass chronological milestones. Connie belonged to the latter group. Less than a month before we were reunited Connie commemorated her thirty-fifth birthday with an event that bore no resemblance to a celebration. A dozen of her closest friends gathered to give her a surprise party. But within hours of opening the champagne, she was despondent. She begged for a ride home and spent the following two weeks in bed either crying or sleeping.

When I began working with her for the second time, I told Connie that I would have to reacquaint myself with her and take a full family history. At the mere mention of the word *family*, she began sobbing. When she regained her composure the first thing she said was "I never wanted a family; it wasn't in the cards." I learned that as an infant Connie had been put in an orphanage. Her mother, a bar girl from Saigon, presumably had no motivation to raise her African American–Asian daughter in a society intolerant of mixed-race children.

The moment I heard about Connie's start in life, why she had been so reluctant to discuss her personal life when we first met, it was clear that Connie suffered more psychic scars than she could bear to allow into consciousness, and that she had done an effective job of suppressing them for twenty-five years. The only memories readily available to her were that her father was a GI who impregnated her teenage mother and that she was adopted at age ten by an American Vietnam War vet and his wife, who raised her in the San Francisco area "with all the love and benefits" of any of her peers.

Since the town Connie grew up in was quite liberal, her mixed race was not cause for concern. She was tall, beautiful, and athletic—not to mention intelligent—and once she mastered the English language and adjusted to her new family (she had two brothers also adopted from Vietnamese orphanages), Connie suffered no social ostracism. Yet it became apparent that she never felt like she belonged to any group. She told me, "I was always a 'star' but never part of the crowd, if you know what I mean. I knew I was loved, but for some reason I never felt it. My entire career has replicated my life in that regard: acclaim for *doing*, not just for being Connie."

Over the next several weeks I learned that Connie had never been in a long-term romantic relationship despite the fact that she enjoyed sex. Her only thought on relationships was "Look, it's great to be put on a pedestal by guys, particularly good-looking ones. The problem is, I always had a voice in me saying, 'Don't get attached.' " When I reminded her how she bade me farewell during our first association (asking for introductions to eligible guys), she nodded. "You've got to appear to be looking for love or people think you're nuts."

This discussion gave me the perfect segue into helping her analyze her current situation: Is it possible that when you built your business incubator you were creating an ersatz family that freed you from facing your conflicts about trying to create a real one?" She agreed, and allowed that she'd had an inkling that her avoidance was beginning to catch up with her when she first refused to allow me to question her about her social life.

After several weeks it occurred to me that I could help Connie break down her barriers to intimate relations by exploiting her business acumen. I had in mind finding a way for her to get involved in an emotionally risky business enterprise without abandoning the safety net afforded by her incubator. I proposed, "Look, one of the things we need to do is familiarize you with being head-over-heels thrilled about something. You've never been out of control in a psychological sense since you entered junior high school. What has the power to move you body and soul?" Instantly she said, "Orphans."

Three weeks later Connie put our psychotherapeutic relationship on hold while she devoted herself full-time to establishing a worldwide agency devoted to placing orphans in American homes. As expected, she dove into this project with abandon. When her enterprise was capable of operating without her full-time involvement, she returned to therapy and began processing the feelings of love, commitment, and belonging she felt as a consequence of "really immersing myself" in this work. In addition, the carryover effects that were predicted as a result of Connie's committing to a labor of love came to fruition: As I complete this manuscript, Connie is celebrating her six-month anniversary with a man she calls "the love of my life."

THE 60 MINUTES CURE

I have watched 60 Minutes for years and concluded that if you examine the motivations of the people featured in the show's most compelling segments you will discover a strategy that can help any-one begin to reclaim the fire. I've named this strategy the *60 Minutes* cure because it exploits the attribute that makes most people featured on this show inspirational role models. Most people fail to appreciate that they have a *60 Minutes* story of their own somewhere in their psyche. This is a large part of the program's appeal: showing that a "little" person with nothing more than passion can change the world. What do you think is responsible for the Anti-Defamation League, the NAACP, ACT UP, MADD, or Barry Scheck's campaign to provide people on death row with DNA testing?

When people suffer midlife crises, experience ennui from shepherding businesses that virtually run themselves, or dread heading to work at a career that once inflamed them with ardor, it seems logical that they would recognize that what is missing from their lives is pure, unadulterated passion. But golden handcuffs and responsibilities to others (and, often, to a reputation) convince most careerists that a flight from tedium to a cause is irresponsible for anyone over the age of twenty-five. Not so. If you hate the fact that there is a social wrong or inequity in the world, fight it. Fight it as Aristotle advised: Be angry with the right person and at the right time and with the right object and in the right way.

When I propose that people consider implementing a *60 Minutes* cure for a been-there-done-that case of career malaise, they typically offer two counterarguments. Counterargument 1 is that they're too old to start anew. This rationale is hollow in the extreme. People will soon be working well into their seventies. Moreover, as Connie demonstrated, most people who suffer Supernova Burnout are financially successful enough to work at part-time pursuits without fear of economic hardship. Even when this is not a certainty, the alternative to not pursuing an avocation that can evoke passion is more dangerous than sustaining the status quo. Resenting a career you feel trapped in virtually guarantees that in time you will extricate yourself from it in some maladaptive manner, making you far less employable than you would have been if you'd opted earlier for a psychologically rewarding pursuit.

The second argument is a variation of shoot the messenger. Many people who are fearful of embarking upon an emotionally risky *60 Minutes* cure attack it as a cheap variation on the money-doesn't-matter-do-what-you-love approach to career rejuvenation. Consider the following points of clarification that I have offered over the years.

1. The *60 Minutes* cure is born of anger, pain, or contempt, not of love of an activity. Doing what we love has far too many narcissistic overtones to be rewarding in a long-term manner that would allow for feelings of generativity. In this same vein, the *60 Minutes* cure, by dint of the fact that it is born of an anger at some societal wrong, is, by definition, generative. When Barry Scheck fights to overturn what he believes are unjust death sentences, there are, obviously, narcissistic rewards derived from a successful outcome. Anyone who brings about a desired end feels a self-esteem boost. But when Scheck works on behalf of the wrongfully convicted, his primary goal is the refinement of the criminal justice system and the betterment of society. When he works on behalf of O. J. Simpson, he is also facilitating his efforts on behalf of indigent inmates while affording himself the opportunity to vacation with his family wherever and whenever he likes. Scheck has combined a *60 Minutes* cure with a profitable vocation in a manner that affords him both material rewards and the psychological gratification born of generativity.

2. George Bernard Shaw, the playwright who had the intestinal fortitude to abandon a successful career in business because it was psychologically unrewarding, maintained, "The true joy in life [is] being used for a purpose that is a mighty one... being a force of nature instead of a feverish selfish little clod of ailments and grievances complaining that the world will not devote it-

self to making you happy."[14] This, as we noted in the discussion of generativity, is what prolongs passion in a career. If you respect what you are doing, not indulging yourself in transient narcissistic gratification, you will derive ongoing psychological rewards, not merely transient relief from nettlesome pains. Far too many people have translated the message of the do-what-you-love-the-money-will-follow school of thought into that Vietnam-era student mantra, "If it feels good, do it." That is narcissism, not passion-fueled commitment to manifesting talent and achieving the rewards of generativity.

3. Expressing anger, outrage, or righteous indignation is liberating. By declaring, "This is who I am, what I feel, what I believe in," you acquire a freedom from the constraints of playing to an audience, which, as the fate suffered by narcissists demonstrates time and time again, can be crippling. Moreover, by dealing honestly with your most fundamental—and at times politically incorrect—emotions, you are freed from the encumbrances of caring how what you do fits with the fashions of the times. All that matters when you express a passion is achieving a gratifying and generative outcome.

In Greek legend, Prometheus wanted to ensure that man would be superior to all the animals. That is why he challenged Zeus's edict, stole the sacred fire from Mount Olympus, and presented it as a gift that would guarantee man's survival and superiority. I see Prometheus's fire as the energy that fuels psychological development and self-reliance. Prometheus's gift of fire made man efficacious, and anyone who has achieved success began his or her career with an overabundance of fire.

One of the most inspiring quotations I have come across, the one I rely on to help explain how people can reverse the effects of Supernova Burnout, comes from Friedrich Nietzsche: "Once one is clear about the 'why?' of one's life, one can let its 'how?' take care of itself."[15] Nietzsche refers, of course, to finding pure intrinsic motivation, or what I have been referring to as passion. This is the motivation that underlies all forms of self-actualization and it is the motivation that enables a person to naturally reclaim the fire.

Asking yourself "how?" implies that an audience is there to judge, evaluate, rank, or approve of what you do. The "why?" questions in life free us from externally mediated rewards and focus us on goals that we are motivated to pursue regardless of the cost or consequence. When we follow the whys, we give gifts back to society anonymously. Those gifts are fulfilling whether they lead to accolades or the fate suffered by Prometheus. If you have the sorts of goals that Nietzsche referred to, intrinsic motivation will never be in short supply and your ability to reclaim the fire will be a natural consequence of giving voice to your passions.

Acknowledgments

Jon Karp contributed to the quality of this book in profound ways. His insights into the subject matter were incredibly penetrating, and I want to thank him for invaluable suggestions, ongoing encouragement and support, and a willingness to say "cut" without equivocation. I could not have designed a better editor and guide for this project.

Jeff Seglin is the person most responsible for my writing career, such as it is. He helped me with every aspect of this book, from writing the proposal to refining the second draft; ever since he was my editor at *Inc.* magazine he has been a devoted mentor and a great friend.

I would also like to thank several people who read the manuscript for this book and were generous with their comments and suggestions. I owe a great debt of gratitude to A. J. Sisk for helping me with the introduction, an effort fraught with anxiety. Janelle Duryea's edits of the entire first draft did much to improve upon my writing, and I thank her for never failing to answer a question with warmth and good humor. Jim Casella made a number of insightful comments on various aspects of the initial draft and was an indispensable resource in several other ways. I would also like to thank Esther Greenglass for providing a number of reprints on the psychology of women, and Ashley Mevi, who gave generously of herself to facilitate the research I conducted after moving to Los Angeles.

A number of people who didn't contribute to the content of this book were, nevertheless, determining factors in my ability to create it. Each of them helped extricate me from a personal hell I was enduring while I labored to complete the manuscript ahead of deadline. I want to thank Alfred E. Osborne, Jr., Ph.D., for giving me a home at the Harold Price Center for Entrepreneurial Studies at UCLA. Because of all Al has done for me, I have never been more excited about research and teaching. Sharon and Doug Brenner were crucial to every aspect of my transition to California. I cannot thank them enough for helping me come to feel that Los Angeles is home as painlessly as they did. Stefano Ongaro of Valentino Restaurant has my undying gratitude for showing me that Italian red wines are the best on earth, for stocking my wine cellar with cases of them, and for making me feel like a cousin every time we dined at his restaurant. Bella Lantsman and Peter Pendl of Chinois have made every visit to their restaurant a special occasion by treating me and my wife like royalty. Finally, I would never have had the peace of mind to leave home with my wife for the dining experiences that mean so much to me were it not for the fact that my daughter, Katie, the co-owner of my heart, was cared for and adored by the best baby-sitter imaginable, my mother-in-law, Kathryn Sisk.

Last, I want to acknowledge the role that my wife, Jennifer, played in developing this book. Most of the ideas that formed the basis of *Reclaiming the Fire* evolved as a result of sharing my insights with her and having them improved by her critical analysis. Everyone who knows me is aware that Jennifer has been my primary source of joy and inspiration since the moment I met her, but rarely do I get an opportunity to say how grateful I am that her mind is as extraordinary as her heart. Without her this book would not exist.

Notes

1. PEOPLE WHO HIT BOTTOM WHEN THEY REACH THE TOP

1. Cited in Erik Erikson (1968) *Identity: Youth and Crisis.* New York: W. W. Norton, p. 143.
2. Throughout this book I will describe people I have worked with in psychotherapy or in my executive coaching practice. To protect their identities, their names, as well as features of their jobs, ethnicity, residence, and the like, have been changed. These changes in no way alter the characteristics of their disorders or the outcomes of their attempts to resolve the conflicts that blocked them from achieving psychological gratification from success.
3. "Wall Street's Deep Throat," *Time,* December 31, 1999. McDermott was ultimately convicted on five counts of security fraud.
4. Steven Berglas (1986) *The Success Syndrome: Hitting Bottom When You Reach the Top.* New York: Plenum, pp. 198–212.
5. See, for example, Steven Berglas (1985) "Self-Handicapping and Self-Handicappers: A Cognitive/Attributional Model of Interpersonal Self-Protective Behavior." In Robert Hogan and W. H. Jones eds., *Perspectives in Personality.* Greenwich, Conn.: JAI Press, vol. 1, pp. 235–270.
6. Steven Berglas and E. E. Jones (1978) "Drug Choice as a Self-Handicapping Strategy in Response to Noncontingent Success," *Journal of Personality and Social Psychology,* 36, pp. 405–417.
7. J. A. Tucker, R. E. Vuchinich, and M. B. Sobell (1981) "Alcohol Consumption as a Self-Handicapping Strategy," *Journal of Abnormal Psychology,* 90, p. 229.
8. This theory was confirmed, albeit without reference to a psychological "disorder," in Jordan's autobiography, published in 1998, in which he indicated that a full year before his first retirement he knew he wasn't mentally committed to continuing his career.
9. See, for example, H. Levinson, "When Executives Burn Out," *Harvard Business Review,* May–June 1981, pp. 73–81.

2. SUCCESS DEPRESSION AND ENCORE ANXIETY

1. Steven Berglas (1986) *The Success Syndrome: Hitting Bottom When You Reach the Top.* New York: Plenum, pp. 198–212.
2. Ibid., p. 21.
3. Angus Campbell (1981) *The Sense of Well-Being in America.* New York: McGraw-Hill.
4. D. G. Meyers (1993) *The Pursuit of Happiness.* New York: Avon.
5. E. Diener, J. Horowitz, and R. A. Emmons (1985) "Happiness of the Very Wealthy," *Social Indicators,* 16, pp. 263–274.
6. Christopher Lasch (1978) *The Culture of Narcissism: American Life in an Age of Diminishing Expectations.* New York: W. W. Norton.
7. See Sigmund Freud (1916/1958) "Some Character Types Met Within Psycho-Analytic Work." In his *Complete Psychological Works: Standard Edition,* vol. 14, ed. and trans. by James Strachey. London: Hogarth Press.
8. See, for example, "From Gold Medal to Nose Dive," *Boston Globe,* July 29, 1996, p. D4.
9. "Ups and Downs," *Newsweek,* June 24, 1996, p. 74.
10. See, for example, " 'Sudden Wealth Syndrome' Brings New Stress," *New York Times,* March 10, 2000, pp. A1, A15; Berglas, *Success Syndrome,* pp. 83–93, 97–109.
11. "Face-to-Face: '1-2-3' Creator Mitch Kapor," *Inc.,* January 1987, pp. 31–38; quotation on p. 31.
12. Ibid., p. 32.
13. G. J. S. Wilde (1982) "The Theory of Risk Homeostasis: Implications for Safety and Health," *Risk Analysis,* 2, pp. 209–225.
14. Steven Berglas, "Your Work Is Never Done," *Inc.,* November 1997, p. 31.
15. See, for a review, W. Heron (1961) "Cognitive and Physiological Effects of Perceptual Isolation." In P. Solomon, P. E. Kubzansky, P. H. Leiderman, et al., eds., *Sensory Deprivation.* Cambridge, Mass.: Harvard University Press.
16. Steven Berglas, "The Case of the Entrepreneurial Arsonist," *Inc.,* December 1996, pp. 76–77.
17. See, for example, John E. Douglas and Mark Olshaker (1995) *Mindhunter.* New York: Scribner.
18. K. Swisher, "Move by Polese Allows Marimba to Shift Focus," *Wall Street Journal,* July 26, 2000, pp. B1, B4; S. Hansell, "Chief Executive of iVillage Gives Up Title to President," *New York Times,* July 29, 2000.
19. Karl Polanyi (1957) *The Great Transformation.* Boston: Beacon Press.
20. Mihaly Csikszentmihalyi (1999) "If We Are So Rich, Why Aren't We Happy?" *American Psychologist,* 54, pp. 821–827.
21. Leon Festinger (1954) "A Theory of Social Comparison Processes," *Human Relations,* pp. 117–140.

22. Csikszentmihalyi, "If We Are So Rich," p. 823.23

23. Staffan Burenstam Linder (1970) *The Harried Leisure Class.* New York: Columbia University Press.

24. Leon Festinger (1942) "Wish, Expectation, and Group Standards as Factors Influencing Levels of Aspiration," *Journal of Abnormal and Social Psychology,* pp. 184–200.

25. As noted earlier, to protect the identity of the people I have worked with, I have changed their names as well as other identifying details.

26. Laurence J. Peter and Raymond Hull (1969) *The Peter Principle.* New York: Bantam Books.

27. Andrew Grove (1996) *Only the Paranoid Survive.* New York: Doubleday.

28. "Ken Olsen's Search for Redemption," *Fortune,* March 16, 1998, pp. 156–157.

29. "Cloudy Days in Tomorrowland," *Newsweek,* January 27, 1997, p. 86.

3. WHY SO MANY BABY BOOMERS SUFFER SUPERNOVA BURNOUT

1. "So You Want to Change Your Job?" *Fortune,* January 15, 1996.

2. "The State of Greed," *U.S. News & World Report,* June 27, 1996, p. 67.

3. "Farewell, Fast Track," *Business Week,* December 10, 1990, pp. 192–200.

4. According to "American Scene," *Time,* June 12, 2000, all Americans are working more and enjoying it less. Between 1995 and 1999, the number of people staying out of work for stress-related complaints more than tripled.

5. William James (1890/1952) *The Principles of Psychology.* Chicago: Encyclopaedia Britannica Press, p. 200.

6. Peter Collier and David Horowitz (1984) *The Kennedys: An American Dream.* New York: Summit Books, p. 357.

7. Ibid.

8. See Steven Berglas and Roy F. Baumeister (1993) *Your Own Worst Enemy: Understanding the Paradox of Self-Defeating Behavior.* New York: Basic Books, p. 78.

9. Ibid., p. 77.

10. Ibid., p. 96.

11. Ibid., p. 122.

12. Abraham H. Maslow (1968, 1999) *Toward a Psychology of Being.* New York: John Wiley.

13. J. W. Brehm (1966) *A Theory of Psychological Reactance.* New York: Academic Press.

14. Maslow, *Psychology of Being,* p. 71.

15. Ibid., p. 72.

4. PYRRHIC REVENGE

1. J. B. Raph, M. L. Goldberg, and A. H. Passow (1966) *Bright Underachievers.* New York: Teachers College Press.
2. Steven Berglas (1986) *The Success Syndrome: Hitting Bottom When You Reach the Top.* New York: Plenum, p. 131.
3. Albert Bandura (1977) "Self-Efficacy: Toward a Unifying Theory of Behavioral Change," *Psychological Review,* 84, pp. 191–215.
4. See, for example, Martin E. P. Seligman (1975) *Helplessness: On Depression, Development, and Death.* San Francisco: W. H. Freeman.
5. Richard Behar, "Wall Street's Most Ruthless Financial Cannibal," *Fortune,* June 8, 1998, p. 212.

5. IF AT FIRST YOU *DO* SUCCEED, TRY THINKING LIKE A WOMAN

1. E. R. Greenglass (1995) "Gender, Work Stress, and Coping: Theoretical Implications," *Journal of Social Behavior and Personality,* 10, pp. 121–134.
2. Jean Baker Miller (1976) *Toward a New Psychology of Women.* Boston: Beacon Press.
3. Ibid., p. 83.
4. E. R. Greenglass (1997) "Gender Differences in Mental Health." In H. S. Friedman, ed., *Encyclopedia of Mental Health.* San Diego: Academic Press.
5. According to the medical models of health, women are seen as being more vulnerable to certain disorders, especially depression, than men are, because of their reproductive function. Women are seen as being particularly at risk for depression during periods of hormonal change, such as menstruation, following childbirth, and at menopause. Three syndromes associated with these stages of women's reproductive cycle—premenstrual syndrome or PMS, postpartum depression, and the menopausal syndrome—are all purportedly determinants of women's depressive symptomatology. Yet because these syndromes are poorly defined, many researchers believe that they merely help justify beliefs in the biological inferiority of women rather than account for the higher incidence of depression in women. Of late a majority of psychiatric professionals have come to accept the theory that differential rates of depression between women and men are social psychological, rather than biologically determined.
6. Greenglass, "Gender, Work Stress, and Coping," p. 124.
7. For a full discussion of the literature on this topic, see Martin E. P. Seligman, (1975) *Helplessness: On Depression, Development, and Death.* San Francisco: W. H. Freeman; L. Y. Abramson, G. I. Metalsky, and L. B. Alloy (1989) "Hopelessness Depression: A Theory-Based Subtype of Depression," *Psychological Review,* 96, pp. 358–372; or L. Y. Abramson, M. E. P. Selig-

man, and J. D. Teasdale (1978) "Learned Helplessness in Humans: Critique and Reformulation," *Journal of Abnormal Psychology,* 87, pp. 49–74.

8. See Ron Chernow (1998) *Titan: The Life of John D. Rockefeller, Sr.* New York: Random House, 1998.

9. "Breaking the Silence," *Newsweek,* May 20, 1996.

10. See E. E. Jones and H. B. Gerard (1967) *Foundations of Social Psychology.* New York: John Wiley, pp. 256–308, for a complete discussion of this topic.

11. See, for example, S. E. Asch (1946) "Forming Impressions of Personality," *Journal of Abnormal and Social Psychology,* 41; pp. 258–290; and H. H. Kelly (1950) "The Warm-Cold Variable in First Impressions of Persons," *Journal of Personality,* 18, pp. 431–439.

12. Ram Charan and Geoffrey Colvin, "Why CEOs Fail," *Fortune,* June 21, 1999, p. 70.

13. "You Snooze, You Lose," *Newsweek,* July 21, 1997, p. 50.

14. See, for example, B. M. Staw and J. Ross, "Knowing When to Pull the Plug," *Harvard Business Review,* 1987, pp. 68–74.

15. Steven Berglas, "Pratfalls," *Inc.,* September 1996, pp. 23–24.

16. See Carol Gilligan (1982) *In a Different Voice: Psychological Theory and Women's Development.* Cambridge, Mass.: Harvard University Press, for a brilliant discussion of this issue.

17. J. Barthel, "Julie Christie: Simply Gorgeous . . . and Awfully Smart," *Cosmopolitan,* February 1986, p. 187.

18. Matina A. Horner (1972) "Toward an Understanding of Achievement-Related Conflicts in Women," *Journal of Social Issues,* 28, pp. 157–175.

19. Matina A. Horner (1968) "Sex Differences, Achievement Motivation and Performance in Competitive and Noncompetitive Situations." Ph.D. diss., University of Michigan, p. 125.

20. G. Sassen (1980) "Success Anxiety in Women: A Constructivist Interpretation of Its Sources and Significance," *Harvard Educational Review,* 50, pp. 13–25.

21. Erik Erikson (1968) *Identity: Youth and Crisis.* New York: W. W. Norton.

22. Greenglass, "Gender Differences in Mental Health."

23. See, for example, Chris Argyris, "Teaching Smart People to Learn," *Harvard Business Review,* May–June 1991, pp. 98–109.

24. Ibid., p. 103.

25. Greenglass, "Gender, Work Stress, and Coping," p. 127.

26. Argyris, "Teaching Smart People to Learn," p. 100.

6. TOWARD RESOLVING THE PARADOX OF SUPERNOVA BURNOUT

1. D. Johnson, "Cheaters' Final Response: So What?" *New York Times,* May 16, 2000, p. A16.

2. Harvey Araton, "At Indiana, the Toadies Are Shocked," *New York Times,* May 16, 2000, p. A27.

3. Ibid.

4. Barbara Goldsmith, "The Meaning of Celebrity," *New York Times Magazine,* December 4, 1983, p. 75.

5. Ibid., p. 76.

6. See, for example, Zick Rubin (1973) *Liking and Loving: An Invitation to Social Psychology.* New York: Holt, Rinehart & Winston, pp. 113–134.

7. *Bartlett's Familiar Quotations,* 15th ed. (1982) Boston: Little, Brown, p. 648.

8. R. M. Huber (1971) *The American Idea of Success.* New York: McGraw-Hill, pp. 11–12.

9. Christopher Lasch (1978) *The Culture of Narcissism: American Life in an Age of Diminishing Expectations.* New York: W. W. Norton, p. 54.

10. See S. N. Eisenstadt, ed. (1968) *The Protestant Ethic and Modernization: A Comparative View.* New York: Basic Books.

11. Lasch, *Culture of Narcissism.*

12. Huber, *American Idea of Success.*

13. Harold J. Laski (1948) *The American Democracy.* New York: Viking Press, p. 39.

14. Benjamin Franklin (1958) *Autobiography and Other Writings,* ed. by Russel B. Nye. Boston: Houghton Mifflin, p. xi.15

15. Huber, *American Idea of Success,* p. 17.

16. Ibid., p. 47.

17. W. D. Ross, ed. (1955) *Aristotle: Selections.* New York: Charles Scribner's Sons, pp. 224–230.

18. Lasch, *Culture of Narcissism,* pp. 58–59.

7. THE GOLDILOCKS DILEMMA

1. R. M. Yerkes and J. D. Dodson (1908) "The Relation of Strength of Stimulus to Rapidity of Habit-Formation," *Journal of Comparative Neurology and Psychology,* 18, pp. 458–482.

2. E. L. Deci (1975) *Intrinsic Motivation.* New York: Plenum.

3. Steven Berglas and Roy F. Baumeister (1993) *Your Own Worst Enemy: Understanding the Paradox of Self-Defeating Behavior.* New York: Basic Books, p. 158.

4. S. Gendron, "Dilbert Fired! Starts New Biz," *Inc.,* July 1996.

5. Christopher A. Bartlett and Sumantra Ghoshal, "Matrix Management: Not a Structure, a Frame of Mind," *Harvard Business Review,* July–August 1990, pp. 138–145.

6. See, for example, Martin E. P. Seligman (1975) *Helplessness: On Depression, Development, and Death.* San Francisco: W. H. Freeman.

8. GENERATIVITY

1. Sigmund Freud (1930/1961) *Civilization and Its Discontents,* trans. by James Strachey. New York: W. W. Norton, p. 11.
2. Christopher Lasch (1978) *The Culture of Narcissism: American Life in an Age of Diminishing Expectations.* New York: W. W. Norton, p. 40.
3. Erich Fromm (1956/1963) *The Art of Loving.* New York: Bantam Books, pp. 1–2.
4. Ibid., p. 12.
5. Erik Erikson (1968) *Identity: Youth and Crisis.* New York: W. W. Norton, p. 138.
6. Ibid.
7. Ibid.
8. Ibid., p. 139.
9. Jeffrey A. Sonnenfeld (1988) *Hero's Farewell: What Happens When CEOs Retire.* New York: Oxford University Press.
10. Erikson, *Identity,* p. 219.
11. Gaston Bachelard (1964) *The Psychoanalysis of Fire,* trans. Alan C. M. Ross. Boston: Beacon Press.
12. *Bartlett's Familiar Quotations,* 15th ed. (1982) Boston: Little, Brown, p. 786.
13. L. Kaufman, "Failed at Your Last Job? Wonderful! You're Hired," *New York Times,* October 6, 1999, p. C12.
14. "Brain Drain," *Business Week,* September 20, 1999, p. 120.
15. K. A. Cameron and M. A. Persinger (1983) "Pensioners Who Die Soon After Retirement Can Be Discriminated from Survivors by Post-Retirement Activities," *Psychological Reports,* 53, pp. 564–566.
16. M. H. Reich (1986) "The Mentor Connection," *Personnel,* 63, pp. 50–56.
17. Jean Baker Miller (1976) *Toward a New Psychology of Women.* Boston: Beacon Press, p. 83.

9. TRUE HAPPINESS IS A VERB

1. B. Stone, "Get a Life!" *Newsweek,* June 7, 1999, pp. 68–69. My analysis is based solely on what appears in *Newsweek,* which could, for a variety of reasons, be omitting significant details of the program that might alter my opinions.
2. L. Kaufman, "Some Companies Derail the 'Burnout' Track," *New York Times,* May 4, 1999, p. C8.
3. Epictetus (1995) *The Art of Living,* trans. S. Lebell. New York: Harper-Collins, p. 103.
4. Steven Berglas, "*Boom!* There's Nothing Wrong with You or Your Business That a Little *Conflict* Wouldn't Cure," *Inc.,* May 1997, pp. 56–57.

5. ReutersNews.com, May 27, 2000.

6. ABCNews.com, May 27, 2000.

7. S. H. Greenberg, "The Karate Generation," *Newsweek,* August 28, 2000, p. 50.

8. See, for example, F. J. Sulloway (1979) *Freud: Biologist of the Mind.* New York: Basic Books, pp. 54–64.

9. H. L. Ansbacher and R. Ansbacher, eds. (1956) *The Individual Psychology of Alfred Adler.* New York: Basic Books.

10. Sigmund Freud (1923/1961) "The Ego and the Id." In his *Complete Psychological Works: Standard Edition,* ed. and trans. by James Strachey. London: Hogarth Press, vol. 19, pp. 3–66.

11. Epictetus, *Enchiridion,* ed. James Fieser (Internet Release, 1966).

12. S. F. Hayward (1998) *Churchill on Leadership.* Rocklin, Calif.: Prima Publishing, p. 121.

13. R. M. Huber (1971) *The American Idea of Success.* New York: McGraw-Hill, p. 9.

14. *Bartlett's Familiar Quotations,* 15th ed. (1982) Boston: Little, Brown, p. 680.

15. Friedrich Nietzsche (1968) *The Will to Power,* trans. by Walter Kaufmann and R. J. Hollingdale. New York: Vintage Books, p. 417.

Index

A

academic achievement, 16–17, 82–83, 85–86, 91, 163–64, 209
accidie, 62–65
achievement:
  academic, 16–17, 82–83, 85–86, 91, 163–64, 209
  Bierce's definition of, 80
  of goals, 15, 22–23, 24, 31–32, 37–38, 176
  motivation for, 140–42, 184
  narcissism and, 93–94
  risk and, 135–39
  Sisyphus of, 90–92, 149
  under-, 82–83, 144
action defenses, 40
Actival, 16–17
Adams, Scott, 145–46
Adler, Gerald, 104
adolescents, 4, 10, 82–83, 114–15, 173–74, 194–96
Adrenaline, 33
advantages, differential, 186, 192–94
aggressiveness, 173–74, 192–201
alcoholism, 9–12, 13, 14, 15, 17, 27, 68, 146, 208, 210
Alger, Horatio, 81, 132, 178, 207
Allen, Woody, 64, 68
ambition, 79, 116–17, 137–38
American dream, 28–30, 35, 130, 133
anger, 192–201
  coping with, 89, 160–62, 164–65, 192–201, 203, 208–10

repression of, 20, 77, 82–83, 87, 93, 160–62, 172–74, 192–201, 203, 208–10
  righteous, 185, 196, 216, 218
anhedonia, 64
Annie Hall, 64
antidepressants, 12, 67
anxiety:
  castration, 175
  encore, 32, 44–46, 48–49, 136
  about failure, 5–6, 107–8, 111, 136–38, 176–78
  illnesses caused by, 9
  medications for, 179
  performance, 5–6, 33, 67, 116–17, 142
Apple Computer, 51
Araton, Harvey, 124
Argyris, Chris, 118–20
Aristotle, 132, 185, 196, 197, 216
Armstrong, Lance, 156–57
arsonists, entrepreneurial, 38–41, 136, 171
Art of Loving, The (Fromm), 167–68
"Art of Money-Getting, The" (Barnum), 133
assessments, psychological, 204–5
athletics, 18–24, 32–34, 52–53, 64, 114, 117, 123–24, 164, 211
authority, challenges to, 57–58, 66–67, 173
Autobiography (Franklin), 131–32
Avery, Sewell, 107, 111
avoidance, 192, 215

B

Baby and Child Care (Spock), 57–59
baby boomers, 35, 54–79
  burnout of, 54–79, 102
  childhood, 56–60
  individualism of, 56–59
  market for, 203, 205
  midlife crises of, 54–55, 68–69
  narcissistic disorders in, 54–55
  opportunities for, 54, 59–62
  silent generation vs., 56, 57, 102, 189
Bachelard, Gaston, 175–76
Bacon, Francis, 177
Baldwin, James, 203
Barnum, P. T., 133
Bartlett, Christopher, 151
Bartlett's Familiar Quotations, 118
basketball, 18–24, 123–24
Bateson, Gregory, 73
Bateson, Mary Catherine, 73, 75
battle fatigue, 20
Bay of Pigs invasion, 108
bears, threat needed by, 36
beauty, 11–15
Begelman, David, 6, 125
Behar, Richard, 89
behavior:
  abusive, 90–92, 93, 168, 192–93, 203–5, 206, 208–10
  acting-out, 19, 99, 164–65, 206
  antisocial, 20, 55, 194–96
  compensatory, 146–48, 161–62, 165, 200–201, 202
  constraints on, 74–75, 80
  devaluing, 20, 161–66
  escapist, 19
  exemplary, 195–96
  illicit, 122–26
  judgmental, 200–201
  politically incorrect, 192–94, 203, 218
  risk-taking, 36–37
  self-affirming, 156–57
  self-destructive, 9, 18, 19–20, 43, 84–90, 93, 114, 144–45, 157, 207–10

self-handicapping, 13–15, 18, 65–69, 119–20, 136, 142, 146, 202, 208
  self-protective, 68–69
Berlin, Irving, 28
Bible, 61–62, 159, 184
Bierce, Ambrose, 80
birds-of-a-feather-flock-together law, 95–96
blame, externalization of, 108, 112, 142, 202
Bok, Derek, 55
bonding, 76
bonsai trees, 121, 149–52
boredom, 18, 36, 129, 143, 170–71, 216
Brand, Myles, 123–24
Branson, Richard, 36–37
Brokaw, Tom, 56, 62
Browning, Robert, 45
Buddha, 193
burnout, *see Supernova Burnout*

C

Calvinism, 127–28
capitalism, 43, 80–81, 128–33
cardiovascular disease, 9
careers:
  abandonment of, 100–101
  adaptation in, 21–22, 24
  "breaking loose" in, 6–7
  building vs. sustaining of, 49–51
  dissatisfaction with, 55–56, 100–101
  diversification in, 51–53, 101, 149, 152–57
  inertia in, 7–8
  nonlinear models for, 149–57
  parallel, 145–46
  path of, 3–5, 74, 100–101, 120–21, 150
  "repotting" of, 149–52
  as vocations, 7–8, 50, 190–91, 215–18
Carpenter, Candice, 40–41
Case, Steve, 6

case studies:
  Adam, 85–93
  A.J., 47–48
  Ashley, 66–67
  Barbara, 172–74
  Connie, 212–15, 216
  David, 112–15
  Don, 108–11, 115
  Doug, 198–201
  Jane, 203–6
  Jeff, 63–65, 68
  Jim, 136–38
  Martha, 7–8
  Patrick, 207–10, 212
  Peter, 146–48
  Roy, 163–66, 171
  Sean, 75–77
  Sharon, 178–81, 184
catastrophizing, 172–73
celebrities, synthetic, 125–26, 132,
  186
Central Park Zoo, 36
challenge-threat curve, 140–42
Champy, James, 46–47
Chandler, Raymond, 88
change:
  catalysts for, 9
  coping with, 143–57
character, 100–101, 201
Charan, Ram, 106
Cheaters, 123
children:
  needs of, 83, 91, 173–74
  play of, 72, 171, 190–91
  raising of, 58–60, 169, 178–79,
    201, 214, 215
  self-esteem of, 161, 163, 173–74,
    201, 209
"choking under pressure," 65–67,
  142
Christie, Julie, 116
Christmas trees, 121, 149
Churchill, Winston S., 210–11
City Slickers, 38
Coca-Cola, 108
Cochran, Johnnie, 45
cognitive therapy, 135, 206

Columbia Pictures, 125
Columbine High School shootings, 82
Colvin, Geoffrey, 106
commitment, escalation of, 107–8,
  111
Compaq Computer Corporation, 51
compensatory retaliation, 88–90
competition, 193–94, 196
connectedness, 98, 111, 114, 115,
  117, 119, 162–63, 183–84
conquerors, 2, 59, 129
consensual validation, 60–62
consumerism, 128
contempt, 20, 161–66
control, 84, 87, 111–15, 118, 144–45,
  156, 173, 195–97
Coors, 155
corporations:
  culture of, 55, 58
  takeovers by, 7–8
"counterdependent," 114
creativity, 4, 25–26, 71, 100, 105–6
crime, 9, 55, 85–90, 93
crisis:
  Chinese symbol for, 4
  midlife, 54–55, 68–69
Csikszentmihalyi, Mihaly, 41, 42
Culture of Narcissism, The (Lasch),
  129–30

D
Dallas, 38, 39
Darling, 116
deception, 207–10
decision-making, 107–8, 111
defense mechanisms, 40, 160–64,
  168–69
delusion, 171
denial, 76, 156, 171, 178
depression:
  accidie vs., 64–65
  causes of, 84, 87, 98, 163, 170
  medications for, 12, 67
  post-Olympic, 31, 32–34
  seasonal, 12
  stigma of, 102
  stress as cause of, 9

depression *(cont'd)*:
  success, 31–32, 37–38, 40, 46, 64
  treatment for, 69
  women and, 98–100, 116, 226*n*
Devil's Dictionary, The (Bierce), 80
Dickinson, Emily, 103
Digital Equipment Corporation
  (DEC), 50–51
Dilbert, 145–46
distress, 9, 22, 47, 157
diversification, chronic, 149, 152–57
divorce, 55, 147–48, 178, 181
DNA, 73–74, 83, 97
Dodson, J. D., 140
Dole, Bob, 129
dot-com millionaires, 34, 40–41
downsizing, 46–48, 145–46
Doyle, Arthur Conan, 44
drug abuse, 11–15, 18
drugs, hallucinogenic, 38
Duke University, 16–17
Dunlap, Al, 47, 112

E
Eastman, George, 37, 49
Eastman Kodak, 37
economy, U.S., 55, 57
ego, 148, 161, 194
Ellis, Havelock, 51
emotions:
  expression of, 20, 77, 119, 192–94,
    199–200, 201
  externalization of, 19, 99, 164–65,
    206
  repression of, 106, 111–12, 114,
    160–62, 172–74, 192–201, 203,
    209–10
  see also anger
empathy, 119
employee assistance programs,
  186–92
employment, 55, 145–46
endorphins, 32–33
ennui, 18, 36, 129, 143, 170–71, 216
entrepreneurs:
  as *"arsonists,"* 38–41, 136, 171

baby boomers as, 58
challenges needed by, 34–37
creativity of, 100
social context of, 96, 130
status quo rejected by, 2, 100
success achieved by, 37–38
Epictetus, 134, 135, 137, 148, 157,
  176–77, 188, 202–3
Epinephrine, 33, 157
Erikson, Erik, 117, 169–71, 175, 181,
  182
euphoria, 32–33
eustress, 22, 24, 36–37, 38, 40, 43,
  139–42, 143, 156–57
Evans, Robert, 125
executives, corporate, 7, 182–83,
  206
exhaustion, 20
expectations:
  baseline for, 61–62
  consensual validation and, 60–62
  meeting of, 5–6, 8, 15, 18–24, 44–46
  of parents, 85–88, 91–92, 93, 114,
    147, 163, 173–74, 200–201, 209
  thwarting of, 68–69, 80–94, 142
  unrealistic, 37–38, 46, 60–62
extramarital affairs, 87, 144, 151

F
failure:
  admission of, 100–101, 108, 120,
    176–78, 181–82
  anxiety about, 5–6, 107–8, 111,
    136–38, 176–78
  consequences of, 118–19, 144–45,
    146
  desire for, 63–65, 68
  as opportunity, 140–42, 178
families:
  nuclear, 57, 98, 174
  raising of, 178–79, 214, 215
  see also children; parents
fathers, expectations of, 85–88,
  91–92, 93, 114, 147, 163,
  173–74, 200–201
Faustian bargains, 68–69, 161–62, 197

fear:
    coping with, 157, 163, 173–74,
      176–78
    irrational, 178–81
    of success, 116–17
    of unknown, 143–46
Federal Bureau of Investigation (FBI),
    39, 93
Finch, Sue, 193–94, 195, 196
fire, as symbol, 24–25
Fisher, Gary, 155
Fitzgerald, F. Scott, 185–86
Five Easy Pieces, 62, 70
flexibility, 69–70, 73–74
Forbes, 63
Forbes, Malcolm, 36
Ford, Henry, 178
Ford Motor Company, 47
Fortune, 50, 89, 106
Fortune 100, 207–8
Fortune 500, 121, 206
Fortune 1000, 7, 47, 101
Foster, Vince, 6
founder's disease, 112–13
Franklin, Benjamin, 40, 43, 81, 127,
    128–33, 135, 203
Freud, Sigmund, 30, 59–60, 64, 77–78,
    93, 147, 159, 169, 175, 192, 198
Freudian slips, 87
Fromm, Erich, 167–68
Fulton, Robert, 98
futility, sense of, 20

G

Gage, John, 187
Gallup Organization, 55
Gates, Bill, 6
generativity, 169–71, 174–76,
    180–84, 217–18
genetics, 73–74, 83, 97
geographic cures, 70–71
Gerstner, Lou, 211–12
gestalt, 153–55, 157
get-a-life programs, 186–92
Ghoshal, Sumantra, 151
Gifford, Kathie Lee, 33–34

Gilbert, William S., 59
goals:
    achievement of, 15, 22–23, 24,
      31–32, 37–38, 176
    commitment to, 74–75
    pursuit of, 22–23, 31–32, 75
    setting of, 51–53, 73, 79, 91–92
Godine, John, 143–44, 145
Goizueta, Roberto, 108, 120
"golden handcuffs," 5, 48–49, 54,
    93–94, 159, 189, 190–91, 216
"golden parachutes," 46, 48
Goldilocks dilemma, 140–49,
    151–52, 153
Goldsmith, Barbara, 125
golf, 22, 65
Greatest Generation, The (Brokaw),
    56, 62
Great Gatsby, The (Fitzgerald),
    185–86
greed, 51–53
Greek mythology, 24–26
Grove, Andy, 50, 156–57
Guernica (Picasso), 152
guilt, 87, 205

H

Hamlet (Shakespeare), 210
Hammer, Michael, 46–47
happiness, 29–30, 127, 158–59,
    185–92
Harris, Eric, 82
Harvard Medical School, 17
Helliwell, Dennis, 89–90
Helmsley, Leona, 124
herd mentality, 211
Herodotus, 134–35
Higher Education Research Institute,
    55
Hill, Napoleon, 133
Hillary, Edmund, 158, 159
hobbies, 187, 190–91
Hock, Dee, 182
Holmes, Oliver Wendell, Jr., 31–32
homeostasis, 36–37, 56
Horner, Matina, 116–17, 119

hubris, 26, 57–58, 202
humiliation, 81–82, 107–8, 159, 171,
    194–95, 201, 208

I
IBM, 211–12
Icarus, 26
identity dependence, 170
idolatry, 161–62
illness, 9, 198–201
impotence, 40
Inc., 34, 35, 37
Inc. 500, 37
incentives, 65–67
income, personal, 29
individualism, 56–59, 129–30, 133
infants, 72, 201
information technology, 35–36,
    50–51
initiative, 139–40
insider trading, 9, 93
insomnia, 13
intellectual performance, 16–17,
    82–83, 85–86, 91, 163–64, 209
intergenerational tension, 174–76
interpersonal conflicts, 38–41,
    192–93, 195–96
intimacy, 170
inventors, 2

J
James, William, 54, 60, 67, 69–70,
    126, 129–30
Jewell, Richard, 39
Jews, 54
Jobs, Steve, 51
Jordan, Michael, 6, 18–24, 191

K
Kapor, Mitch, 35–36, 49
Kennedy, John F., 61, 108, 120, 175
Kennedy, Joseph P., Sr., 61
Kennedy, Robert F., 61–62
Kennedy, Rose, 61–62
King, Martin Luther, Jr., 186
Klebold, Dylan, 82
Knight, Bob, 123–24

Koch, Ed, 111
Kroc, Ray, 122, 129

L
Lake Worth, Fla., shooting in, 194–96
Lasch, Christopher, 30, 129–30, 132,
    133, 138, 163
Laski, Harold, 131
Lawrence, T. E., 142
lawyers, 44–45, 150–51
layoffs, 46–48
leadership, 136–38, 206
legacy, 174–76, 183–84
Leno, Jay, 33
Lenzi, Mark, 31, 32–34, 49, 52–53
Lerner, Alan Jay, 95
libido, 30, 201
Lombardi, Vince, 30, 117
Looking Out for #1 (Monsky), 167
Lotus Development Corp., 35–36
love, 162, 167–68, 175, 214–15
Luke, Gospel of, 61–62

M
McDermott, James, 9
McDonald's, 129
Machiavelli, Niccolò, 79, 88
managers, 107, 112–15, 145–46, 151,
    203–6, 208–12
manipulation, 84
Marcus Aurelius, 26
Marine Midland Bank, 89
marriage, 55, 108–11, 147–49, 178,
    181
martial arts, 114–15, 196
Marx, Groucho, 162
Maslow, Abraham, 71, 75, 77, 78, 79
Masters of the Universe, 29
Mather, Cotton, 127, 130–31
Matthew, Gospel of, 184
Maxwell, Robert, 6
Mead, Margaret, 73, 95, 115
men:
    gender identity of, 98, 116, 117
    success as defined by, 100–103,
        111–12, 121, 176
Menninger, Karl, 196–97

mentoring, 180–84
methaqualone, 11–15, 27
Michigan, University of, 29
midlife period, 49–50, 54–55, 68–69, 216
Miller, Arthur, 211
Miller, Jean Baker, 97, 98, 120, 184
Millionaire Next Door, The (Stanley and Danko), 34
models, fashion, 11–15, 16, 61, 74
Monsky, Mark, 167
Montgomery Ward & Co., 107
morale, 20, 150–51, 193
mothers, expectations of, 163, 173–74, 209
"musical chairs" game, 193–94
musicians, 18, 74–75
mutuality, 175–76
"my career = my self" predicament, 138–39
My Fair Lady (Lerner), 95

N
narcissistic disorders, 160–69
   in baby boomers, 54–55
   defense mechanisms of, 160–69
   generativity impeded by, 176, 217–18
   "injuries" in, 146–48, 168–69
   in parents, 84–85, 90–94
   self-esteem and, 66–67, 93–94, 133, 146–48, 168–69
National Basketball Association (NBA), 18–19, 23
needs:
   acknowledgment of, 111, 159–60
   of children, 83, 91, 173–74
   emotional, *see* emotions
   hierarchy of, 71–72, 77
   meeting of, 160–61, 163
Nehru, Jawaharlal, 135
New Deal, 46
Newsweek, 187
New York Times, 42, 123–24, 178
Nicholson, Jack, 62
Nicomachean Ethics (Aristotle), 132
Nietzsche, Friedrich, 218–19

Norman, Greg, 65
Nye, Russel B., 131

O
obedience, 83
obligations, 190–91
obsession, 122–33, 160, 170–71
Oedipus complex, 175
Olsen, Ken, 50–51, 52
Olympics, 31, 32–34, 39, 52–53
opportunities:
   for baby boomers, 54, 59–62
   failure as, 140–42, 178
   initiative and, 139–40
   limitation of, 41–45, 46
   risk vs., 4–5, 140–42, 178
optimism, 56–57, 156–57
Organization Man, The (Whyte), 58
"out of the box" thinking, 100, 105–6
overextension, 171, 174

P
Pacific Bell, 145–46
Pandocrin, 16–17
panic attacks, 108–11, 179
paradoxical incentive effects, 65–67
parents:
   abusive, 90–92, 93
   expectations of, 85–88, 91–92, 93, 114, 147, 163, 173–74, 200–201, 209
   influence of, 83, 175
   narcissistic disorders in, 84–85, 90–94
"passing the torch," 174–76
passion, 212–19
Pavarotti, Luciano, 44
Peace Corps, 182
peak experiences, 77, 79
Peck, M. Scott, 41, 46
People, 125
perfectionism, 174, 176
performance:
   anxiety and, 5–6, 33, 67, 116–17, 142
   baseline, 44–46

performance *(cont'd)*:
  risk-avoidance in, 135–39, 145
  standards of, 18–24
personalism, 59
personality:
  choke-prone, 65–67, 142
  domineering, 104–5, 111–12, 115
  implicit theory of, 103–5, 106
  self-made, 81, 132, 169, 178, 207
  successful, 105–7, 118–19
  traits of, 49–51, 100–101, 151, 201
  Type A, 75, 146–48
Peter Pan syndrome, 69
Peter Principle, 48
Philbin, Regis, 33, 34
phobias, 178–81
Picasso, Pablo, 4, 152
placebo effects, 188–90
play, 72, 171, 190–91
Polese, Kim, 40–41
political correctness, 192–94, 203,
  218
Ponzi, Charles, 89
Ponzi schemes, 89–90, 183
Poor Richard's Almanack (Franklin),
  81, 129, 131–33
predestination, 127–30
Princess Ida (Gilbert), 59
Prinze, Freddie, 6
"process," 58
projection, 160, 209–10
Promethean complex, 175–76
Prometheus, 24–26, 58, 100, 175–76,
  218, 219
promotions, 47–48
*Protestant Ethic and the Spirit of
  Capitalism, The* (Weber), 128
Proverbs, Book of, 159
provider paradox, 190–91
pseudo-intimacy, 170
"Psychology of the Entrepreneurial
  Spirit," 34
psychosomatic illness, 198–201
public speaking, 135
Publilius Syrus, 118
Puritanism, 80–81, 126–30, 132, 133
Pyrrhus, King of Epirus, 88

Q
Quaaludes, 11–15, 27

R
rage, *see* anger
Rashad, Ahmad, 155
reactance, psychological, 74–75
Reaganomics, 29
recruitment, 181–82
Reengineering the Corporation
  (Hammer and Champy), 46–47
relationships:
  conflict in, 38–41, 192–93, 195–96
  development of, 53, 76, 159–62,
    163, 164, 170, 183–84, 213–15
  perseverance in, 95–97
  retaliation and, 89–90
  in social groups, 95–96
reputation, 21–22, 177
rerum novarum cupidus, 153
retaliation, 88–90
retirement, 18–24
return on investment (ROI), 43–44,
  52, 53
Reuters, 193
revenge, Pyrrhic, 80–94, 144, 146,
  168
risk:
  achievement and, 135–39
  avoidance of, 135–39, 145
  homeostasis vs., 36–37, 56
  management of, 36–37, 134–39
  opportunity vs., 4–5, 140–42, 178
  safety vs., 36, 71, 72–73, 114–15,
    165, 215
RJR Nabisco, 211–12
Road Less Traveled, The (Peck), 41
Robards, Jason, 9, 10
Rockefeller, John D., 100
Rocker, John, 124
role models, 216–18
Roosevelt, Eleanor, 177
Roosevelt, Franklin D., 46
Rudolph, Wilma, 25–26
Rummel, William James, 125
"runner's high," 32–33
Russell, Bertrand, ix

S

safety, psychological, 36, 71, 72–73, 114–15, 165, 215
Sallust, 158–59
Sanderson, Derek, 10
Saving Private Ryan, 56, 62
Scheck, Barry, 216, 217
Scholastic Aptitude Test (SAT), 16
self:
  gestalt of, 153–55, 157
  professional, 138–39, 153–57, 170
  sense of, 4, 60–61, 68–69, 71, 72, 77, 88–89, 115–16, 152, 196–97
self-actualization, 69–79, 75, 77–78, 159, 171, 219
self-assessment, 49–51, 159, 160–61, 202–3, 210–12
self-consciousness, 65–67, 72, 142, 156
self-efficacy, 84–85
self-esteem:
  of children, 161, 163, 173–74, 201, 209
  diversification and, 152–53, 155–56
  establishment of, 59–60, 71, 75, 80, 83, 91, 114–15, 166, 171, 183, 188, 196, 201–2
  formula for, 60–61
  material success and, 29–30, 79, 126–33
  narcissistic disorders and, 66–67, 93–94, 133, 146–48, 168–69
  professed, 57–58
  reaffirmation of, 22–23, 33, 156–57, 163–64, 210–12
  threats to, 20–21, 31, 76–77, 90–92, 135–36, 140–42, 160–62, 201–3, 206, 208–10
  of women, 99
self-help ethos, 80–81
self-help psychiatry, 166–68, 208
sensory deprivation, 38–39
Service Corps of Retired Executives (SCORE), 182–83
sexuality, 108–11, 148–49, 198, 214
Shakespeare, William, 210, 212

shame, 87, 101–2, 107–8, 178–79, 194–95, 201
Shaw, George Bernard, 6–7, 26–27, 100–101, 178, 217–18
"Sign of Four, The" (Doyle), 44
silent generation, 56, 57, 102, 189
Sisyphus, 90–92, 149
60 Minutes cure, 215–18
sloth, 63
social comparison, 42–43, 73
social life, 213–15
social policy, 46
social service workers, 20
Socrates, 202
Solomon, 54
specialization, 99
Spock, Benjamin, 57–59
Sports Illustrated, 124
stagnation, 170–71
Starr, Marylin, 9
status quo, 2, 25, 58, 100, 210–11
Steiger, Rod, 102
Steinbeck, John, 27
Steinmetz High School, 123, 124
stigmatization, social, 82–83, 84
stimulation, 139–40
stress:
  causes of, 108–11, 172–74
  coping with, 119, 135, 157, 172–74
  distress, 9, 22, 47, 157
  eustress, 22, 24, 36–37, 38, 40, 42, 139–42, 143, 156–57
  women and, 99–100
success:
  accoutrements of, 6, 28–29, 34–35, 159, 161–62, 163, 165, 168–69, 177, 190
  active vs. passive, 14, 15, 16–17
  as common goal, 8, 28–30, 81–82, 126–33
  cultural standards for, 100–101, 122–33, 203
  definitions of, 28–30, 98
  depression caused by, 31–32, 37–38, 40, 46, 64
  drive for, 75–77, 79, 139–42, 146–48, 202

success *(cont'd)*:
  fear of, 116–17
  feminine definition of, 17, 95–121
  financial rewards of, 6, 28–29
  happiness vs., 29–30, 127, 158–59,
    185–92
  ironies of, 3–5
  linear model of, 142–43
  masculine definition of, 100–103,
    111–12, 121, 176
  material, 28–30, 41–43, 54–55, 79,
    81, 126–33, 160, 168–69,
    185–86
  morality of, 122–26
  motivation for, 140–42, 219
  noncontingent, 16–17, 205–6,
    207
  nonlinear, 149–57
  obsession with, 122–33, 160,
    170–71
  obstacles to, 3–5, 106–7, 135,
    140–42, 192
  opportunities limited by, 41–45, 46
  paradox of, 3–5, 75, 137–38
  self-actualization vs., 77–78
  social approval and, 21–22, 98,
    177, 211
  striving for vs. sustaining of, 22–23,
    31–32, 37–38, 43–44, 51–53
  as trap, 25–27
  victims of, 15, 26
sudden wealth syndrome, 34–35
suicide, 6, 37
Sullivan, Harry Stack, 60
sundae fallacy, 192
Sun Microsystems, 187, 189
Supernova Burnout:
  definition of, 18–19
  generic, 20
  prevalence of, 6–7
  prevention of, 149, 150, 158, 176,
    190–91, 197–98
  revenge and, 82, 88, 94
  as syndrome, 5–10, 17
  treatment of, 49, 78–79, 101–2,
    115, 207, 212–19
Supreme Court, U.S., 125

T
Taoism, 69, 72, 73–74, 78
tarot cards, 4
Tennyson, Alfred Lord, 122, 129
therapy:
  goals of, 167
  referrals to, 3–5, 172, 213
  stigma of, 101–2
Think and Grow Rich (Hill), 133
"threat zone," 142–43
trauma, 165–66
triage, 53
Trump, Donald, 43
trust, 161
turnover, associate, 150–51
Twain, Mark, 190, 201–2

U
"Ulysses" (Tennyson), 122, 129
unemployment, 46–48, 145–46
unemployment insurance, 46
Unilever, 151
University of Michigan, 29

V
Ventura, Jesse, 155–56
Viagra, 129
vocations, 7–8, 50, 190–91, 215–18
vulnerability, 101–3, 108–11, 112,
    115, 118, 138, 159–60, 163, 178

W
Wall Street Journal, 46
Way to Wealth, The (Franklin),
    131–32
wealth:
  accumulation of, 28–30, 36–37,
    41–43, 55, 56, 61, 79, 81,
    126–33
  hierarchy of, 29–30
  inherited, 63–65, 73
  necessary, 131–33
  psychological, 182–83
  sudden, 34–35
Weber, Max, 128
Wells, H. G., 126
Who Wants to Be a Millionaire, 34

Whyte, William, 58
Wilde, Oscar, 28
Will, George, 191
Wilson, Flip, 14–15
Winfrey, Oprah, 6
wishful thinking, 119
women, 95–121
    career, 99
    depression and, 98–100, 116,
        226*n*
    gender identity of, 97–100, 115–16,
        117, 184
    as homemakers, 99
    nurturing nature of, 97, 99
    relationships sustained by, 95–97
    self-esteem of, 99
    social role and stress of, 99–100
    success as defined by, 17, 95–121

Woods, Tiger, 22
workaholism, 49–50, 146–48
work ethic, 81, 126–33
World War II, 56–57, 189, 210–11
Wozniak, Steve, 51
Wriston, Walter, 182
writer's block, 66

Y
Yeager, Chuck, 26, 134
Yerkes, R. M., 140
Yerkes-Dodson law, 140
Young Presidents' Organization
    (YPO), 112
yuppies, 55

Z
Zeus, 24–25, 100, 218

DR. STEVEN BERGLAS is a clinical psychologist and adjunct faculty member at Harvard Medical School. He formerly wrote the "Entrepreneurial Ego" column for *Inc.* magazine, and his work has been profiled in *The New York Times, Fortune, Time, The Wall Street Journal,* and *People.* A counselor to hundreds of executives and industry leaders on the perils of success-induced burnout, Dr. Berglas currently resides in Los Angeles, where he teaches at the John E. Anderson Graduate School of Management at UCLA.

ABOUT THE TYPE

This book was set in Sabon, a typeface designed by the well-known German typographer Jan Tschichold (1902–74). Sabon's design is based upon the original letter forms of Claude Garamond and was created specifically to be used for three sources: foundry type for hand composition, Linotype, and Monotype. Tschichold named his typeface for the famous Frankfurt typefounder Jacques Sabon, who died in 1580.

RECLAIMING
THE FIRE